THE SANCTITY OF LOUIS IX

The Sanctity of Louis IX

Early Lives of Saint Louis by Geoffrey of Beaulieu and William of Chartres

Translated by Larry F. Field

Edited and Introduced by
M. Cecilia Gaposchkin and Sean L. Field

Cornell University Press
Ithaca and London

Copyright © 2014 by Cornell University

All rights reserved. Except for brief quotations in a review, this book, or parts thereof, must not be reproduced in any form without permission in writing from the publisher. For information, address Cornell University Press, Sage House, 512 East State Street, Ithaca, New York 14850.

First published 2014 by Cornell University Press

First printing, Cornell Paperbacks, 2014

Printed in the United States of America

Library of Congress Cataloging-in-Publication Data

    The sanctity of Louis IX : early lives of Saint Louis by Geoffrey of Beaulieu and William of Chartres / translated by Larry F. Field ; edited and introduced by M. Cecilia Gaposchkin and Sean L. Field.
       pages cm
    Includes bibliographical references and index.
    ISBN 978-0-8014-5137-9 (cloth : alk. paper)
    ISBN 978-0-8014-7818-5 (pbk. : alk. paper)
    1. Louis IX, King of France, 1214–1270. 2. France—Kings and rulers—Biography. 3. Christian saints—France—Biography. I. Field, Larry F., translator. II. Gaposchkin, M. Cecilia (Marianne Cecilia), 1970– editor of compilation. III. Field, Sean L. (Sean Linscott), 1970– editor of compilation. IV. Geoffrey, of Beaulieu, died approximately 1274. Vita et sancta conuersatio piae memoriae Lvdovici quondam Regis Francorum. English. V. William, of Chartres, approximately 1225–approximately 1280. De vita et actibus inclytae recordationis Regis Francorum Ludouici. English. VI. Title: Life and comportment of Louis, former King of the Franks, of pious memory. VII. Title: On the life and deeds of Louis, King of the Franks of famous memory, and on the miracles which declare his sanctity.

    DC91.A2S26   2014
    944'.023092—dc23   [B]   2013023199

Cornell University Press strives to use environmentally responsible suppliers and materials to the fullest extent possible in the publishing of its books. Such materials include vegetable-based, low-VOC inks and acid-free papers that are recycled, totally chlorine-free, or partly composed of nonwood fibers. For further information, visit our website at www.cornellpress.cornell.edu.

Cloth printing   10 9 8 7 6 5 4 3 2 1
Paperback printing 10 9 8 7 6 5 4 3 2 1

Discipulis nostris

Contents

List of Figures and Maps ix
Preface xi
List of Abbreviations xiii
Note on Sources and Translation Policies xv

Introduction 1
1. Three Early Letters on the Sanctity of Louis IX 61
2. Geoffrey of Beaulieu's *Life and Saintly Comportment of Louis, Former King of the Franks, of Pious Memory* 69
3. William of Chartres' *On the Life and Deeds of Louis, King of the Franks of Famous Memory, and on the Miracles That Declare His Sanctity* 129
4. Pope Boniface VIII's Bull *Gloria Laus* 160

Appendix: The Manuscript and Printing Histories of the Texts 173
Select Bibliography 185
Index 191

Figures and Maps

Figures

1. Louis IX carrying the Crown of Thorns   5
2. Autograph letter of William of Chartres   35
3. The opening page of Geoffrey of Beaulieu's *vita*   70
4. The opening page of William of Chartres' *vita*   130
5. The sealed original of Boniface VIII's canonization bull   161

Maps

1. Thirteenth-century France and the Ile-de-France region   xviii
2. Europe and the Mediterranean   12
3. Paris about 1270   28

Preface

Louis IX of France (r. 1226–70) is one of the iconic figures of the European Middle Ages, among the most famous kings and best-known saints of the high medieval period. This volume offers the first English translations of two of the earliest and most important accounts of his life: the *vitae* (saint's lives) by the Dominicans Geoffrey of Beaulieu (written around 1274–75) and William of Chartres (written shortly thereafter). The *vitae* are preceded by translations of three closely associated letters: one relating Louis IX's death, written by his successor Philip III from North Africa on 12 September 1270 and entrusted to Geoffrey of Beaulieu and William of Chartres to carry back to the churches of France; a second in which Pope Gregory X on 4 March 1272 asked Geoffrey to send him his recollections of Louis; and a third from the Dominican Provincial Chapter of France (the province to which Geoffrey and William both belonged as friars) to the College of Cardinals dated 8 September 1275 urging Louis' canonization. Taken together, these *vitae* and related texts demonstrate how Louis IX was being remembered and promoted in the years immediately following his death, before the formal canonization proceedings of 1282–83 that led to his official enrollment in the catalogue of saints in 1297. For purposes of thematic and chronological comparison the volume also includes Boniface VIII's canonization bull itself, here translated into English for the first time.

The introduction provides background information on Louis IX and his two Dominican biographers, analysis of the historical context of the 1270s, and a thematic analysis of the texts. Although this material is geared toward students, much of it should be of interest to specialists as well, since Geoffrey and William are little-known figures and this early period in the development of Louis' hagiographic legend has often been overlooked. Finally, in an appendix (aimed at specialists) we include an essay on the manuscript and early printing histories of our texts.

We would like to thank Peter Potter at Cornell University Press for his support from the beginning of this project, the press's anonymous readers for corrections and critiques, and Gavin Lewis for expert copy editing. Sean Field thanks the College of Arts and Sciences at the University of Vermont for a Lattie Coor Faculty Development Award, and Cecilia Gaposchkin thanks the Nelson A. Rockefeller Center for a Faculty Research Grant; these awards made possible essential manuscript-checking trips to Paris. Sean Field would also like to thank his students in History 195 and 224 in 2011–12 for testing out the translations and critiquing the introduction. Our particular thanks are due to Elizabeth A. R. Brown, Adam Davis, Xavier Hélary, Anne E. Lester, Patricia Stirnemann, and Simon Tugwell, O.P., for their expert help, to William Chester Jordan for years of encouragement (and for reminding us of Louis' dark side), and to Charlotte Denoël and Ghislain Brunel for kindly facilitating access to manuscripts and documents at the Bibliothèque nationale de France and the Archives nationales de France. Finally, our deepest thanks goes to each of our families, for years of understanding support.

A final word about how this co-authored book took shape. Larry Field handled the initial work of translation, while Sean Field checked existing editions of the texts against extant manuscripts. Cecilia Gaposchkin and Sean Field then edited, revised, and provided notes for the translation, and wrote the introduction and appendix. Everything was then passed back and forth between all three contributors in multiple drafts, until everyone could live with the result. Sean and Cecilia, however, would like to credit any particularly inspired translation choices to Larry Field's original rendering of the Latin, while hoping that the editing process did not introduce an excessive amount of clunky literal-mindedness.

Abbreviations

AD	Archives départementales
AN	Paris, Archives nationales de France
BL	*Beatus Ludovicus*, in *Blessed Louis, the Most Glorious of Kings: Texts Relating to the Cult of Saint Louis of France*, ed. M. Cecilia Gaposchkin, trans. with Phyllis Katz (Notre Dame, Ind.: University of Notre Dame Press, 2012), 106–51
BnF	Paris, Bibliothèque nationale de France
HLF	*Histoire littéraire de la France*, 41 vols. (Paris: Imprimerie nationale, 1832–1974)
Kaeppeli, SoP	Thomas Kaeppeli, with Emilio Panella, *Scriptores ordinis Praedicatorum*, 4 vols. (Rome: Ad S. Sabinae, 1970–93)
om.	Omitted (words in one version of a text that occur in another version)
PL	J.-P. Migne, ed., *Patrologiae cursus completus … Series latina*, 221 vols. (Paris: Migne, 1844–64)
Quétif and Echard, SOP	Jacques Quétif and Jacques Echard, eds., *Scriptores ordinis Praedicatorum recensiti*, 2 vols. (Paris, 1719–21; reprint, New York: Burt Franklin, 1959)
RHGF	M. Bouquet et al., eds., *Recueil des historiens des Gaules et de la France*, 24 vols. (Paris, 1738–1876). (Individual volumes in this series are cited by volume number in the introduction and appendix, but without volume numbers in chapters 2, 3, and 4, where only one volume is cited throughout each chapter. For full bibliographical details, see the Note on Sources and Translation Policies below.)

WSP, *Vie*   William of Saint-Pathus, *Vie de saint Louis,* ed. H. François Delaborde, Collection de textes pour servir à l'étude et à l'enseignement de l'histoire 27 (Paris: A. Picard, 1899)

WSP, *Miracles*   Percival B. Fay, ed., *Guillaume de Saint-Pathus, confesseur de la reine Marguerite: Les miracles de saint Louis* (Paris: Champion, 1932)

Note on Sources and Translation Policies

For a more substantial treatment of the manuscript and printing histories of these texts, and further details on editorial policies behind our translations, the reader should consult the appendix. The editions and manuscripts that served as the base texts for our translations must be listed here briefly, however, to explain references in the notes.

Philip III's letter is based on the version printed in Guérard, *Cartulaire de l'église Notre-Dame de Paris*, vol. 1 (Paris: Crapelet, 1850), 189–92 (#CCLVII), compared with BnF ms. lat. 5526, fols. 138r–139v (the basis for Guérard's edition), and lat. 9376, fols. 65rb–65vb.

For Gregory X's letter we have compared the two printed texts known to us: Ripoll, *Bullarium Ordinis Fratrum Praedicatorum*, vol. 1 (Rome: Ex Typographia Hieronymi Mainardi, 1729), 503; and Chapotin, *Histoire des Dominicains de la Province de France, Le siècle des fondations* (Rouen: Cagniard, 1898), 648 n. 1.

For the letter of Jean of Châtillon and the French Dominicans, we have compared Jean de Rechac, *La vie du glorieux patriarche S. Dominique*, vol. 1 (Paris: Huré, 1647), 652–54, and Chapotin, *Histoire des Dominicains de la Province de France*, 648–49 n. 2.

The base text for Geoffrey's and William's *vitae* is the most recent edition, found in *RHGF*, vol. 20 (Paris: Imprimerie royale, 1840), 3–27 (Geoffrey), and 28–41 (William) [= *RHGF* in the footnotes to chapters 2 and 3], compared against BnF ms. lat. 13778 [= *A* in the footnotes, the manuscript used for the *RHGF* edition] and (for Geoffrey) lat. 18335 [= *B* in the footnotes, unknown to the *RHGF* editors].

Boniface VIII's bull is translated from the edition in *RHGF*, vol. 23 (Paris: Welter, 1894) [= *RHGF* in the footnotes to chapter 4], 154–60, compared against AN J 940 no. 111.

In the translations, we have sought a balance between fidelity to the Latin phrasing and production of idiomatic English prose. For most of the *vita* by Geoffrey of Beaulieu and all of Boniface VIII's bull, we have had the benefit of Louis Carolus-Barré's earlier French renderings. Carolus-Barré, however, translated only pars. 7–14 and 16–44 of Geoffrey and omitted chapter headings (interestingly, he worked from Ménard's 1617 edition, not from the 1840 *RHGF* edition).[1] His omission of Geoffrey's lengthy comparisons of Louis with the biblical King Josias highlights the fact that our authors tend to begin with elaborate rhetorical flourishes foreign to modern sensibilities. The three preliminary letters, in fact, stick to a highly emotional style throughout. Geoffrey, William, and Boniface, by contrast, each settle into more straightforward narration. Geoffrey continually refers to his charge to omit nothing, repeatedly offering slightly apologetic notes that various traits of the king "should not be passed over." William is more direct in his Latin and more concrete in his overall style as a storyteller, while Boniface (in spite of a typically elaborate brand of papal Latin) in fact provides the most straightforward chronological narrative of Louis' life. Readers will likely detect some of these shifts of register as the authors move from preliminary rhetoric to core narration, since we have tried to allow our English to follow the authors' lead in this regard.

Paragraph breaks generally follow the base editions, except that in Boniface's bull we have broken the text up into a greater number of paragraphs. Paragraph numbers (and any other text) within square brackets, however, are always our editorial insertion. The *RHGF* editions put overt biblical quotations in italics, but neglect to identify most other biblical citations and echoes. Translations of biblical passages (also in italics in our translation) are based on the Douay-Rheims translation, but modernized and taking account of differences between the manuscript renderings and the Vulgate. Psalm numbering follows the Vulgate. We generally employ English rather than French forms of first names (e.g. William rather than Guillaume) but have chosen to use Jean rather than John, in order to preserve the more familiar forms Jean of Joinville and Jean Tristan.

---

[1] Boniface's bull has also recently been reprinted from the *RHGF* edition, along with Carolus-Barré's French translation, as an appendix to Prosper Guéranger, *Saint Louis et la papauté* (Paris: Association Saint-Jérome, 2008) (this work by Guéranger, who died in 1875, had not previously been published; the modern editors added the papal documents and translations).

THE SANCTITY OF LOUIS IX

Map 1. Thirteenth-century France and the Ile-de-France region, showing cities, regions, and religious houses mentioned in the texts. © M. Cecilia Gaposchkin.

INTRODUCTION

The Life, Reign, and Crusades of Louis IX

Louis IX was born in 1214, during the reign of his grandfather Philip II "Augustus" (r. 1180–1223).[1] This was a propitious decade for Paris and France. Philip Augustus had presided over the rapid growth of the prestige and power of the Capetian kings that followed his seizure of Normandy and neighboring counties from King John of England. In the very year of Louis' birth, Philip won the battle of Bouvines, defeating the combined forces of other northern powers (England, Flanders, and a claimant to the German Imperial throne). Between 1210 and 1220, the

---

[1] The literature on the life of Saint Louis is immense (often verging on the hagiographical). Sébastien Le Nain de Tillemont's seventeenth-century study, edited by J. De Gaulle as *Vie de Saint Louis, Roi de France*, 6 vols. (Paris: J. Renouard et cie, 1847–51), remains indispensable for serious students of Louis' life. The best modern treatments are William Chester Jordan, *Louis IX and the Challenge of the Crusade: A Study in Rulership* (Princeton, N.J.: Princeton University Press, 1979); Jean Richard, *Saint Louis: Crusader King of France*, trans. Jean Birrell (Cambridge: Cambridge University Press, 1992); and Jacques LeGoff, *Saint Louis*, trans. Gareth Evan Gollrad (Notre Dame, Ind.: University of Notre Dame Press, 2009). On Louis' canonization, the crucial work is Louis Carolus-Barré, *Le procès de canonisation de Saint Louis (1272–1297): Essai de reconstitution*, ed. Henri Platelle, Collection de l'Ecole Française de Rome 195 (Rome: Ecole Française de Rome, 1994); on the formation of Louis' cult see M. Cecilia Gaposchkin, *The Making of Saint Louis: Kingship, Sanctity, and Crusade in the Later Middle Ages* (Ithaca: Cornell University Press, 2008); and eadem, ed., *Blessed Louis, the Most Glorious of Kings: Texts Relating to the Cult of Saint Louis of France* (Notre Dame, Ind.: University of Notre Dame Press, 2012). For political uses of Louis' memory, Colette Beaune, *The Birth of an Ideology: Myths and Symbols of Nation in Late-Medieval France*, trans. Susan Ross Huston, ed. Frederick L. Cheyette (Berkeley: University of California Press, 1991), 90–125; Daisy Delogu, *Theorizing the Ideal Sovereign: The Rise of the French Vernacular Royal Biography* (Toronto: University of Toronto Press, 2008), 22–57; Anja Rathmann-Lutz, *"Images" Ludwigs des Heiligen im Kontext dynastischer Konflikte des 14. und 15. Jahrhunderts* (Berlin: Akademie Verlag, 2010); and Anne-Hélène Allirot, *Filles de Roy de France: Princesses royales, mémoire de saint Louis et conscience dynastique (de 1270 à la fin du XIVe siècle)* (Turnhout: Brepols, 2010). There is some possibility that Louis was actually born in 1215, but 1214 seems more likely. See Tillemont, *Vie*, 1:422–26.

new mendicant orders—the Dominicans and the Franciscans—arrived in Paris, the great west façade of Notre Dame was erected, and the first statutes of the University of Paris were promulgated. More broadly, the barons of northern France had partnered with Pope Innocent III to invade the Languedoc under the banner of the Albigensian Crusade (started 1209; resumed in 1213), and Innocent's epoch-making Fourth Lateran Council in 1215 gave new definition to church doctrine and practice. On the wider political front, Alfonso VIII of Castile advanced Christian power on the Iberian peninsula with a decisive victory against the Almohad army at the battle of Las Navas de Tolosa in 1212; Henry III began his long but troubled reign (1216–72) in England; and Frederick II (d. 1250) loomed as the most impressive but controversial emperor of the Middle Ages. Within this larger context, the Capetian dynasty emerged as the preeminent political power in Europe, with Paris as its intellectual and cultural capital.[2]

Louis IX was the second son of Prince Louis (the future Louis VIII) and his princess, Blanche of Castile (d. 1252). The death of their oldest son Philip in 1218 left Louis as the new heir to the throne. Louis VIII was busy in these years running military campaigns in his father's name in England and in the south of France. Louis IX's formative influence seems to have been his strong-willed mother, Blanche, the Spanish princess who had come to France to marry Prince Louis in 1200 and whom much later Geoffrey of Beaulieu would describe as having the "the heart of a man" (ch. 4). She also seems to have been sincerely devout and to have instilled in the young Louis a set of religious values that would remain with him all his life. Later hagiographers noted that she recruited religious men of learning to oversee Louis' education, and Geoffrey of Beaulieu recounted the story that she would rather Louis die than that he commit a mortal sin (ch. 4).

Philip Augustus died in 1223 and was succeeded by Louis VIII. The new king was just thirty-six at the time and probably anticipated a long reign, but he ruled for only three years, dying unexpectedly from illness in 1226 as he was returning from a military campaign in the south. Louis IX was only twelve, and he was rushed to Reims to be crowned and anointed king

---

[2] For the period immediately before Louis's reign a perfect introduction is John W. Baldwin, *Paris, 1200* (Stanford, Calif.: Stanford University Press, 2010).

as soon as possible to secure the succession. Although the Capetian dynasty by this point was well entrenched,[3] the vacuum left by the succession of a young, untried king invited some northern princes, jealous of the growth of Capetian power under Philip Augustus and unhappy about the prominence of a foreign queen, to mount a rebellion. It was the foreign queen, Blanche, who quashed it, established a settlement, and then effectively ruled as regent during her son's minority. A series of religious foundations that were later credited to Louis were probably initiated by Blanche in this period—most notably the Cistercian monastery at Royaumont that later became one of Louis' favorite retreats; she must also have played a significant role in the early reception of the Franciscans and Dominicans in Paris.

In 1234 Louis married Marguerite of Provence, the count of Provence's eldest daughter. This alliance was desirable given the expansion of Capetian power south into Languedoc in the wake of the Albigensian Crusade. It was thus a political marriage, arranged by Blanche, but one which seems to have suited Louis. The sources sometimes suggest tensions in the relationship, but all in all it seems to have been a good match.[4] Marguerite bore Louis eleven children, took command and defended Damietta during Louis' captivity in Egypt (see below), and displayed moments of tenderness and affection toward the king, even if she was sometimes frustrated by his extreme expressions of piety.[5]

That piety demonstrates Louis' participation in (and later, as a saint, his representation of) some of the trends in thirteenth-century lay spirituality often associated with the rise of the mendicant movement, most importantly the Dominicans (*Fratres praedicatores*, Order of Preachers or Preaching Brothers) and Franciscans (*Fratres minores*, Brothers Minor

---

[3] Philip II was the first of the Capetian kings not to feel the need to "co-crown" his heir before he died. This was a practice established by the first of the Capetians, Hugh Capet (r. 987–96) when he crowned his heir Robert the Pious (r. 996–1031) before his own death, and followed by every later king up to Louis VII (d. 1180), who had Philip Augustus co-crowned in 1179.
[4] See Jordan, *Louis IX and the Challenge*, 5–8.
[5] Marguerite of Provence is not as well studied as she should be. The only full length biography, Gérard Sivéry, *Marguerite de Provence: Une reine au temps des Cathédrales* (Paris: Fayard, 1987), leaves a good deal of room for future research. Nancy Goldstone, *Four Queens: The Provençal Sisters Who Ruled Europe* (New York: Viking, 2007), is an engaging recent work of popular history.

or Lesser Brothers).[6] The wild success of the mendicant orders in the first half of the century grew out of broader shifts in lay religiosity characterized by a new valorization of personal penitence and humility and active participation in the world through charity, away from an older monastic model that prioritized contemplation and ascetic retreat from the secular world. These forces also affected the evolving portrait of lay sanctity. While clerics and monks continued to be revered as saints, now lay men and women who had embraced practices of self-denial and active charity were increasingly also considered worthy of sainthood. Louis was particularly attracted to and influenced by the new mendicant movement, and it is no accident that his earliest biographers, Geoffrey of Beaulieu and William of Chartres, were both Dominicans attached to his court.

Louis' religious ideals were also in evidence when, in 1238, he purchased from Baldwin II, emperor of Constantinople, the Crown of Thorns which Christ was believed to have worn during his Passion, and then in subsequent years other Passion relics. To house these relics he rebuilt the royal chapel in the palace on the Ile de la Cité in Paris, the Sainte-Chapelle. The Crown of Thorns was a potent symbol of Christic and sacral kingship, underscoring the Capetians' understanding that they were "Most Christian Kings," ruling by grace of God, heirs to the Old Testament kings such as David and Solomon, and that France was the new Israel. The Crown of Thorns represented at once the Passion of Christ, and thus the humility and humanity that resonated strongly with the spiritual trends of the thirteenth century, and also the kingship of Christ, from which the institution of kingship took its authority and sacral quality. These ideas were woven into the iconographic scheme of the Sainte-Chapelle, and the Crown of Thorns became central to the development of the mystique and authority of the king—what historians have come to call "the cult of kingship."[7]

---

[6] A good summary is found in André Vauchez, "Lay People's Sanctity in Western Europe: Evolution of a Pattern (Twelfth and Thirteenth Centuries)," in *Images of Sainthood in Medieval Europe*, ed. Renate Blumenfeld-Kosinski and Timea Szell (Ithaca: Cornell University Press, 1991), 21–33. Much of this is also treated in Vauchez, *Sainthood in the Later Middle Ages*, trans. Jean Birrell (Cambridge: Cambridge University Press, 1997), and idem, *The Laity in the Middle Ages: Religious Beliefs and Devotional Practices*, ed. Daniel Ethan Bornstein (Notre Dame, Ind.: University of Notre Dame Press, 1993).

[7] Daniel Weiss, *Art and Crusade in the Age of Saint Louis* (Cambridge: Cambridge University Press, 1998); Alyce Jordan, *Visualizing Kingship in the Windows of the Sainte-Chapelle*,

Figure 1. Louis IX carrying the Crown of Thorns, from the *Hours of Jeanne de Navarre*. BnF ms. nouv. ac. lat. 3145, fol. 102. Reproduced by permission of the Bibliothèque nationale de France.

International Center of Medieval Art Monograph Series (Turnhout: Brepols, 2002); Meredith Cohen, "An Indulgence for the Visitor: the Public at the Sainte-Chapelle of Paris," *Speculum* 83 (2008): 840–83; Beat Brenk, "The Sainte-Chapelle as a Capetian Political Program," in *Artistic Integration in Gothic Buildings*, ed. Virginia Raguin, Kathryn Brush, and Peter Draper (Toronto: University of Toronto Press, 1996), 195–212; Chiara Mercuri,

Another element of the prestige and identity of the kings of France was their support of the papacy's crusading goals. The crusades had begun in 1095 when Pope Urban II enjoined the warriors of Western Christendom to go to the Levant and recapture Jerusalem, and, in the language of the time, return Christ's inheritance to Christian rule. No king had participated in the First Crusade, though Hugh of Vermandois (d. 1101), brother of King Philip I of France (r. 1060–1108), did so. Beginning, however, with the (disastrous) Second Crusade (1145–49), which Louis VII (r. 1137–80) led along with Conrad III of Germany, the Capetians had been heavily involved in crusade leadership. Philip Augustus had gone on the Third Crusade (1189–92), participating in the siege of Acre, and Louis VIII had died during the last stages of the Albigensian Crusade. In their roles as the defenders of the Church and of Christendom, the kings of France had imbibed the ideal of crusade. So, in 1244, when Louis became violently ill, he made a vow to God that should he recover he would mount a new crusade. Blanche of Castile was aghast, and saw to it that he could legally renounce his vow, but Louis held steadfast, planning steadily over the next few years for what would be the largest and best-prepared crusade yet.[8] This vow was, in a sense, Louis' attempt to free himself from his mother's tutelage; yet he nevertheless put her in charge as regent when he left in 1248 and Blanche again proved herself an able ruler and sophisticated politician during her son's absence.[9]

In the event, the crusade was a catastrophe.[10] Louis left in 1248 from Aigues-Mortes on the southern shores of the newly incorporated

---

Corona di Cristo corona di re: La monarchia francese e la Corona di Spine nel Medioevo (Rome: Edizioni di storia e letteratura, 2004); Edina Bozoky, "Saint Louis, ordonnateur et acteur des rituels autour des reliques de la passion," in *La Sainte-Chapelle de Paris: Royaume de France ou Jérusalem céleste? Actes du colloque (Paris, Collège de France, 2001)* (Turnhout: Brepols, 2007), 19–34.

[8] The system of numbering the crusades breaks down after the Fifth Crusade. Some scholars join the crusade of Frederick II with the Fifth Crusade, while others separate it. Consequently, the crusade of 1249–50 is sometimes called the Sixth Crusade, and sometimes the Seventh.

[9] Jordan, *Louis IX and the Challenge*, 3–13, 105–33.

[10] On Louis' crusades, in addition to studies cited in note 1 see Joseph R. Strayer, "The Crusades of Louis IX," in *Medieval Statecraft and the Perspectives of History: Essays by Joseph R. Strayer* (Princeton, N.J.: Princeton University Press, 1971): 159–92, and the sources translated in Peter Jackson, *The Seventh Crusade, 1244–1254: Sources and Documents* (Aldershot: Ashgate, 2009).

province of the French kingdom, and wintered in Cyprus. The war council had decided to head for Cairo, the political and power center of the Ayyubid dynasty, which controlled the Levant and threatened the (exiled) kingdom of Jerusalem now stationed in Acre.[11] The crusading forces began by landing and taking the coastal city of Damietta. The city had been besieged during the Fifth Crusade (1218–21), but this time the garrison panicked and fled after an initial skirmish, delivering the city to the crusaders. Louis' army then turned south to head up the Nile toward Cairo. But at the city of Mansura, a fortified outpost protecting the capital, the vanguard, which was made up of the Templars and led by Louis' brother, Robert of Artois, was lured into the city and promptly cut down. The losses were immense, particularly because the Templars—the elite fighters of the crusading host—were wiped out. Louis was deeply grieved by the death of his younger brother, though others would later blame Robert for foolishly making the catastrophic decision that cost the crusade. Louis finally ordered retreat, and it was during this retreat that the crusaders met the Ayyubid forces at the battle of Fariskur (1250); the king took refuge in the house of a local Frenchwoman, presumably someone who had settled there after the Fifth Crusade, where his foes came and took him into captivity (6 April).

During a month of captivity, the negotiations for Louis' release got caught up in a dynastic rupture in Cairo. Louis and what was left of his army were ultimately ransomed for 400,000 bezants (about 200,000 *livres tournois* in French money, a vast sum only a little less than the crown's annual income)—though Louis later negotiated the remission of a second scheduled payment of the same amount.[12] After returning Damietta to Muslim control, Louis was allowed to leave Egypt and head for Acre. In August, he wrote a pained letter to his subjects, where he narrated the initial campaign, its failure, the negotiations, and his decision to remain in the Levant.[13] It is hard to imagine that this was anything but the biggest personal, spiritual, and political crisis of his entire life. He named his son,

---

[11] The Khorizman Turks, fighting in the service of the Ayyubid rulers of Egypt, had taken the city of Jerusalem in 1244.
[12] See Strayer, "The Crusades of Louis IX," 177–80.
[13] For the Latin text, see André Duchesne, *Historiae Francorum scriptores coaetanei ...*, 5 vols. (Paris: Cramoisy, 1636–49), 5:428–32. For English translations see Jean of Joinville,

to whom Marguerite of Provence had given birth in Damietta just days after Louis had been taken into captivity, Jean Tristan—Tristan meaning "sadness" or "grief"—because of the tragic circumstances of his birth.

Yet instead of returning to France, Louis remained for four years in the Levant to do what he could for the ailing kingdom of Jerusalem. His hagiographers would recall how he worked to ransom Christians still in captivity, to refortify cities that were in Christian hands, and otherwise to secure the rump kingdom's stability and security. In 1252 he received the news of his mother's death. In spite of his grief (touchingly recorded by Geoffrey of Beaulieu), he stayed on another year to finish the work he had begun, before setting sail for France.

By all accounts, Louis was a thoroughly changed man when he returned to France, profoundly moved by the events of the crusade, and deeply penitent for the remainder of his life.[14] His aim, it seems, was to perfect himself and his kingdom in order to become worthy of furthering God's cause with a new crusade. Failures in crusading had long been attributed to the sins of the crusaders themselves, and throughout the thirteenth century one of the pillars of preparing for crusading in the East had been the moral and penitential reform of Christians at home.[15] Upon returning to France in 1254, Louis quickly initiated a series of political reforms designed to ensure the purity and ethical integrity of the agents of the crown. The immediate cause was a series of reports he had received from his *enquêteurs* (investigators sent out prior to leaving in 1248 to settle any claims or complaints against the crown)[16] which included popular criticism of the king for exploiting his subjects and despoiling the Church of funds in his zeal to collect resources for the crusade. In response, Louis

---

The Life of St. Louis, trans. René Hague (New York: Sheed and Ward, 1955), 247–54; and Jackson, *The Seventh Crusade,* 108–14.

[14] Jordan, *Visualizing Kingship.* LeGoff, *Saint Louis,* has interpreted the crusades as less of a change than a point on a continuum, as a moment when earlier devotional attitudes were sharpened by the experience of the crusade.

[15] See for instance Christopher Tyerman, *God's War: A New History of the Crusades* (Cambridge, Mass.: Belknap Press of Harvard University Press, 2006), and for criticisms Elizabeth Siberry, *Criticism of Crusading, 1095–1274* (New York: Oxford University Press, 1985).

[16] A common part of leaving for crusading was making sure secular and moral debts were settled.

issued the Great Reform Ordinance of 1254 to insist on upright behavior from royal agents, and soon expanded it to include the moral conduct of his subjects, outlawing such stains as prostitution, gaming, and blasphemy.[17] He also followed a policy of peacemaking within Christendom, for instance, giving away lordship over substantial parts of his territory in the interest of peace.[18] Personally, he became increasingly ascetic and penitent, donating enormous sums of money as alms, supporting all kinds of religious foundations, and engaging in harsh and debilitating practices of personal asceticism and discipline. This stern bent was part of Louis's developing reputation for godly rule, even as it helped foster "a genuinely repressive regime based on a narrow sense of what was morally permissible."[19]

Much of his legislation after 1254 seems to have been guided by his ethical principles. In 1260 he sought to outlaw the duel, as part of his larger effort to staunch private warfare and bring conflict resolution into the king's court.[20] Around 1269 he issued a kingdom-wide ban on blasphemy. He also moved decisively against the Jews in France by reissuing and strengthening earlier legal restrictions on them and co-opting their wealth (though unlike his grandfather and grandson, he did not actually expel all Jews from his lands).[21] As with the crusade, from a modern perspective these anti-Jewish actions are deplorable. They were treated by some contemporaries, however, as causes of celebration and praise. William of Chartres, for example, clearly approved of Louis' prejudicial actions (par. 21).

---

[17] Louis Carolus-Barré, "La grande ordonnance de 1254 et la réforme de l'administration et la police du royaume," in *Septième centenaire de la mort de saint Louis: Actes des colloques de Royaumont et de Paris (21–27 mai 1970)* (Paris: Les Belles Lettres, 1976), 85–96.

[18] Two classic examples are the Treaty of Corbeil (1258) with James I of Aragon, and the Peace of Paris (1259) with Henry III of England. In both instances, Louis ceded territorial rights to lands within the kingdom in exchange for formal recognition of his suzerain overlordship.

[19] William Chester Jordan, *Men at the Center: Redemptive Governance Under Louis IX* (Budapest: Central European University Press, 2012), 101.

[20] William of Chartres, par. 24. J.-P. Babelon, "L'abolition du duel judiciaire," in *Le siècle de Saint Louis* (Paris: Hachette, 1970), 218–19. Louis also tried to limit private warfare in 1245 and 1257: *Ordonnances des roys de France de la troisième race, recueillies par ordre chronologique*, ed. Eusèbe Laurière et al., 21 vols., vol. 1 (Paris: Imprimerie royale, 1723), 56–58, 84–85.

[21] William Chester Jordan, *The French Monarchy and the Jews: From Philip Augustus to the Last Capetians* (Philadelphia: University of Pennsylvania Press, 1989).

Thus the king's rule in these years seems to have been animated by a sense of repentance, and a commitment to serve God, justice, and the obligations of Christian kingship. These obligations were essential to Louis' perspective on his own rule and his contemporaries' later perception of him as a saint, and in turn reflect a long literary tradition of ideal kingship. The argument had been developed since Saint Augustine that the institution of kingship in the first book of Samuel (1:8–10) was a response to the Fall (that is, the expulsion of Adam and Eve from the Garden of Eden). In Eden there had been no need for secular authority to restrain the impulses of men; only after the Fall had God allowed the Israelites to elevate a king. The first was Saul, then David, and then Solomon. The king's legitimacy lay in God's sanction, which was confirmed, following biblical practice, by the king's consecration with holy oil at the beginning of his reign.[22] In the ninth century, with the renewal of temporal authority under the Carolingians, a number of churchmen wrote about the qualities of the ideal king, arguing repeatedly for the critical necessity of the king's individual piety. In a corrupt world, secular leadership had to be utterly free of moral stain, pure and just in order to do the work of constraining rabid elements of society. The only way a king could function for good was to be himself beyond reproach, self-restrained, and conscious always of his own humility. The principle that the justice of the king was defined by his protection of the poor, the weak, and the Church was elaborated by these ecclesiastical writers in the ninth century and carried forward into the coronation liturgies, which included an oath sworn by the king or emperor. The oath changed somewhat over the course of the centuries, but when Louis himself was crowned and anointed, he probably vowed to protect and preserve the law, justice, and peace for both the Church of God and the people subject to him.[23] The theoretical writing on

---

[22] See 1 Kings 10.1–2; 2 Kings 5.5.

[23] It is not known precisely which coronation *ordo* was used for Louis in 1226. An *ordo* of about 1200 is probably closest to the text used in Louis' coronation; given that it took place so soon after his father's death, it is unlikely that there was time to revise the ceremony for the occasion. The next known liturgical rite, the "Ordo of Reims," is thought by its most recent editor to date to "ca. 1230." Richard A. Jackson, ed., *Ordines Coronationis Franciae: Texts and Ordines for the Coronation of Frankish and French Kings and Queens in the Middle Ages*, 2 vols. (Philadelphia: University of Pennsylvania Press, 1995–2000), 2:292. But in any event it includes only instructions for the ceremony and not the texts themselves (and is

kingship evolved alongside developments in political and social history, but always remained grounded in the framework of the king's personal virtue and self-governance inherited from the Carolingians. Louis himself commissioned a number of treatises on kingship by churchmen—all Dominicans and Franciscans—which, though making room for the newer exigencies of rulership, belonged to this long tradition.[24]

Perhaps our best evidence for Louis' understanding of Christian kingship is his own writings and legislation. The Great Reform Ordinance can be read as Louis' effort to institute the imperatives of Christian kingship in the practical terms of his own reign. And a few years later he wrote an extraordinary letter of instruction (known as the *Enseignements*) to his son and heir Philip, detailing the theoretical principles of Christian kingship.[25] Not surprisingly, many of his hagiographers (including Geoffrey of Beaulieu) included the *Enseignements* to demonstrate Louis' commitment to the sublime ideals of his own vocation. Fulfilling these ideals of defending the faith and protecting the weak were core elements of what defined the "just king," though as the mechanism of government and the dependence of royal administration on the workings of judicial and legal frameworks increased, the "just king" became increasingly tinged with the functions of the king doing justice—that is, the judicial functions of the crown. And, as the power of the king became more complex and buttressed by royal institutions, the old ideal of the just king took on newer qualities of rulership.

---

thus not strictly speaking an *ordo*). The next known *ordo*, that of 1250, was not intended for actual liturgical use, but rather as a kind of commemoration of the *sacre*, and includes the oath found in the *ordo* of 1200. The "Last Capetian Ordo" (ca. 1250–70) also includes the king's promise, which essentially duplicates the *ordo* of 1200. The texts and commentary can all be found in Jackson's collection.

[24] For analysis see Jacques Krynen, *L'Empire du roi—Idées et croyances politiques en France, XIIIe–XVe siècle* (Paris: Gallimard, 1993).

[25] See David O'Connell, *The Teachings of Saint Louis: A Critical Text* (Chapel Hill: University of North Carolina Press, 1972); for Louis' related set of instructions to his daughter Isabelle, see idem, *The Instructions of Saint Louis: A Critical Text*, North Carolina Studies in the Romance Languages and Literatures 216 (Chapel Hill: U.N.C. Department of Romance Languages, 1979). On the political impact of the *Enseignements* see most recently Frédérique Lachaud, "The Knowledge and Use of the 'Teachings of Saint Louis' in Fourteenth-Century England," in *Contact and Exchange in Later Medieval Europe: Essays in Honour of Malcolm Vale*, ed. Hannah Skoda, Patrick Lantschner, and R. L. J. Shaw (Woodbridge, UK: Boydell, 2012), 189–209.

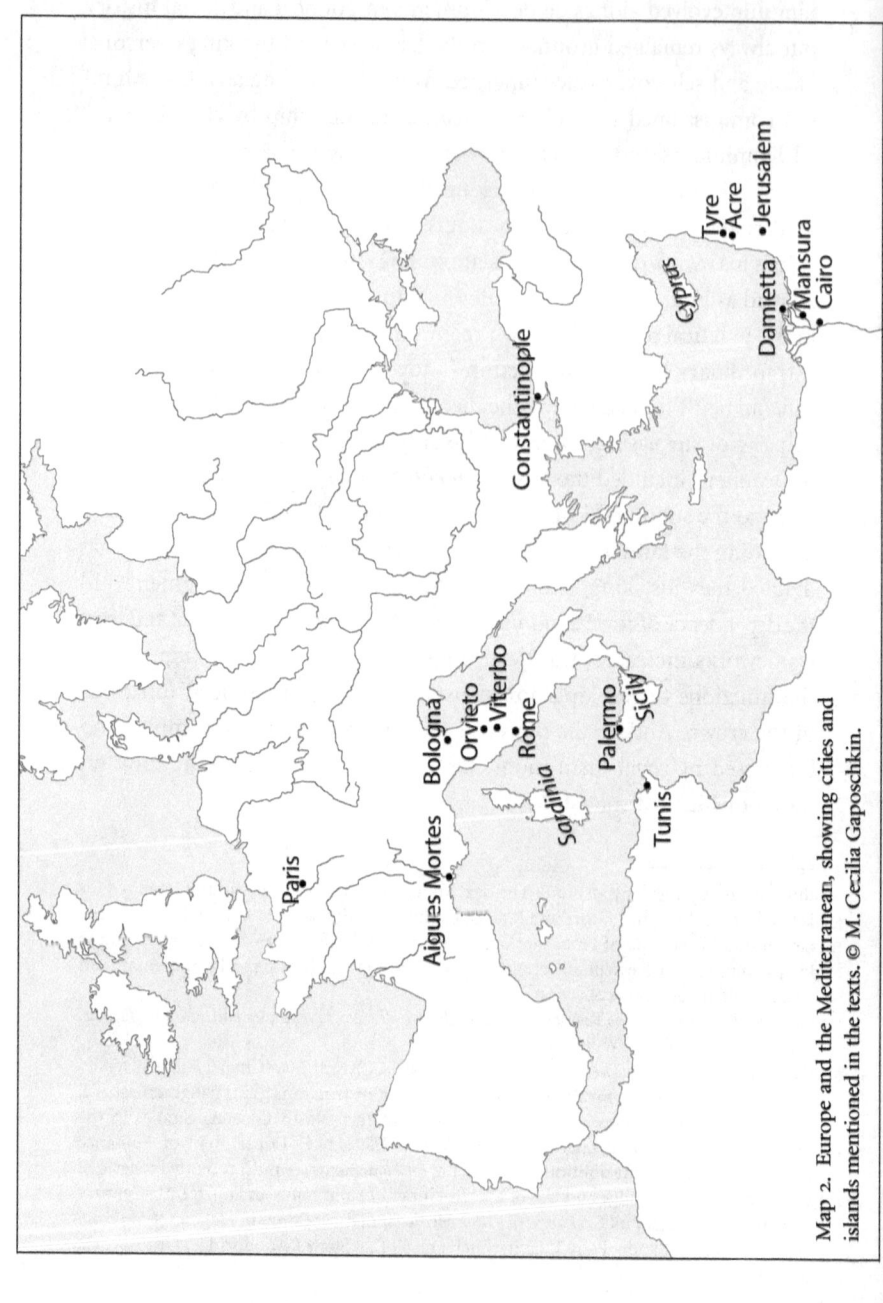

Map 2. Europe and the Mediterranean, showing cities and islands mentioned in the texts. © M. Cecilia Gaposchkin.

These imperatives of Christian kingship were certainly on Louis' mind in the years between his two crusades. Louis probably always planned to launch a second crusade. When he finally did take the Cross again in 1267, he faced a fair amount of resistance. Jean of Joinville—an enthusiastic participant in Louis' first crusade—would famously condemn all those who had encouraged the king's second crusading venture.[26] Geoffrey of Beaulieu takes great pains to explain the odd decision to go to Tunis instead of to Egypt or the Levant. This was a new strategy, and the reasons behind it remain a subject of historical debate.[27] In any event, the crusade sailed from Aigues-Mortes on 1 July 1270, landed in north Africa on 17 July, and set up camp outside Carthage. But the king, with much of the army, became gravely ill in the weeks following, and died on 25 August.

Louis' death threw the invading Christian forces into crisis, but his brother Charles of Anjou arrived the same day and assumed leadership of the crusade. Charles negotiated a settlement with the sultan of Tunis and the larger effort effectively dissipated. Louis' heart and entrails were given over to Charles to be buried in Palermo. But Louis had requested to be buried at the abbey church of Saint-Denis, the traditional burial place of French kings. And so his body was boiled down in order to separate the flesh (which, in the summer heat, could not be long preserved) from the bones. The latter were transported back to Saint-Denis and buried in the crossing at the abbey church, next to the tombs of Louis' father and grandfather which had been placed there as part of the grand dynastic burial scheme that had been concocted in the 1260s at Louis' command.[28] Only after he was canonized would his bones be moved to the high altar, from the fellowship of his secular family to that of the church's saints.

---

[26] Jean de Joinville, *Vie de Saint Louis*, ed. Jacques Monfrin (Paris: Garnier, 1995), pars. 734–37.
[27] Most recently, see Michael Lower, "Conversion and St Louis's Last Crusade," *Journal of Ecclesiastical History* 58 (2007): 211–31; idem, "Louis IX, Charles of Anjou, and the Tunis Crusade of 1270," in *Crusades—Medieval Worlds in Conflict*, ed. Thomas F. Madden, James L. Naus, and Vincent Ryan (Burlington, Vt.: Ashgate, 2010), 173–93.
[28] On the burial, see William Chester Jordan, *A Tale of Two Monasteries: Westminster and Saint-Denis in the Thirteenth Century* (Princeton, N.J.: Princeton University Press, 2009), 136–38. On the dynastic burial scheme, Georgia Sommers Wright, "The Royal Tomb Program in the Reign of St. Louis," *Art Bulletin* 56 (1974): 224–43; and Elizabeth A. R. Brown, *Saint-Denis: La basilique* (Paris: Zodiaque, 2001), 360–93.

The Challenges of Royal Canonization in the Thirteenth Century

The road to canonization, however, was long.[29] The Capetians very much wanted Louis' formal canonization, since it would cement several claims that were becoming increasingly central to their legitimacy and ideology: the claim of sacral kingship (not unique to the French kings but confirmed through the holy unction modeled on Old Testament king-making); the claim that they were "the Most Christian Kings" (*reges christianissimi*, a title employed by the Capetians in particular); and increasingly the claim that the Capetian lineage itself was holy.[30] And yet, despite the many examples of kings and other royalty elsewhere in Christendom who had been made saints—most galling, perhaps being

---

[29] William of Saint-Pathus narrates the canonization history in his prologue. The seminal institutional narrative of the process of Louis' canonization is Louis Carolus-Barré, "Les enquêtes pour la canonisation de Saint Louis de Grégoire X à Boniface VIII et la bulle *Gloria Laus*, du 11 août 1297," *Revue d'histoire de l'Eglise de France* 57 (1971): 19–31, which is included in the first chapter of Carolus-Barré, *Le procès*.

[30] A large literature exists on these themes. Most influential have been Joseph R. Strayer, "France: The Holy Land, the Chosen People, and the Most Christian King," in *Medieval Statecraft and the Perspectives of History*, 300–315; Andrew Lewis, *Royal Succession in Capetian France: Studies on Familial Order and the State*, Harvard Historical Studies 100 (Cambridge, Mass.: Harvard University Press, 1981); Marc Bloch, *The Royal Touch*, trans. J. E. Anderson (New York: Dorset Press, 1989); Elizabeth A. R. Brown, "La notion de la légitimité et la prophétie à la cour de Philippe Auguste," in *La France de Philippe Auguste: Le temps de mutations. Actes du Colloque international organisé par le C.N.R.S.* (Paris, 29 septembre—4 octobre 1980), ed. Robert-Henri Bautier (Paris: Editions du Centre Nationale de la Recherche Scientifique, 1982); eadem, "La généalogie capétienne dans l'historiographie du Moyen Age: Philippe le Bel, le reniement du *reditus* et la création d'une ascendance carolingienne pour Hugues Capet," in *Religion et culture autour de l'an mil: Royaume capétien et Lotharingie: Actes du colloque Hugues Capet 987–1987, La France de l'an Mil, Auxerre, 26 et 27 juin 1987—Metz, 11 et 23 septembre 1987*, ed. Dominique Iogna-Prat and Jean-Charles Picard (Paris: Editions Picard, 1990); Percy Ernst Schramm, *Der König von Frankreich: Das Wesen der Monarchie vom 9. zum 16. Jahrhundert, ein Kapitel aus der Geschichte des abendländischen Staates*, 2 vols. (Weimar: H. Böhlaus Nachfolger, 1960); Ernst H. Kantorowicz, *Laudes Regiae: A Study in Liturgical Acclamations and Mediaeval Ruler Worship*, ed. G. H. Guttridge, R. J. Kerner, and F. L. Paxson, University of California Publications in History (Berkeley: University of California Press, 1946); Kantorowicz, *The King's Two Bodies: A Study in Mediaeval Political Theology* (Princeton, N.J.: Princeton University Press, 1957); John W. Baldwin, *The Government of Philip Augustus: Foundations of French Royal Power in the Middle Ages* (Berkeley: University of California Press, 1986), 355–93. Most recently see Allirot, *Filles de roy de France*, and Julien Théry, "Le pionnier de la théocratie royale: Guillaume de Nogaret et les conflits de Philippe le Bel avec la papauté," in *Guillaume de Nogaret: Un Languedocien au service de la monarchie capétienne*, ed. Bernard Moreau (Nîmes: Lucie-éditions, 2012), 101–27.

Edward the Confessor of England (d. 1066)—the Capetians could not boast a saint among them.[31] Efforts had earlier been made for Philip Augustus's canonization, but they did not go far, in part due to his long-running battle with the papacy over the legitimacy of his marriages.[32] Nor did moves toward having Louis' sister, Isabelle of France (d. 1270), canonized find success.[33] By the thirteenth century it had become increasingly difficult for any king to achieve canonization since, in the wake of the Gregorian reforms, the papacy's enthusiasm for legitimizing the holy quality of a secular ruler had been dampened. In fact, no king had been canonized since 1161.[34] Yet Louis had earned a widespread reputation during his lifetime as pious, just, and even "saintly," and there could be no better confirmation of the dynasty's special role in God's order than for the most respected king in Europe to be formally recognized as a saint.

Thus from the moment of Louis' death the royal entourage began to make concerted claims for his sanctity. The earliest evidence comes from a series of letters written following the king's death. On 4 September the royal cleric Peter of Condé wrote from North Africa to the treasurer of Saint-Frambaut in Senlis (a position earlier held by William of Chartres) and related how "our lord king Louis of most faithful memory gave up his most holy spirit."[35] Then on 12 September Philip, the king designate, sent

---

[31] On the earlier tradition of saint kings and saint queens, see Robert Folz, *Les saints rois du Moyen Age en occident (Vie–XIIIe siècles)*, Subsidia hagiographica 68 (Brussels: Société des Bollandistes, 1984); idem, *Les saintes reines du Moyen Age en Occident: VIe–XIIIe siècles*, Subsidia hagiographica 76 (Brussels: Société des Bollandistes, 1992); Gábor Klaniczay, *Holy Rulers and Blessed Princesses: Dynastic Cults in Medieval Central Europe*, trans. Eva Pálmai, ed. Lyndal Roper and Chris Wickham, Past and Present Publications (Cambridge: Cambridge University Press, 2002).
[32] Jacques LeGoff, "Le dossier de sainteté de Philippe Auguste," *L'Histoire* 100 (1987): 22–29.
[33] Sean L. Field, *Isabelle of France: Capetian Sanctity and Franciscan Identity in the Thirteenth Century* (Notre Dame, Ind.: University of Notre Dame Press, 2006); idem, *The Writings of Agnes of Harcourt: The Life of Isabelle of France and the Letter on Louis IX and Longchamp* (Notre Dame, Ind.: University of Notre Dame Press, 2003); Allirot, *Filles de roy de France*, 255–92; William Chester Jordan, "Isabelle of France and Religious Devotion at the Court of Louis IX," in *Capetian Women* (New York: Palgrave, 2003), ed. Kathleen Nolan, 209–23.
[34] Or 1165, if one accepts the legitimacy of the canonization by an antipope of Charlemagne. Edward the Confessor had been canonized by Alexander III on 7 February 1161. See Robert Folz, *The Coronation of Charlemagne, 25 December 800* (London: Routledge & Kegan Paul, 1974).
[35] "Volo enim, quod sciatis, quod fidelissimae memoriae dominus Rex noster Ludovicus die Lunae in crastino beati Bartholomaei circa horam nonam sanctissimum emisit spiritum."

his own letter (discussed below) to all the churches of France, showering praise on his pious father and asking for prayers for his soul "though many believe it needs no outside intercession." On 24 September, Louis' son-in-law Thibaut of Navarre (husband of Louis' daughter Isabelle) wrote in French to Cardinal Eudes of Châteauroux, Louis' long-time associate and companion (as papal legate) on his first crusade,[36] reporting that Louis had prayed for his people for twenty hours straight as he lay dying. Thibaut's testimony agrees with Geoffrey of Beaulieu's and William of Chartres' later recollections, that Louis' final prayers were from the offices of Saint Denis and Jacob the Apostle and that his very last words were drawn from Psalms 5 and 137. But Thibaut also specified that Louis called on Saint Geneviève, and the Latin phrases Thibaut provides in his otherwise vernacular letter make it clear that Louis recited his prayers in that language. Moreover, Thibaut wished Eudes to "know that we and all those who are in the army have very great hope that his prayers will benefit us with Our Lord ...," and that the archdeacon of Palermo had already reported that miracles had begun to occur there at the burial place of Louis' heart.[37] In a very tangible way, family members expressed their

---

Printed in Luc d'Achery, ed., *Spicilegium sive Collectio veterum aliquot scriptorum qui in Galliae bibliothecis delituerant*, vol. 3 (Paris: Montalant, 1722; reprint, Farnborough: Gregg, 1968), 667. On this group of letters see Jean Richard, "Un recueil de lettres sur la huitième croisade," *Bulletin de la Société des Antiquaires de France* (1960): 182–87; Louis Carolus-Barré, "Un recueil épistolaire composé à Saint-Denis sur la Croisade (1270–1271)," *Comptes-rendus des séances de l'Académie des Inscriptions et Belles-Lettres* 110, no. 4 (1966): 555–68; and now importantly Xavier Hélary, "'L'épistolaire politique' en XIIIe siècle: Autour d'un recueil de lettres relatives à la croisade de Tunis (1270)," forthcoming in *L'Epistolaire politique*, ed. Laurent Vissière and Bruno Dumézil (Paris: Presses de l'Université Paris-Sorbonne). We thank Prof. Hélary for a prepublication copy of this work. For further use of these letters, see Richard Sternfeld, *Ludwigs des Heiligen Kreuzzug nach Tunis 1270 und die Politik Karls I. von Sizilien* (Berlin: E. Ebering, 1896); and more briefly Jordan, *A Tale of Two Monasteries*, 132–34, 146–47.

[36] For the career of Eudes (who reappears in several of our texts) see Alexis Charansonnet, "Du Berry en Curie: La carrière du cardinal Eudes de Châteauroux (1190?–1273) et son reflet dans sa prédication," *Revue d'histoire de l'Eglise de France* 86 (2000): 5–37.

[37] The text is printed by Antoine-Jean Lettrone in "Sur l'authenticité d'une lettre de Thibaud, roi de Navarre, relative à la mort de Saint Louis," *Bibliothèque de l'Ecole des chartes* 5 (1843–44): 105–17; for corrections to Lettrone's understanding of the manuscript tradition see Leopold Delisle, *Instructions adressées par le comité des travaux historiques et scientifiques aux correspondants du ministère de l'Instruction publique et des Beaux-arts, Littérature latine et histoire du moyen-âge* (Paris: Ernest Leroux, 1890), 72–73. Lettrone's edition is from Le

belief that Louis was already at the right hand of God, ready to act as advocate and intercessor for those who offered supplication and prayer. These sentiments were quickly echoed by officials back in France. For example, in an undated letter probably composed in the last months of 1270, the regents Matthew of Vendôme (abbot of Saint-Denis) and Simon of Nesle wrote to Philip acknowledging news of Louis' death and urging the new king to return quickly to his realm.[38] As a preamble, they included profuse praise of the late king, who "with the help of divine grace," had extended and preserved and solidified his kingdom, which was "blessed by the Lord."[39]

The royal entourage, however, knew these claims would have to be confirmed by the papacy on the evidence of popular sentiment and documented miracles. Sanctity was in a sense an objective quality—in its purest meaning a saint was someone who had led such a Christian life that he or she immediately entered the court of heaven and could thus intercede with God for his or her devotees on earth. But it was also a status established by the Church. By 1270 only the pope could confer official canonization, which had come to involve a decades-long process of collecting and testing the evidence of sanctity.[40] Successful candidates for canonization needed a strong and deep-pocketed lobby committed to seeing the process through.

Canonization required proof both of the quality of the saint's life and evidence of his or her miracles.[41] These were documented by a formal inquiry (*inquisitio*) which was itself commissioned by the pope upon the receipt of reliable reports of popular veneration. In general, those reports would be relayed to the papacy through the local authorities, usually

---

Nain de Tillemont's notebook B, BnF ms. fr. 13747, fol. 483, which, as Delisle demonstrated, was in turn copied from the manuscript now known as BnF ms. lat. 9376.
[38] On Simon see Jordan, *Men at the Center*, 71–99; on Matthew, see idem, *A Tale of Two Monasteries*.
[39] D'Achery, *Spicilegium*, 3:670.
[40] Vauchez, *Sainthood in the Later Middle Ages*. For the institutional history of canonization, see Eric Waldram Kemp, *Canonization and Authority in the Western Church* (London: Oxford University Press, 1948; reprint, New York: 1980).
[41] Kemp, *Canonization and Authority*, 82–106; Vauchez, *Sainthood in the Later Middle Ages*, 33–84. For a recent wider survey see Ronald C. Finucane, *Contested Canonizations: The Last Medieval Saints, 1482–1523* (Washington, D.C.: Catholic University of America Press, 2011), 13–32.

the bishop. If the pope was amenable, he established an inquest at the place of the emerging cult in order to collect "direct evidentiary proof" of the candidate's sanctity and miracles.[42] In this way, the process took on a quasi-legal character, in which "inquisitors" took depositions and questioned witnesses, who had to be trustworthy and take an oath for their testimony to be valid. Other documentation might be proffered to make the case, including *vitae*—saints' lives such as the two presented here—written to showcase the nature and quality of the saint's comportment or manner of living. These materials were collected and made available to the papal curia. Only then, if the pope so deemed, would the new saint be formally canonized with a bull disseminated throughout Christendom instructing churches to add his or her commemoration to the calendar.

Geoffrey of Beaulieu, William of Chartres, and the "Dominican Moment," 1270–1276

The first two properly hagiographic lives of Louis were by two Dominicans who had served the king for at least two decades.[43] Geoffrey of Beaulieu and William of Chartres knew each other well, and William self-consciously constructed his *vita* as an addendum to Geoffrey's. Moreover, a third early Dominican text, a letter from the Provincial Chapter of France to the College of Cardinals, shares ideas and phrases with both early Dominican *vitae*. Although the three texts also diverge in important thematic and ideological ways, taken together they represent a concerted effort by the Dominicans of France to record their memories of the king. By the middle of the thirteenth century Dominicans (and Franciscans) were acting as Louis's *enquêteurs* and royal confessors, and exerting increasing influence as masters of theology at the University of Paris and as popular preachers. These early writings about Louis' life highlight the fact that the

---

[42] Vauchez, *Sainthood in the Later Middle Ages*, 39.
[43] On Dominicans as hagiographers (though with no reference to Geoffrey and William), see most recently Agnès Dubreil-Arcin, *Vies de saints, légendes de soi: L'écriture hagiographique dominicaine jusqu'au* Speculum sanctorale *de Bernard Gui (†1331)* (Turnhout: Brepols, 2011).

Order of Preachers provided some of the men closest to the man destined for sainthood.[44]

Little is known about Geoffrey of Beaulieu or William of Chartres before they sailed in 1248 with Louis on his first crusade. Geoffrey's origins are obscure (there are many towns called Beaulieu in France) but presumably he was from northern France[45] and entered the Order of Preachers before 1248. As a young Dominican, he would have received a solid education in arts and theology.[46] Indeed, a certain intellectual sophistication is apparent in the way his *vita* would echo Peter Lombard at one point and allude to a logical maxim of Aristotle at another (chs. 28, 42). William's family origins were presumably in Chartres.[47] He may perhaps have been the "William of Chartres, cleric, scholar at Verceil" who stood surety for other French scholars studying in Lombardy in 1231,[48] and was surely a secular cleric in the king's employ by 1248.

---

[44] Jordan, *Men at the Center*, 17–18, briefly treats William of Chartres as typical of the figures in Louis IX's inner circle.

[45] Quétif and Echard, *SOP*, 1:170 (based on report by Nicolas le Febvre in his 1637 *Praedicator Carnuteus*), considered the possibility that Geoffrey was from Chartres, because his death was recorded in a martyrology from the Dominican house there (on le Febvre's notes see Auguste Molinier, *Obituaires de la diocèse de Sens*, vol. 2 [Paris: Imprimerie nationale, 1906], 310; indeed William's death was also recorded in a breviary of Dominican usage from Poissy, see ibid.). Carolus-Barré agrees in his "notice biographique" in *Le procès*, 209–10. But Daunou, "Geoffroi de Beaulieu," *HLF* 19 (1838): 234–37, raised justifiable doubts. Xavier de la Selle, *Le service des âmes à la cour: Confesseurs et aumôniers des rois de France du XIIIe au XVe siècle* (Paris: Ecole des chartes, 1995), 261, says Geoffrey's origins were in the diocese of Rouen, apparently following the Abbé Oroux, *Histoire ecclésiastique de la Cour de France*, vol. 1 (Paris: Imprimerie royale, 1771), 295, who gave no evidence for this claim, which was also repeated in Marie-Dominique Chapotin, *Histoire des dominicains de la province de France. Le siècle des fondations* (Rouen: Cagniard, 1898), 336. M.-H. Laurent, *Le bienheureux Innocent V (Pierre de Tarentaise) et son temps* (Vatican City: Biblioteca Apostolica Vaticana, 1947), 82, calls Geoffrey "bourguignon." Kaeppeli, probably wisely, simply says Geoffrey was from the Dominican province of France. Kaeppeli, *SoP*, 1:15.

[46] See M. Michèle Mulchahey, *"First the Bow is Bent in Study": Dominican Education before 1350* (Toronto: Pontifical Institute of Mediaeval Studies, 1998).

[47] Quétif and Echard, *SOP*, 1:381; Daunou, "Guillaume de Chartres, historien," *HLF* 19 (1838): 359.

[48] Heinrich Denifle, *Die Universitäten des Mittelalters bis 1400*, vol. 1 (Berlin: Weidmannsche Buchhandlung, 1885), 292 n. 278. Louis Carolus-Barré, "Guillaume de Chartres clerc du roi, frère prêcheur, ami et historien de saint Louis," *Collection de l'Ecole française de Rome* 204 (1995): 51, accepted this as a reference to our William. This short article is the most detailed biographical look at William's career, and we are indebted to it as a starting point; unfortunately its posthumous publication did not include any documentation or notes, but

Both men entered the king's inner circle during the course of the crusade. William of Chartres actually endured captivity by the king's side in spring 1250, remaining "almost always with him at all times and places" (pars. 6–7). Perhaps in gratitude for this loyalty, Louis made a gift of rents to William's two sisters and their eldest sons in March 1251.[49] Geoffrey, for his part, was by Louis' side at Jaffa in the Holy Land when Louis received the news of his mother's death at the end of 1252 (ch. 28). He was surely acting as Louis' confessor by this point. He himself states that he held the position of confessor "for twenty years or so" (ch. 5), indicating that he assumed the office at least by 1250, if not when the crusade sailed in 1248.

Geoffrey is in fact the first man who can be identified as holding an acknowledged, long-term office as confessor to any king of France, beginning a string of Dominicans who filled this position.[50] Before this, it would simply have been impossible for a churchman to have written a life of a French king based on the kind of intimate, detailed confessions that Louis must have made to Geoffrey over the course of two decades. Indeed, many of Geoffrey's stories involve Louis' relationship to unnamed "confessors" (particularly in chs. 10, 16–17, 21) and in at least some of these cases Geoffrey is surely invoking his own testimony. William of Chartres' recollections are equally personal and detailed, but necessarily less concerned with spiritual unburdenings.

Between the crusades, various bits of evidence offer glimpses of Geoffrey and William acting as trusted royal agents. William was made a canon of Saint-Quentin by the time the royal entourage returned to France in autumn 1254. Over a period of months in 1254–55 "lord William of Chartres, canon of Saint-Quentin" acted on royal behalf to buy up houses and properties on the Left Bank that then went to help with the foundation of the Sorbonne (in one of these documents William is labeled "chaplain of the lord king of France").[51] "Lord" William of Chartres

---

we have been able to trace and augment most of the biographical data given by Carolus-Barré.
[49] Carolus-Barré, "Guillaume de Chartres," 51. In this instance we rely on Carolus-Barré, having been unable to verify his source.
[50] De la Selle, *Le service des âmes à la cour*, 96.
[51] Palémon Glorieux, *Aux origines de la Sorbonne*, vol. 2 (Paris: Vrin, 1965), no. 87 (July 1254, sale to "Domino Guillelmo de Carnoto canonico sancti Quintini ... ad opus cuiusdam amici sui"). Similar in documents nos. 90 to 104 (all November 1254), nos. 109–11, 113–33,

also appears in the fragmentary royal records that survive for 1255–56, receiving funds for a small horse, a new cape, and other unspecified expenses.[52] Geoffrey, in his role as royal confessor, helped with the king's charitable bequests and hence appears repeatedly in these accounts. He dispensed royal alms in July 1256 to the *Filles-Dieu* in Domfront, to the nuns of "Beaulieu" (in Paris), and to "three poor women" in Paris. He distributed funds to the beguines of Senlis in September (to allow them to buy a house), and traveled on unspecified royal business to Peronne the same month.[53] When Geoffrey would later write about Louis' charity and support for communities of beguines, other semireligious institutions, and the poor—all women here, interestingly—he was working from first-hand experience.

By the late 1250s Geoffrey and William were advancing into ever more rarified political circles. As William would later recall, Louis awarded him a remunerative position as treasurer of a church (par. 11), in fact Saint-Frambaut in Senlis. William must have gained this position by early 1259, because in February of that year "William of Chartres, treasurer of Saint-Frambaut in Senlis" is mentioned in a royal letter as having been empowered (with Ralph the treasurer of Saint-Martin of Tours) to act as a royal arbitrator in a dispute over rents involving William, bishop of Olenos and former abbot of Cluny, Yves the new abbot of Cluny, and the prior and convent of Lihons.[54] In 1261 "lord W. of Chartres, priest" was part of a group of royal counselors that adjudicated a petition from the brothers of Grandmont asking that the king restore to them

---

and 135–36 (December 1254 to January 1255). No. 133, however, refers uniquely to "domino Mattheo et domino Guillermo de Carnoto capellanis domini regis Francie," removing any doubt about whether this "lord" and canon of Saint-Quentin is the same as the royal clerk. For other transactions involving William see ibid., no. 144, and Léon Brièle, *Archives de l'Hôtel-Dieu de Paris* (1157–1300) (Paris: Imprimerie nationale, 1894), 307 (nos. 610 and 611) for sale of two properties on the Petit-Pont in December 1254 handled by lord William of Chartres, canon of Saint-Quentin.
[52] *RHGF*, 21:323, 331, 343, 354, 355, 357, 368, 391, 392.
[53] See the "Tabulae ceratae Johannis Sarraceni, in thesauro cartarum servatae," edited ibid., 355–57, nos. 206, 207, 208.
[54] Alexandre Bruel, ed., *Recueil des chartes de l'abbaye de Cluny,* vol. 6 (Paris: Imprimerie nationale, 1903), 467–70, no. 5004. The surviving document is a letter from Louis IX to the *bailli* of Amiens explaining the settlement.

certain rights in the bois de Vincennes.⁵⁵ And on 6 July 1262, at the time of the marriage of the future Philip III to Isabelle of Aragon, "William of Chartres, treasurer of Saint-Frambaut of Senlis" subscribed to the act pledging friendship between Louis IX and James of Aragon.⁵⁶ In the latter two cases William's name appears at or near the end of an impressive group of ecclesiastical and secular leaders, headed both times by Eudes Rigaud, the Franciscan archbishop of Rouen.

Geoffrey of Beaulieu was also rising in reputation by this time. In 1264 Pope Urban IV appointed him to a three-man commission (with the bishop of Troyes and the abbot of Marmoutier) charged with resolving a dispute between the abbot of Cîteaux and other leaders of the Cistercian Order.⁵⁷ Perhaps he was chosen in order to assure Louis IX's cooperation in making peace, since in May the king called the abbots concerned to Paris. In July Geoffrey was still participating in these talks (at Langres), but he was not present when the other commissioners wrote up their report, being called away to the king's side at Boulogne-sur-mer.⁵⁸ Indeed, the sense that Louis liked to keep Geoffrey near at hand is reinforced by a homely anecdote later reported by William of Saint-Pathus (in his own later life of Saint Louis, written 1302–3), which mentions Louis' desire for

---

⁵⁵ Le Comte Beugnot, *Les Olim, ou registres des arrêts rendus par la cour du roi*, vol. 1 (Paris: Imprimerie royale, 1839), 503–4; Ch.-V. Langlois, *Textes relatifs à l'histoire du Parlement depuis les origines jusqu'en 1311* (Paris: Picard, 1888), 63. The initial is actually "G." presumably for "Guillaume." The label "presbyter" is unique in these sources, but because this "dominus G. de Carnoto" occupies the same place in the list as the William of Chartres, treasurer of Saint-Frambaut in the next document (1262), they seem to be the same person. In turn, the documents related to purchases for the Sorbonne show that the man referred to as the canon of Saint-Quentin and royal chaplain is later labeled treasurer of Saint-Frambaut. Thus all of these references must be to the same man. It is true that a secular nobleman "William of Chartres, knight" appears in other contemporary documents, but all of the cases above clearly involve the clerk in the king's employ. In reexamining this question, we have reached the same conclusion as Carolus-Barré.
⁵⁶ Elie Berger, ed., *Layettes du Trésor des Chartes*, vol. 4 (Paris: Plon-Nourrit et Cie, 1902), 43, no. 4775, where last on the list of signers is "Guillelmus de Carnoto thesaurarius Sancti Frambaldi Silvanectensis."
⁵⁷ Jean Guirard, ed., *Registres d'Urbain IV*, vol. 2 (Paris: Thorin et fils, 1901), pp. 415–18, no. 862 (dated 15 March 1264).
⁵⁸ The episode is explicated in Laurent, *Le bienheureux Innocent V*, 81–83. For the resolution of this affair see Edouard Jordan, *Les registres de Clément IV (1265–1268)*, vol. 1 (Paris: Thorin et fils, 1893), 26, no. 114.

Geoffrey of Beaulieu's company when taking a simple walk in the woods near the Loire in 1260.[59] It was probably in 1264 that William of Chartres abandoned his promising secular career to enter the Order of Preachers. William would later recall that Louis had predicted this.[60] As Louis Carolus-Barré has noted, in joining the Dominicans William was turning his back on a clear path to ecclesiastical advancement, since his predecessor and two immediate successors as treasurer of Saint-Frambaut all became bishops of Evreux.[61] Even after converting to the Dominican life, however, William remained attached to the royal court—possible since leading Dominicans moved easily between the Left Bank house of Saint-Jacques and the royal palace a short walk away on the Ile de la Cité. Not only is William's continuing association with the king clear from the recollections contained in his *vita*, but on 30 December 1269, as Louis prepared to depart on crusade, "Brother" William of Chartres helped produce a royal letter to the bishop of Clermont sending him relics of the Passion and asking for prayers in exchange.[62]

---

[59] WSP, *Vie*, 83–84. In this tale, the king was at Châteauneuf-sur-Loire in September 1260 and wanted to go amuse himself (*esbatre*) in the woods, so he summoned Geoffrey to accompany him. Geoffrey declined because he was waiting for a group of Dominicans coming up the Loire by boat to Orléans for a provincial chapter meeting, so Louis insisted on accompanying Geoffrey on the long walk to the river and on then lodging the brothers at his own expense. William of Saint-Pathus mentions Geoffrey of Beaulieu by name numerous times, but this seems to be the only independent anecdote that is not simply drawn from Geoffrey's own text. The anecdote is dated to 1260 in Chapotin, *Histoire des dominicains de la province de France*, 498, and Carolus-Barré, "Le procès," 253.

[60] A document issued by Louis IX in May 1263 refers to the house near the "Palatium Termarum" that "our beloved and faithful clerk, William of Chartres, treasurer of Saint-Frambaut of Senlis, holds from us." See Glorieux, *Aux origines de la Sorbonne*, vol. 2, no. 219. See also no. 231, dated December 1263, showing William still in possession of this house. By August 1267, however, the house was referred to as "formerly belonging to William of Chartres, formerly treasurer of Saint-Frambaut in Senlis" (ibid., no. 266). Thus these documents show that William left the secular world between 1264 and August 1267. William later remarked (par. 11) that Louis' prediction that he would remain treasurer for only five or six years had come true, since he entered the Dominican Order five and a half years later. If this is taken literally, it would suggest that William became treasurer just before February 1259 (the first documented use of that label) and entered the Dominican Order in 1264 (since he was still being called treasurer in December 1263).

[61] Carolus-Barré, "Guillaume de Chartres," 52.

[62] "Per fratrem G. de Carnoto" is written on the fold at the bottom of the parchment, indicating he prepared the letter in the king's name. See L. Delisle, "Lettre de Saint Louis expédiée par Guillaume de Chartres," *Bibliothèque de l'Ecole des chartes* 65 (1904): 310–12.

Geoffrey and William witnessed first-hand the king's preparations for his second crusade, with Geoffrey in particular offering an insider's account of the factors that contributed to the controversial decision to attack Tunis (ch. 41). Both men sailed with the crusade, and thus were there for the landing in North Africa and the disastrous events of late summer 1270. When the king fell ill, both were at his side. Louis' son Jean Tristan died on 3 August, but the news was kept from the ailing king for a week until at last, at the king's insistence, Geoffrey himself told him.[63] William of Chartres assumed guardianship of the royal seal when the archdeacon of Paris died on 20 August.[64] As it became clear that the king himself was nearing the end, Geoffrey offered him last rites, recited psalms with him, and heard him sing dying prayers to Saint Denis and Saint James (ch. 44). William was also at hand, and therefore later able to confirm the outlines of Geoffrey's account while adding other details about Louis' last words, prayers, and actions.

As Philip III took up the obligations of rule, he turned to these men whom his father had trusted, choosing them (along with the Franciscan Jean of Mons) to return to France bearing the letter dated 12 September that announced Louis' death and asked religious houses of the kingdom to pray for his soul.[65] Geoffrey reports (ch. 46) that Philip had considered sending Louis' bones with them as well, but thought better of it after consulting Charles of Anjou, preferring to keep this (assumed) source of holy power close to the army while it remained in North Africa. Geoffrey and William were evidently also entrusted with three further letters that Philip dated 12 September. One was to Matthew of Vendôme and Simon of Nesle, confirming their continued authority to act as regents until Philip's return, and instructing them to continue using the same seal with only the name of the reigning king changed. The second informed all the kingdom's ecclesiastic and secular leaders of this fact.[66] The third

---

The document is now AD du Puy-de-Dôme, 3 G Suppl. 38a. Reproductions can be seen ibid., and Carolus-Barré, "Guillaume de Chartres."

[63] This fact was reported in a letter of 21 August 1270 from Peter of Condé to Matthew of Vendôme. Edited in Delisle, *Littérature latine et histoire du moyen age*, 73–75.

[64] Ibid.

[65] Jean was confessor to Louis' wife Marguerite of Provence, and may perhaps have acted as Louis' confessor too.

[66] D'Achery, *Spicilegium*, 3:666.

was again addressed to Matthew and Simon directly and noted that "full assurance will be given to you concerning our new seal by means of our beloved brother William of Chartres and our other letters."[67] On 4 October, Philip wrote again to Mathew and Simon, repeating his earlier instructions because, he said, he feared that Geoffrey and William might have been impeded in their travels.[68] Philip's uncle Charles of Anjou, king of Sicily, had meanwhile arranged for Louis IX's heart and internal organs to be buried at Palermo, and when Geoffrey and William passed through Palermo on their return journey sometime shortly after September 12, Geoffrey reported hearing of miracles already occurring in that spot (ch. 47).[69]

Geoffrey and William left North Africa well before hostilities had ended (a treaty was signed 28 October), and thus avoided the trail of death that followed the French back across the Mediterranean. By the time Philip III wrote again to Matthew of Vendôme from Italy on 11 February 1271, he had lost not only his father and his brother, but also his brother-in-law Thibaut of Navarre (at Tripani in Sicily in November) and his own wife Isabelle of Aragon (at Cosenza in Calabria, 28 January 1271), who was injured falling off a horse and died after giving birth to a stillborn son.[70] The new king reached Viterbo in March, where the College of Cardinals had been already for two years laboring to elect a new pope following the death of Clement IV.

As the royal entourage made its way across the Alps, Geoffrey and William must have been occupied with delivering the request for prayers on behalf of Louis IX's soul "to the various parts of the realm" as Philip had commanded. For instance, a letter dated 6 May 1271 from the prior of the Cistercian abbey of Vaux-de-Cernay (some fifty kilometers southwest

---

[67] Ibid., 667.
[68] Ibid., 666.
[69] Geoffrey does not say he was with Philip III when the king returned with Louis' bones, though he gives a vivid depiction of the crowds that came to witness the procession across Italy. The inclusion of a new chapter heading (47*bis*) in our translation, found only in BnF ms. lat. 18335, helps to emphasize the distinction between what Geoffrey actually saw and what he merely described. Natalis de Wailly, in defending Geoffrey's overall reliability, suggested the possibility that Geoffrey had gone to Paris, returned to North Africa, and then passed through Sicily with the royal entourage. See "Examen critique de la *Vie de saint Louis* par Geoffroy de Beaulieu," *Bibliothèque de l'Ecole des chartes* 5 (1844): 205–31. There is really no evidence, however, for this idea of a return to Africa.
[70] D'Achery, *Spicilegium*, 669.

of Paris) assures the king that in Geoffrey of Beaulieu's presence twelve masses had already been instituted in Louis' memory, and that masses were now being instituted for the rest of Philip's recently deceased family members.[71] Two weeks later, on 21 May 1271, King Philip entered Paris. Louis IX's bones were interred at Saint-Denis the next day, after which Philip (according to William of Chartres, par. 48) retreated to the royal residence at Saint-Germain-en-Laye.

It is not clear how long or in what capacity William or Geoffrey remained tied to Philip III's court. But William, at least, was keeping an eye on reports of Louis' miracles. The seventeen miraculous episodes that William records are the earliest extant gathering of these.[72] They break down into several distinct groups, analysis of which reveals something

---

[71] AN J 462, layette 27, no. 39. This is an original letter to Philip III from Thomas, prior of Vaux-de-Cernay (writing in the absence of his abbot), with remains of the seal still attached. It replies to Philip's request for prayers, not only for Louis but also for Jean Tristan, Thibaut of Champagne, and Isabelle of Aragon. Carolus-Barré (Le procès, 14) incorrectly gave the date of the letter as 27 April (it is dated 1271, Wednesday, the feast of Saint John before the Latin Gate), and he believed it showed that Geoffrey of Beaulieu was actually at Vaux-de-Cernay on that date. In fact, however, Prior Thomas described a two-part process, whereby masses had earlier been established for Louis in Geoffrey's presence, and were now (6 May) also being established for Jean, Thibaut, and Isabelle, in the presence of Philip III's chaplain (who is referred to earlier as having brought Philip III's letters to the abbey): "Scientes quod in presencia fratris Gaufridi de Bello Loco, ex parte vestra ad nos destinati, pro bone memorie Ludovico genitore vestro duodecim missas iniunximus in nostro capitulo ... modo autem ad peticionem vestram pro animabus bone memorie Ysabelli illustris regine Francie quondam uxoris vestre et domini J. quondam comitis Nivenensis fratris vestri et domini Theobaldi quondam regis Navarre sororii vestri sex missas, presente predicto capellano vestro, iniunximus ..."

[72] The importance of William's miracle collection has generally been overlooked, with the literature tending to focus on the later, more extensive collection produced by William of Saint-Pathus. See in general Nicole Chareyon, "Représentation du corps souffrant dans la Vie et les Miracles de Saint Louis," Cahiers de recherches médiévales (XIIe–XVe s.) 4 (1997): 175–87; Sharah Chennaf and Odile Redon, "Les Miracles de Saint Louis," in Les Miracles Miroirs des Corps (Paris: Université de Paris VIII, 1983), 53–85; Jacques LeGoff, "Saint de l'Eglise et saint du peuple: Les miracles officiels de saint Louis entre sa mort et sa canonisation (1270–1297)," in Histoire sociale, sensibilités collectives et mentalités: Mélanges Robert Mandrou (Paris: Presses Universitaires de France, 1985), 169–80; Hannah Skoda, "Representations of Disability in the Thirteenth-Century Miracles de Saint Louis," in Disability in the Middle Ages: Reconsiderations and Reverberations, ed. Joshua Eyler (Burlington, Vt.: Ashgate, 2010), 53–66; M. Cecilia Gaposchkin, "Place, Status, and Experience in the Miracles of Saint Louis," Cahiers de recherches médiévales et humanistes/Journal of Medieval and Humanistic Studies 19 (2010): 249–66; Sharon Farmer, Surviving Poverty in Medieval Paris: Gender, Ideology, and the Daily Lives of the Poor (Ithaca: Cornell University Press, 2002).

of William's own role in gathering them. The very first miracle William records (par. 44) occurred just as word of Louis' death reached Paris, which must have been at the very end of September or the beginning of October. A woman in Paris had a vision of Louis and Jean Tristan, and then immediately learned from her husband, who had some position at the royal court, of their deaths. Since William says she told this story to him directly, he may have heard it as early as October 1270, and certainly well before Philip III's return to Paris (the following May).

The next six miracles all seem to have occurred in conjunction with Philip III's return and the burial of Louis' bones at Saint-Denis:

2   (22 May 1271) the day of Louis' burial at Saint-Denis a blind woman regained her sight. Master William of Mâcon, canon of Paris, reported this.

3   ("shortly thereafter") a deaf-mute from Burgundy came to Saint-Denis and had his speech and hearing restored. People who knew him reported this.

4   ("about that time") a cleric got sick at Chartres, prayed to Louis, and recovered.

5   (24 May 1271) The physician Dudo was at Saint-Germain-en-Laye with King Philip, got very sick, and traveled to the royal palace in Paris. Louis appeared to him in a vision, removed a tumor from his head, and Dudo recovered. Dudo told William about this the next morning, and also gave him a longer written account.

6   (undated) The knight Peter of Laon was cured, at the Louvre, through the power of some of Louis' hairs he had preserved.

7   ("about this time") Two Dominicans walking near Saint-Denis met a woman who had just been cured of blindness by Louis.

The two miracles given precise dates occurred on the very day of and two days after Louis' burial. The others were "about this time" (the one concerning Peter of Laon has no indication of date but can probably be assumed to have occurred about then). Most specifically, William was apparently at the royal palace on the Ile de la Cité on 25 May 1271—just three days after Louis' burial at Saint-Denis—to hear the story of Dudo,

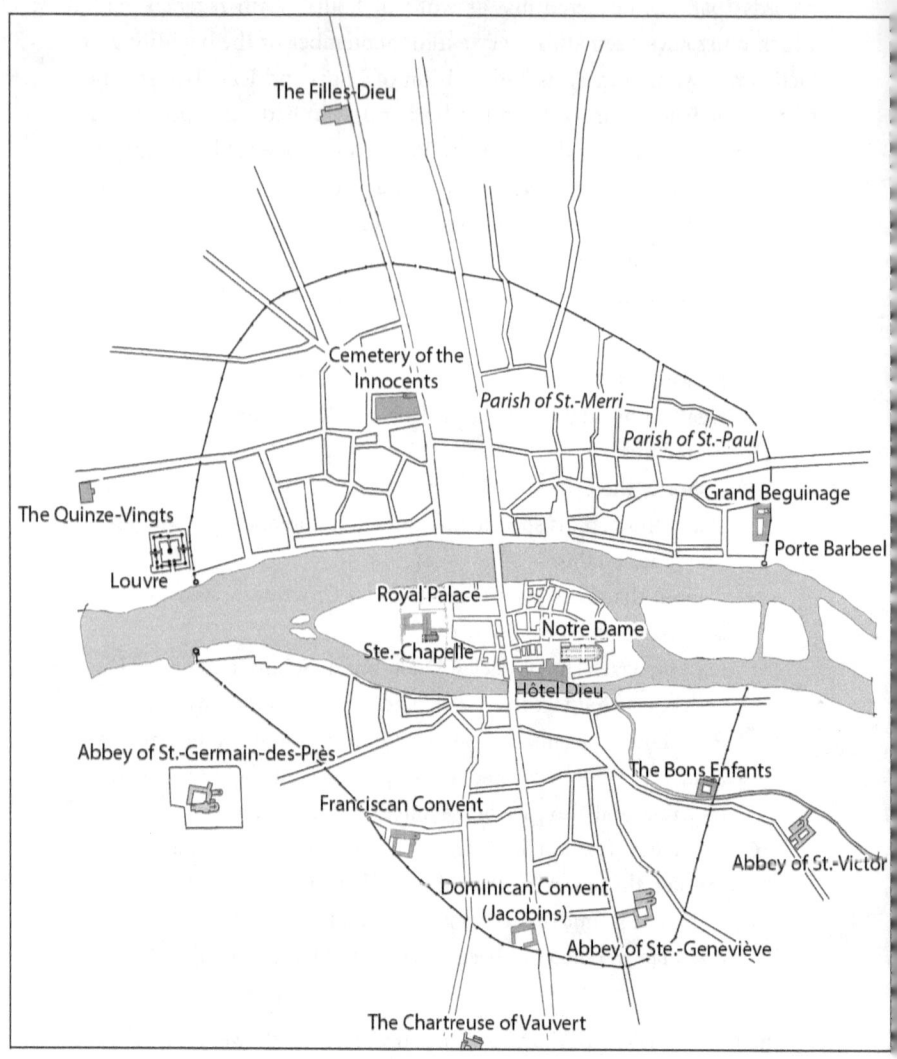

Map 3. Paris about 1270, showing buildings and parishes mentioned in the texts. © M. Cecilia Gaposchkin; adapted from Hercule Géraud, *Paris sous Philippe-le-Bel, d'après des documents originaux et notamment d'après un manuscrit contenant le rôle de la taille imposée sur les habitants de Paris en 1292* (Paris: Crapelet, 1837).

the physician. William also says that Dudo entrusted him with a lengthier version of the miracle, written in his own hand, which highlights the way those around the court were preparing evidence in anticipation of hearings into Louis' sanctity.

Certainly William himself was an active part of this process. The canon William of Mâcon told his story directly to him and presumably William of Chartres would have heard the experience of his Dominican brethren from their lips as well. Moreover the miracle involving a cleric at Chartres concerned a man "well known to the bishop of Saint-Malo." This bishop, Simon of Clisson, was a Dominican and former prior of the Parisian house, and so it seems that William must have heard this story through the local Dominican grapevine. Several of the miracles took place at the royal court, the royal castle of the Louvre, or on William's home turf of Chartres; and several of the reporters were tied to the royal court (Dudo, Peter of Laon, the woman whose husband was associated with the court) or were Dominicans. Thus William was on some level himself an early gatherer of testimony at Paris concerning Louis' miraculous claims to sanctity.[73]

The final ten miracles all involved cures at Saint-Denis, but also reveal some further patterns.

8   (26 May 1271) Emeline from Chambly was healed at Saint-Denis.
9   (29 May 1271) Petronilla, a resident of Saint-Denis, was cured there.
10 (4 June 1271) Agnes who had been staying in Paris near the Grand Béguinage (Parish of Saint-Paul) was cured at the tomb.
11 (3 June 1271) Hodierne, from a village near Saint-Denis, was cured at the tomb.
12 (6 June 1271) Michael, living in Paris (Parish of Saint-Paul), was cured at the tomb.

---

[73] According to the chart in WSP, *Miracles*, xxv–xxvii, miracles nos. 3, 5, 8, 9, 10, 11, 12, and 15 were later taken up by William of Saint-Pathus. Since his account was based on the canonization hearings at Saint-Denis in 1282–83, it seems likely that these miracles were known and noted as part of the Dionysian tradition. Of the first seven miracles discussed here, the two—the deaf mute from Burgundy and the physician Dudo—later pursued at Saint-Denis were among the most spectacular and hence the most likely to be spread by word of mouth. The other five seem particularly likely to have been gathered by William himself.

13   (23 August) Jeanette, living in Paris (Parish of Saint-Paul), was cured at the tomb.
14   (23 August) Jean, living in Paris (Parish of Saint-Merri), was cured at the tomb.
15   (13 June 1271) Emeline, living in Paris (Parish of Saint-Merri), was cured at the tomb.
16   (9 June 1271) Gila, living in Paris (Parish of Saint-Paul), was cured at the tomb.
17   (7 June 1271) Alice was cured at the tomb.

The first two of these miracles, still in May 1271, involved women well known in Saint-Denis (Emeline was "known to many trustworthy people" there, and Petronilla was a resident). A third (miracle no. 11) involved a woman from a village near Saint-Denis, and a fourth (no. 17) does not specify where the woman who experienced the cure was living. The other six, however, all follow a consistent pattern. Four women and two men, all of whom lived in the Right Bank parishes of Saint-Merri or Saint-Paul, experienced illness of some kind, traveled to Saint-Denis, and were cured at the king's tomb. In terms of chronology, of these final eight miracles, six occurred between 3 and 13 June, still within a few weeks of Louis' burial. The other two are dated 23 August. The association here was evidently with the anniversary of Louis' death (25 August) but perhaps also reflected heightened enthusiasm as Philip III's coronation approached (30 August).

At Saint-Denis, the monks were also keeping track of Louis' miracles. Abbot Matthew of Vendôme arranged for a man named Thomas Hauxton to watch over and regulate pilgrims' access to Louis' tomb. The monks also kept a record of Louis' miracles,[74] probably in preparation for a later inquest, and certainly in sincere hopes that the abbey, whose fortunes were closely tied to the crown, would find itself in possession of the relics of a saint-king. Later testimony shows that recipients of miracles were quickly ushered to Hauxton to tell their story.[75] It is certainly possible that William had access to this miracle list at Saint-Denis, perhaps

---

[74] Gaposchkin, "Place, Status, and Experience in the Miracles of Saint Louis," 257–58.
[75] WSP, *Miracles*, 19.

drawing on it for some of the cures he reports at the king's tomb.[76] But it is also striking that so many of these cures were experienced by people living in Right Bank Parisian parishes, who went north to Saint-Denis and then returned home. Perhaps their stories were being noted in Paris; if not by William in the first instance, then by other churchmen who passed them along.[77]

William of Chartres in Paris and the monks at Saint-Denis were thus already making a record of Louis' local reputation for miraculous sanctity when Pope Gregory X wrote to Geoffrey of Beaulieu on 4 March 1272 and asked him to quietly assemble his recollections of the king and send them by messenger. This was in fact the first step toward a formal canonization proceeding, building on local reputation (*fama*) by collecting preliminary anecdotal evidence of sanctity. Gregory X, however, was already well acquainted with Louis' piety. At the time of the king's death, the papal throne had been vacant for nearly two years (since the death of Clement IV, 29 November 1268) and would remain so for another year. When the cardinals at last elected Tebaldo Visconti on 1 September 1271, they chose a man long familiar with France and Louis IX, and with a commitment to crusading. Tebaldo had attended the First Council of Lyon in 1245 (at which Louis' first crusade was discussed and approved), studied in Paris for several years, and enjoyed positions as a canon of Lyon and as archdeacon of Liège.[78] He had in fact intended to join Louis IX on the crusade of 1270, but when he learned of the king's death he went instead to Palestine with Edward, Prince of England. He was notified of his election to the papacy while in Acre, and returned to Italy only in early 1272. His first papal letters are dated 4 March from Viterbo and

---

[76] Four of these miracles (nos. 13, 14, 16, 17) did not enter the collection by William of Saint-Pathus. This could be taken as evidence that none of these miracles were recorded at Saint-Denis, but it might be more likely that they simply were not interesting enough to be followed up at the canonization hearings, or that the witnesses were no longer alive by that time.

[77] The miracles do not follow a strict chronological order, so it would not seem that William was keeping a running account. Nor do they follow a clear grouping by parish. Yet it is striking that the two concerning residents of the parish of Saint-Merri are grouped together, surrounded by those from the parish of Saint-Paul, so perhaps those were reported separately to William, who was otherwise noting events in the parish of Saint-Paul.

[78] For a sketch of Gregory X's career see Ghislain Brunel, "Gregory X," in *The Papacy: An Encylopedia*, ed. Philippe Levillain, vol. 2 (New York: Routledge, 2001), 656–58.

include letters to Philip III and Marguerite of Provence, as well as the one to Geoffrey of Beaulieu translated here. This batch of letters centers on Gregory's concern for the Holy Land and desire to launch a new crusade.[79] His requested account of Louis IX's life must have been seen as potential propaganda in this cause.

Geoffrey presumably began work on his life of Louis soon after March 1272, less than two years after the king's death. He was certainly still based in Paris, since there is evidence for his preaching there later in 1272. Of his two extant sermons, the one preached on the theme "Behold, your king comes!" (*Ecce rex tuus venit,* Matt. 21:5) at the Grand Béguinage in Paris on 27 November 1272 is particularly worthy of note.[80] The sermon used remarkable examples pertaining to the king of France to stress the even greater majesty of the King of Heaven. Geoffrey noted the way towns must prepare in advance for the entrance of a new king (surely recalling the crowning of Philip III the previous year), to stress how one should prepare for the coming of Christ. He further explained how the kings of France could cure scrofula, because God had given them, and them alone, this power. But "the king of France cures only one illness, while the King of Paradise has the power to cure all illnesses …." Similarly, new kings customarily show mercy by liberating prisoners, but the Lord will liberate everyone when he comes; the king gives alms to the poor out of mercy, but the Lord is more merciful still. And perhaps most concretely in drawing on his experience at the royal court, Geoffrey asserts that just as *baillis* come before the king to render their accounts, everyone must render account to the Lord eventually; and just as a *bailli* who frequently adds up

---

[79] Xavier Hélary, "Les rois de France et la terre sainte, de la croisade de Tunis à la chute d'Acre (1270–1291)," *Annuaire-Bulletin de la Société de l'histoire de France* 118 (2005): 27.
[80] BnF ms. lat. 16481, fols. 27vb–29ra. See Nicole Bériou, *L'avènement des maîtres de la Parole: La prédication à Paris au XIIIe siècle,* vol. 1 (Paris: Institut d'Etudes Augustiniennes, 1998), 547, and for a partial transcription Jean Leclercq, "Le sermon sur la royauté du Christ au Moyen age," *Archives d'histoire doctrinale et littéraire du moyen age* 14 (1943–45): 165–66. Geoffrey's other extant sermon was copied down by Jean of Essômes, master at the university of Paris and member of the Sorbonne, but without a date. It is found in BnF ms. lat. 16499, fols. 278ra–279vb (on the theme *Mulier cum parit*). Kaeppeli, *SoP,* 2:15, no. 1206. On the manuscript see Bériou, *L'avènement des maîtres de la Parole,* 1:87; and Madeleine Mabille, "Les manuscrits de Jean d'Essômes conservés à la Bibliothèque nationale de Paris," *Bibliothèque de l'Ecole des chartes* 130 (1972): 231–34. To our knowledge, however, this sermon has never been edited or studied in detail.

his accounts will give a more certain reckoning than one who waits until the last minute, Christians would be wise to confess often rather than putting it off. Thus when Geoffrey wrote—at just about this time—about Louis' innovations to rituals around the "royal touch" or his scrupulous choice and oversight of *baillis*, he was repeating themes he deployed from the pulpit. And we see again Geoffrey's first-hand contact with beguines and familiarity with careful record keeping, both of which had previously been documented in the royal accounts from 1255 to 1256.

William of Chartres was also resident in Paris at least into 1273, since he also gave a string of recorded sermons on 2, 12, and 19 February 1273; the first at the parish church of Saint-Leufroy on the right bank near the Grand Châtelet, the other two at Sainte-Madeleine at the heart of the Ile de la Cité. Although these sermons are unedited and have yet to be properly studied, they offer a glimpse of William as a regular part of Parisian parish life at this time, again suggesting his ability to collect miracles he might have heard as he made his rounds for these Sunday sermons.[81]

Geoffrey of Beaulieu died within a few years, on 9 or 10 January in an unrecorded year.[82] Further precision rests on William of Chartres' remark that "at the close of his own life ... bidden by our lord pope Gregory, [Geoffrey] wrote down his text and left it to be given to our lord pontiff" (par. 2). This passage seems to indicate that Geoffrey worked on the *vita* up to the very end of his life, and left it then to be sent on to Gregory X, whom he believed to still be alive at that time. Since Gregory died on 10 January 1276, Geoffrey must therefore have died on 9 or 10 January, in a year between 1273 and 1276.[83] Since he was still active as a preacher at the end of November 1272, it seems relatively unlikely (though not impossible) that he died only a little more than a month later in January 1273. On

---

[81] All are found in BnF ms. lat. 16481 (fols. 111va–113va; 119va–120rb; 127ra–129rb). See Bériou, *L'avènement des maîtres de la Parole*, 2:707. For small excerpts from these sermons transcribed by Bériou, see ibid., 1:234 n. 63; 263 n. 192; 306 n. 51; 339 n. 176; 347 n. 208; 390, n. 22; 392 n. 28; 399 n. 59; 492 n. 61; 495 n. 78; 549 n. 264. See also Kaeppeli, *SoP*, 2:95–96. We have examined these sermons only superficially, to verify that nothing directly relating to William's relationship with the king appears there.
[82] 9 January according to the necrology of Dominicans of Chartres; 10 January according to breviary of Dominicans of Poissy. See note 45 above.
[83] 1276 remains technically possible by this logic, since Geoffrey would not yet have known of the pope's death if they died within a day of each other.

the other hand, if Geoffrey had died within a day of Pope Gregory in 1276, one would think that William might have mentioned that fact. January of 1274 or 1275 therefore seem the most probable dates for Geoffrey of Beaulieu's death.

William of Chartres' text was written only after Geoffrey's death. It could have therefore been begun as early as 1273,[84] but (based on the reasoning above) more likely William set himself to the task after January 1274 or 1275. William himself has been presumed to have died before 1282 because there is no trace of him at the canonization hearings that then took place at Saint-Denis, and surely he would have testified had he been alive.[85] Yet, in the passage just cited, William speaks of Geoffrey's death, but does not describe Gregory X as the late or former pope (a common practice when this was the case). While this omission is not definitive, it suggests that Gregory was still alive when William wrote. We therefore think it most likely that Geoffrey of Beaulieu died in January 1274 or 1275 and that William composed his additional text in the interval before Gregory X's death in January 1276.

One scrap of evidence may suggest that William of Chartres was himself still alive in autumn 1277. Sometime after his entry into the Dominican Order, William wrote a letter—by extraordinary good fortune the autograph is still extant today—to his sister's husband, Gilles de la Chaussée, noting that he had secured royal letters asking the abbot of Saint-Denis to receive his nephew Matthew.[86] William also mentions his niece, and asks Gilles to remember him to his sister. This is one of six letters to or mentioning Gilles de la Chaussée, *châtelain* of Pacy, which are still preserved in carton J 1030 of the Archives nationales. Those that are dated (three of the six) are from September and October 1277. The modern inventory of this carton therefore assigns William's letter a tentative

---

[84] He certainly wrote after Eudes of Châteauroux's death in January 1273 (see par. 9, where Eudes is clearly referred to as no longer alive).

[85] A William of Chartres is mentioned in a document of 1286 as clerk of the royal chapel, but surely this is another man; see Daunou, "Guillaume de Chartres, historien," 360.

[86] This letter, apparently in William's own hand, survives as AN J 1030 no. 59. A reproduction and short analysis can be found in Carolus-Barré, "Guillaume de Chartres." The letter is not dated, but because William calls himself "frater" it is virtually certain that it postdates his entry into the Dominican Order. In that case, the abbot of Saint-Denis in question would have been Matthew of Vendôme.

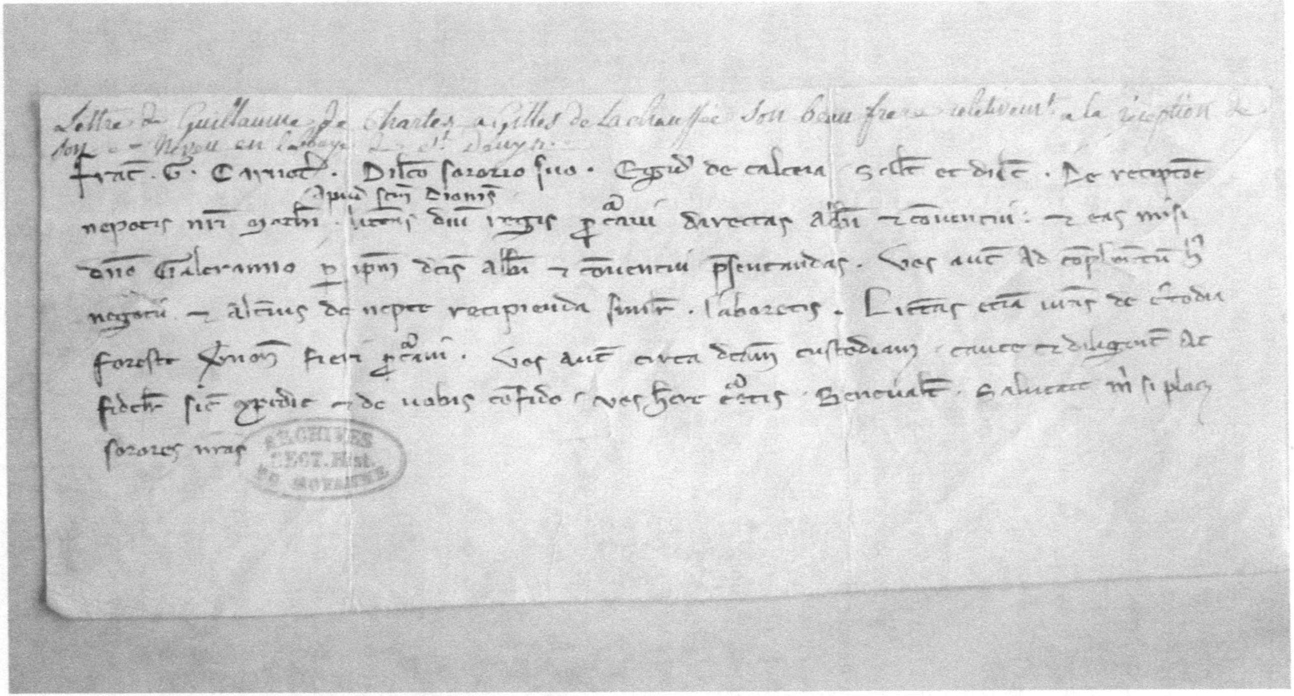

Figure 2. Autograph letter of William of Chartres to his brother-in-law Gilles de la Chaussée. AN J 1030 no. 59 (the French cursive at the top of the document is a later addition). Photograph by Sean Field. Reproduced by permission of the Archives nationales, Paris.

date of 1277; the inference seems likely enough, though not completely certain.[87] If this dating is correct, this letter would be William of Chartres' last known appearance in the documentary record.

The period 1272–75 when Geoffrey's and (we believe) William's texts were composed witnessed wider efforts to jump-start Louis' canonization. Philip III met with Pope Gregory in 1274 and may have pushed the matter.[88] Then, in 1275, elite churchmen from the region around Paris mounted a campaign to formally advocate for it. Between June and September a series of letters addressed to the College of Cardinals and to the Pope urged the curia to declare Louis a saint.[89] The letters that have survived came from the archbishops of Sens (June) and Reims (July) in the name of their suffragans, and from Jean of Châtillon, the Dominican prior for the province of France (September), in the name of the Dominican Provincial Chapter. We know of other such letters that have not survived, but this may not matter in substance since the letters were highly coordinated. Those that came in from the archbishops of Reims and Sens were essentially identical. The one from Jean of Châtillon and the Dominicans used different language but was similar in tone and advanced the same overall argument, which was that Louis should be canonized a saint because he had died as a martyr on crusade. Yet the incipit (first Latin words) of the Dominican Provincial Chapter's letter

---

[87] This information is drawn from Série J, Trésor des chartes, supplément: Inventaire, par Henri de Curzon. J 1028 à J 1034. Enquêtes et informations. Dactylograpié par Alain Ganeval. Relu et complété par Jean-Pierre Brunterch et Bruno Galland (available at http://www.archivesnationales.culture.gouv.fr). Nos. 33 (10 October 1277) and 42 (14 October 1277) are from Philip III to R. de Yvemesnil, chanter of the church of Rouen, and Gilles de la Chaussée, châtelain of Pacy, asking them (no. 33) to inquire into a dispute between the convent of Saint-Ouen of Rouen and a knight, and (no. 42) to question witnesses in a process between the count of Périgord and the chamberlain of Tancarville; no. 53 (undated) is from the count of Périgord to Philip III referring to R. de Yvemesnil and Gilles de la Chaussée; no. 47 (13 September 1277) is from Peter of Condé to Gilles "au sujet du service du roi"; no. 58 (undated) is from Jean de Benco to Gilles regarding a debt the former has not yet paid; and no. 59 (no date) is our letter from William. We have examined the original of only this last letter. Evidently Gilles was a trusted royal functionary with excellent connections himself. For further references, see also Joseph Reese Strayer, *The Administration of Normandy Under Saint Louis* (Cambridge, Mass.: Mediaeval Academy of America, 1932), 72 n. 7 and 94.

[88] Carolus-Barré, *Le procès*, 2.

[89] Gaposchkin, *The Making of Saint Louis*, 30–33 (with full references). The letter from the suffragans of the province of Reims was addressed to the pope himself; the letters from the suffragans of Sens and from the Dominicans were addressed to the College of Cardinals.

is the same as that of William's *vita*, which, we have argued, was probably written at about this same time; this can hardly be a coincidence, and suggests the coordinated nature of the Dominican efforts to argue for Louis' canonization. Moreover, the letter specifically appeals to the evidence of things "seen or heard by some of the brothers of our order who were close by his side in life and in death." These brothers certainly included Geoffrey and William, showing the way this letter builds on the hagiographic efforts emanating from the Order of Preachers. Read together, our two *vitae* and the contemporary letter in the name of all Dominicans in France represent the influence of a "Dominican moment" in the move toward Louis's canonization.

Gregory X certainly favored this move. Besides commissioning Geoffrey of Beaulieu's initial *vita*, Gregory, "desiring the honor of the royal house," also asked the Franciscan Simon of Brie—cardinal priest of Saint Cecilia, papal legate to France, and another former associate of Louis—to undertake a secret and careful investigation into Louis' sanctity.[90] Gregory himself was in Lyon from November 1273 through April 1275 for the Second Council of Lyon, then in Beaucaire into early September and in Lausanne through October, as he made his way back to Italy. Thus it is quite possible that he was on the borders of France while Geoffrey and William were working on their *vitae*, and the Dominican letter (though addressed to the College of Cardinals) might have reached his attention in Beaucaire, before the pope returned to Italy at the end of 1275 and died shortly thereafter on 10 January 1276.[91]

Moreover, Gregory and Philip III were actively planning for a new crusade throughout this period. Philip took the Cross 24 June 1274 at the Sainte-Chapelle (at the time of the crowning of his second wife, Marie of Brabant), along with his brothers and brothers-in-law. The king even paid for a contingent of French knights to go to the immediate aid of the Holy Land, and lent money to Gregory X for the same purpose.

---

[90] We know this from a letter that one of his successors, Nicolas III, wrote to Philip III in 1278. Jules Gay, ed., *Les registres de Nicolas III (1277–1280): Recueil des bulles de ce pape*, 5 vols. in 1 (Paris: E. de Boccard, 1898–1938), 146–47, no. 394. Carolus-Barré supposed that Gregory commissioned Simon of Brie to begin this investigation after he received the letters of 1275.

[91] Laurent, *Le bienheureux Innocent V*, notes the relevant fact that the previous Dominican provincial for France, Peter of Tarentaise, was now a cardinal (and the future Innocent V) and hence part of the body addressed in this letter.

This plan for a new French-led crusade remained a serious proposal up through about 1277, before fading in the face of more pressing political concerns.[92] The Dominican texts thus fit neatly into this window when money and manpower were again being directed toward the Holy Land by the French king.

The Formal Hearings and Canonization, 1277–1297

The momentum for Louis IX's canonization temporarily stalled after the death of Gregory X.[93] After several short pontificates, Nicholas III was elected in November 1277, and Philip III sent a delegation to Rome to urge the new pope to establish a public commission to investigate Louis' merits and miracles.[94] Nicholas, however, wanted Louis' sanctity fully documented so as to meet the high evidentiary standards that had been established for canonization over the course of the past century and a half. Simon of Brie, still papal legate, was again charged with the task of collecting evidence (and was aided by the Franciscan and Dominican priors of the province of France, the Franciscan Jean of Samois, and the prior at Saint-Denis).[95] The results were apparently sent to the curia and examined by members of the College of Cardinals. But Nicholas III died in 1280 with the canonization still in the balance. The cardinals in turn elected as pope no less an advocate of Louis' sanctity than Simon of Brie himself, who took the name of Martin IV. Yet another delegation of ecclesiastics from France was sent to press the cause, demanding with great urgency that the papacy institute a "public inquisition into the miracles and merits of the King Louis."[96] In 1281, the pope ordered another—this time public—inquest. In a letter of 23 December 1281 Martin commis-

---

[92] Hélary, "Les rois de France et la terre sainte," 29–41, summary at p. 93; idem, *L'armée du roi de France: La guerre de Saint Louis à Philippe le Bel* (Paris: Perrin, 2012), 22–23.
[93] On this paragraph, see Carolus-Barré, "Les enquêtes."
[94] Gay, *Les registres de Nicolas III (1277–1280)*, 146, no. 393.
[95] Ibid., 147, no. 394. The detail about Simon being assisted by other prelates including the priors of the Dominican and Franciscans and Jean of Samois relies on Carolus-Barré, *Le procès*, 21.
[96] F. Olivier-Martin et al., eds., *Les registres de Martin IV*, 3 vols. (Paris: Bibliothèque des Ecoles françaises d'Athènes et de Rome, 1901–1935), 1:32, no. 84.

sioned William of Flavacourt, William of Grez, and Roland of Parma (bishops of Rouen, Auxerre, and Spoleto) to undertake a public inquest into the "new miracles as well as the life and comportment of king Louis." Another letter, dated the same day, informed the French ecclesiastical establishment of the commission.[97]

The inquest was held between March 1282 and May 1283 in the newly constructed high gothic abbey church of Saint-Denis, where Louis' earthly remains were buried and thus where most of the miracles attributed to him had occurred. Witnesses who were still alive offered their testimony about Louis' life—the medieval term here (which is used frequently in our sources) is *conversatio*—that is, "comportment," "manner of living" or "conduct."[98] They included many of the elites of the realm, including Philip III himself and his brother Peter of Alençon; Simon of Nesle, a chief advisor; Jean of Joinville, who would later write the vernacular *vie* of Louis for Philip IV's queen, Jeanne of Navarre, sometime before 1308; Matthew of Vendôme, abbot of Saint-Denis; Adam of Saint-Leu, abbot of Royaumont; and Nicholas of Auteuil, bishop of Evreux.[99] But the commissioners also questioned men and women of lesser stature, in particular about the miracles Louis had effected at his tomb. At the end of the inquest two copies of the testimony were made; one was sent to the curia, and the other lodged in the Franciscan convent in Paris. A provisional *vita*—a *vita curia approbata* (a life that had been papally approved)—was also composed at this stage.[100]

---

[97] Ibid., 33–34, no. 85 and 32–33, no. 84.
[98] On the inquest of 1282–83 see William of Saint-Pathus's prologue; Jordan, *A Tale of Two Monasteries*, 202–3; Gaposchkin, *The Making of Saint Louis*, 36–43; and most fully Carolus-Barré, *Le procès*.
[99] Charles of Anjou offered testimony, but not at Saint-Denis. Paul Edouard Didier Riant, "Déposition de Charles d'Anjou pour la canonisation de saint Louis," in *Notices et documents publiés pour la Société de l'histoire de France à l'occasion du cinquantième anniversaire de sa fondation* (Paris, 1884): 155–75. Partially translated in Jackson, *The Seventh Crusade*, 115–20. For those who testified at Saint-Denis in 1282–83, see Carolus-Barré, *Le procès*.
[100] Referred to in a sermon by William of Saint-Pathus. See H.-François Delaborde, "Une oeuvre nouvelle de Guillaume de Saint-Pathus," *Bibliothèque de l'Ecole des chartes* 63 (1902): 278 (Delaborde's discussion, 270–71).

With the exception of a few fragments, both copies, as well as the *vita approbata*, have been lost.[101] And yet, we have a good idea of the contours of what they contained, because in 1302–3 the Franciscan William of Saint-Pathus, who had been the confessor of Queen Marguerite of Provence and subsequently of her and Louis' daughter Blanche, used these materials to write (at Blanche's request) a new life of Louis. William in fact wrote two books: a life comprising twenty chapters, and a work detailing the sixty-three miracles for which the commission believed they had reliable testimony.[102] William incorporated a great deal from Geoffrey of Beaulieu and cited him repeatedly (and oddly, cited very little from William of Chartres, suggesting this account was unknown to those at the inquest). William of Saint-Pathus's works are thus our best evidence for how, in 1282 and 1283, people were advocating for Louis' sanctity.

Despite this crucial step, canonization was still well more than a decade away. Martin IV and Philip III both died in 1285. In France, the king was succeeded by his son, the indomitable Philip IV ("the Fair," r. 1285–1314), who pursued the cause with equal zeal and immediately wrote to Rome demanding the "expediting of the work of the canonization of the lord King Louis of holy memory."[103] In Rome, Martin was succeeded by Honorius IV, Nicholas IV, (briefly) Celestine V, and finally Boniface VIII. It was Boniface who, in August of 1297, would at last canonize Louis, probably as much out of political exigency as from a belief in Louis' sanctity. Relations between Boniface and Philip the Fair were tense, and Boniface acceded to Philip's desire for Louis' canonization as part of a package of concessions the papacy made to the crown, following a protracted dispute regarding their relative authority over taxing

---

[101] For the fragments of actual testimony, see Henri-François Delaborde, "Fragments de l'enquête faite à Saint-Denis en 1282 en vue de la canonisation de saint Louis," *Mémoires de la Société de l'histoire de Paris et de l'Ile-de-France* 23 (1896): 1–71; Louis Carolus-Barré, "Consultation du cardinal Pietro Colonna sur le IIe miracle de saint Louis (Arch. du Vatican, A.A. Arm. C, 493)," *Bibliothèque de l'Ecole des chartes* 117 (1959): 57–72; Riant, "Déposition."
[102] WSP, *Vie*; WSP, *Miracles*.
[103] In February 1286, Philip the Fair sent a delegation to the court of the newly elected Honorius IV. Georges Alfred Laurent Digard, *Philippe le Bel et le Saint-Siège de 1285 à 1304*, vol. 2 (Paris: Librairie du Recueil Sirey société anonyme, 1936), 218.

the French church.¹⁰⁴ During this process, Boniface had asked one of his cardinals to produce a summary (recently rediscovered) of the case for Louis' canonization.¹⁰⁵ Boniface preached two sermons in Louis' honor on August 6 and 11, and issued his formal bull of canonization (*Gloria Laus*) on the latter date. These texts drew heavily on material from the canonization proceedings and thus also reflect the influence of Geoffrey of Beaulieu. *Gloria Laus* constituted a concise hagiography and as such was later incorporated into collections of *vitae sanctorum* (lives of saints), including the popular *Legenda Aurea (The Golden Legend)* originally written in the 1260s by the Dominican Jacob of Voragine.¹⁰⁶

With Louis' enrollment in the catalogue of saints, the formal business of the canonization process was complete. At Saint-Denis, the following year, Louis' remains—now confirmed as sacred relics—were elevated in a solemn ceremony and placed upon the high altar in the crossing in a ceremony choreographed by Philip the Fair. And at this stage a series of new texts were written. Louis' daughter, Blanche, now living as a pious widow at the female Franciscan community of Saint-Marcel (or Lourcines), commissioned the life by the Franciscan William of Saint-Pathus. Jeanne of Navarre (d. 1305), the wife of Philip the Fair, asked Louis' old friend and companion in arms Jean of Joinville to write "a book of the saintly words and good deeds" of Louis, a work Joinville finished after Jeanne had died and that he dedicated to her son and the heir to the throne, the future Louis X. Joinville consulted a vernacular history composed at Saint-Denis (a version of the *Grandes chroniques de France*) which had itself incorporated some of Geoffrey of Beaulieu's text.¹⁰⁷ And

---

¹⁰⁴ This has been frequently narrated. A good introduction is Charles T. Wood, *Philip the Fair and Boniface VIII: State vs. Papacy*, 2d ed. (New York: Holt, Rinehart and Winston, 1971). Highly relevant is also J. Marrone and C. Zuckerman, "Cardinal Simon of Beaulieu and Relations between Philip the Fair and Boniface VIII," *Traditio* 31 (1975): 195–222. The classic study is Digard, *Philippe le Bel et le Saint-Siège*.
¹⁰⁵ Peter Linehan and Francisco J. Hernández, "'Animadverto': A Recently Discovered *Consilium* Concerning the Sanctity of King Louis IX," *Revue Mabillon* 66 (1994): 83–105.
¹⁰⁶ See Gaposchkin, *The Making of Saint Louis*, 51 n. 18. *Gloria Laus* was also used by the Dominican Bernard Gui in composing his entry on Saint Louis for his collection of saints' lives, the *Speculum Sanctorale*. See BnF ms. lat 5046, fols. 152r–155r.
¹⁰⁷ The old French is best accessed in the edition by Jacques Monfrin (see note 26 above). Geoffrey's indirect influence (through William of Nangis and then the *Grandes chroniques de France*) can be most clearly seen in pars. 720–26. The most recent English translation

several other lesser-known lives of Louis were composed at this stage, probably for use in a liturgical or paraliturgical context: *Gloriosissimi Regis* and *Beatus Ludovicus*.[108] Their authors remain anonymous, but they too drew on the materials from the 1282–83 inquest, and thus, ultimately, on Geoffrey of Beaulieu. *Beatus Ludovicus* in particular became an enormously important text, being reproduced in redacted form dozens of times as part of the most popular of the liturgical offices written for Louis, and constituting the text that preachers most frequently consulted when composing sermons on the saint-king.[109] Although William of Chartres' *vita* was generally less influential than Geoffrey of Beaulieu's, *Beatus Ludovicus* picked up most of the miracles reported by William and incorporated them directly into the text, thus passing them on to medieval audiences.[110]

The Texts and their Themes

These early texts written before 1282 represent both individual interpretations of Louis' saintly characteristics and the development of increasingly honed arguments designed to push him through the canonization process. The first of these interpretations was arguably the letter that Louis' son and successor dispatched to all the churches in France on 12 September 1270. Although the letter's ostensible purpose was to announce Louis' death and ask for prayers and masses to be said for the sake of his soul, it also claimed that Louis probably had no need of such

---

is Joinville and Villehardouin, *Chronicles of the Crusades*, trans. Caroline Smith (London: Penguin, 2008). The dating of the text is complicated; for recent assessments see Caroline Smith, *Crusading in the Age of Joinville* (Burlington, Vt.: Ashgate, 2006), 48–58, and Gaposchkin, *The Making of Saint Louis*, 182–85.

[108] Edited and translated in Gaposchkin, *Blessed Louis*, 105–52.

[109] This process is described ibid., 16–17, and the redacted text is presented and translated as part of the liturgy, 168–95.

[110] For William's miracles 1–12, the order is respected in *BL* (see Gaposchkin, *Blessed Louis*, 141–51, nos. 12.2 to 12.13); for William's miracles 13–17, they appear in the order 17, 14, 16, 13, 15 in *BL* nos. 12.14 to 12.18. There seems no clear reason why William's original order was respected for the first twelve miracles and then abandoned. Although *BL* was probably written after 1297, it does not include any other miracles beyond those given by William of Chartres, nor does it omit any of those included by William.

prayers and called his acts *sanctissimos* (most saintly), suggesting that he was already at God's right hand, in heaven. The letter was thus making an immediate claim for Louis' sanctity, while also stressing his qualities as a king. It recounted the reason that Louis was in Africa when he died—his desire to eradicate the "wicked filthiness" of the "barbaric Saracen race" from Africa and to dedicate the land to the Christian faith—and his landing, capture of the coastal city of Carthage, and siege of (somewhat inland) Tunis. Finally the letter detailed Louis' good, devout, and faithful death. This was critical, since the good death was a prerequisite of sanctity, both as evidence of true devotion and as a trope of hagiography. Philip spoke of his own grief, and also of his aim of following in his father's footsteps, imitating his example, and fulfilling his ideals. Indeed, Philip was here setting Louis out as an extraordinary exemplar of Christian kingship, calling him the "the pious king, the peaceful king, the father of the poor, the refuge of the miserable, the consolation of the oppressed, the particular champion of all religion and innocence, the zealous supporter of justice, the defender of faith and the Church." Philip's 1270 letter thus laid down the basic assertion that Louis' sanctity was rooted in his extraordinary fulfillment of ideal Christian kingship. Perhaps most importantly, given the context of his second crusade, Louis' crusading ideals represented the sublime expression of his defense of the Church. His good death, suffering from illness, receiving the last rites, lying on sackcloth and ashes, and leaving this world at the "very hour" that Christ himself died on the Cross, simply confirmed that this all meant he was a saint.

Similarly, when Gregory X wrote to Geoffrey of Beaulieu in March 1272 to ask him to compose a new life of the late king, he described Louis as "a model of blessed living to other orthodox rulers." Evidently, the pope agreed with Philip III that the model of Christian kingship Louis represented was at least part of what made him a potential saint.

Geoffrey of Beaulieu's response to this request is the first, and arguably most important of the *vitae* for Louis in the medieval period. Like William of Chartres a few years later, Geoffrey composed a work of hagiography—a medieval genre designed specifically to show how an individual fulfilled the tropes and expectations of sainthood; this was not biography in a modern sense and thus Geoffrey neglected all manner of information that we might expect from a modern account of an individual's life.[111] Instead, Geoffrey clearly set out the principal themes of Louis' sanctity as well as the basic narrative structure for describing how that sanctity was manifest in his life that clearly influenced later accounts. The modern interpretation of Louis, which sees the failure of 1250 in Egypt as a personal and spiritual turning point that deeply affected his attitude towards his kingship and his sense of penitential responsibility for his kingdom and his people before God, was in fact first advanced by Geoffrey himself (ch. 31, as well as chs. 8, 16, 30).[112] In this sense, it is critical to note that Geoffrey's reports on Louis' pre-crusade piety are largely second hand; it was only with his assumption of the confessor's role around 1248 that he himself really gained access to Louis' innermost thoughts.

Geoffrey framed his text with a comparison to the biblical King Josias, son of King David. In 2 Kings 22–23, Josias discovers the book of Deuteronomy, after which he implements a series of religious reforms to the Law, reforms the Temple, and restores the observance of Passover.[113] The comparison between kings and their biblical forebears was a common precept of royal biography and hagiography, but the way in which Geoffrey deploys the comparison to set up his entire *vita* is instructive.[114] The biblical passages describing Josias with which Geoffrey opens (and which he says are equally fitting to Louis) praise the Old Testament king thus: God directed him to the "repentances of the nation" and he "took away the abominations of wickedness"; he "directed his heart toward the Lord"; and even as a boy he was pleasing to God; he restored the Temple and the House of the Lord; he returned his entire heart and soul to

---

[111] On the expectations of hagiography see Thomas J. Heffernan, *Sacred Biography: Saints and Their Biographers in the Middle Ages* (New York: Oxford University Press, 1988); Alison Goddard Elliot, *Roads to Paradise: Reading the Lives of the Early Saints* (Hanover, N.H.: published for Brown University Press by University Press of New England, 1987); Felice Lifshitz, "Beyond Positivism and Genre: 'Hagiographical' Texts as Historical Narrative," *Viator* 25 (1994): 95–113; and Gaposchkin, *The Making of Saint Louis*, 43–44.

[112] The best scholarly account representing this interpretation is Jordan, *Louis IX and the Challenge*, whose framework has been highly influential for subsequent authors, including most notably Jean Richard. LeGoff claims to argue against this view, but really only insists on Louis' commitment to kingship as well as crusade.

[113] See: 4 Kings 22–23; Par. 34; Ecclus. 49; 1–5; Jer. 1, 3, 22, 25, 26.

[114] For an extended discussion of the comparison between Josias and Louis, see LeGoff, *Saint Louis*, 309–14.

the Lord; and finally, he observed Passover as kings before him had not. Thus Geoffrey saw in Josias the model of the pious king, devout from boyhood, whose utmost priority throughout his life was the proper worship of the Lord's cult, observance of His rites, and "repentance of his people" (*poenitentia gentis*); in so far as his kingship was concerned, what was noteworthy was the removal of vice and promotion of repentance on a social, rather than individual, scale. Geoffrey's early chapters (2–4) are a pointed explanation of how these qualities applied to Louis. From there, he moves on to newer—more contemporary—themes, but themes that fit into the overarching scheme that he has set up with the comparison to Josias. These revolved around Louis' charity, his religiosity, and ultimately his crusades. Kingship is a pervasive theme, in that Geoffrey sets out to describe Louis as a saint-king (a term he uses several times explicitly),[115] but it is rarely understood in terms of the exercise of power (or rulership); kingship is instead represented here as personal piety, charity, and ensuring the public observance of the cult of the Lord (*cultus domini*, the Old Testament term for proper worship).

The early chapters deal directly with the most obvious tropes of sanctity: Louis' love and compassion, and his deep religiosity. At the end of the thirteenth century—the century of Saints Dominic and Francis—it would have been very difficult to make a case for sanctity without these qualities being front and center. Geoffrey highlights these with examples from his own experience, as Louis' confessor and member of his household. Louis' personal religiosity and devotion took recognizable forms—prayer, masses (chs. 21, 22, 23), sermons (13, 21), confession (16), chastity (11), bodily austerities and disciplines (16, 16*bis*, 17, 18). Geoffrey emphasizes the "religious" way in which Louis raised his children (13, 14, 15) and takes pains to emphasize that he engaged in forms of humbling charity "with his own hands": he personally fed the poor at his own table; he personally washed the feet of the poor (9); he gave out alms "with his own hand" (19); a particularly charming story has him, while at sea, volunteering to hold the line of a sailor with his own hands if that sailor needed to make confession (23). Louis' religiosity is exemplified by his reverence

---

[115] Chs. 18, 37, and 49.

for religious men. A theme that appears several times is his equal love for both Franciscans and Dominicans (12, 13, 16*bis,* 23). Geoffrey also describes his purchase of the Crown of Thorns and the other Passion relics (24), his devotion to the Cross (35, 36), and his pilgrimage to Nazareth (22). Louis was of course personally humble (8, 9, 10, 12, 30*bis*). Folded into these examples of his personal religiosity are descriptions of his institutional expressions of his piety and his sense of the obligations of his kingship. He gave many alms to individuals and institutions (19). He founded and supported religious houses, including Royaumont, hospitals, the *Filles-Dieu,* beguinages, and other identifiable institutions (19)—whereas nuns are largely absent from Geoffrey's picture, semireligious such as beguines and other poor women are important recipients of Louis' charity. He fed large numbers of the poor at his palace (19). Abhorring blasphemy, he banished it from his kingdom (32). In this he marshaled the obligations of his royal status and the resources of his kingdom toward the instincts of personal devotion.

Exemplifying these tropes of piety, compassion, and religiosity are the anecdotes that made Louis personally attractive to the people who were arguing for his sainthood. Geoffrey records for us some singularly charming moments and several memorable remarks that Louis made. The most famous was actually about his mother, who said that she would rather see her son, whom she loved above all other creatures, lie sick to the point of death, than that he would be cured by sinning only once with a woman who was not his wife; and she would sooner see him die than offend his Creator even once by mortal sin (ch. 4). But others seem worth noting, as they have not, despite the long availability of these texts in Latin, entered the array of stories that most commonly represent *Saint Louis* in the scholarly and popular imagination. These include the story that, impressed on hearing of a Muslim sultan who had copies made of the important works of "Saracen philosophy," Louis began to build his own library (or, as Geoffrey said, his own "book cupboard") of the writings of the Church Fathers, and he wished his books to be copied anew rather than purchased, so that "this way the total number of holy books was increased" (ch. 23). Or the (newly recovered) story of how Louis was so discomfited by the sumptuous reception he received from Paris in 1254 upon his return from the crusade that he immediately fled to his retreat at Vincennes (ch. 30*bis*). Or Louis' comment, when criticized for his harsh punishment of a blasphemer at a time when he was sponsoring some unspecified but expensive project for public benefit, that "he was anticipating greater reward from God for all the evil words he had received for the branding incident than for all the blessings that came his way [for his good works]" (ch. 33).

A close reading of Geoffrey also suggests some between-the-lines observations about Louis' character and some of the tensions that animated his personal life and relationships with members of the court. For instance, he was self-deprecatingly relieved after the death of one of his confessors, who imposed the discipline a bit *too* harshly (ch. 16*bis*); he "agreed" to let up on some abstinences and self disciplines because of "bodily weakness" or "delicate skin," on the advice of counselors and confessors, and, in exchange, simply asked his almoner to give out more money. He was frustrated not to be able to devote his children to religious orders but understood the value of political marriages (ch. 14). He endured criticisms by his familiars (ch. 33). His queen sometimes became exasperated with his pious projects (chs. 12, 30). If while in bed with his wife he was inappropriately "moved by the flesh," he would straightaway get up, pace about, and walk it off (ch. 11). Geoffrey, himself his confessor, may have sometimes found his need for immediate confession—say, in the middle of the night—a bit tedious (chs. 15, 16, 16*bis*).

Although all of this was to make the case that Louis was a saintly *king*, his kingship was subordinated to his proper religiosity. This presented no problem in so far as the ideal of good kingship had long been rooted in a tradition of the king's personal propriety, self-restraint, and piety. Yet the fact that Geoffrey rarely employs the word "justice" (*iustitia*), the paradigmatic royal virtue, demonstrates that kingship per se was not really his focus.[116] To be sure, Geoffrey discusses some elements of Louis' reign: his oversight of officials (ch. 5), his management of subordinates (ch. 6); his handling of church temporalities, and his conferral of benefices (ch. 20).

---

[116] The word appears in chs. 2 (in a biblical quotation), 4 (generically, and in praising Blanche for her governance during Louis' youth), 5 (in discussing royal agents who might be "slow in the exercise of justice"), and frequently in 15, in Geoffrey's translation of Louis' own writings. Geoffrey never applies it to Louis as a trope of his sanctity or of his kingship.

But these paled within the greater scheme, and even the chapter that compares Louis to Solomon and speaks of him as a peacekeeper (ch. 20) models this in terms of his "piety and compassion."

Rather than exemplifying the exercise of kingship, for Geoffrey, Louis' crusades were central to the case for his sainthood. This too was tied up with the broader view of Louis' saintly kingship insofar as the Capetians had taken on crusading as their particular responsibility. Geoffrey devotes much of the second half of the *vita* to them, treating Louis' first crusade (1248–54) in chapters 25–30 and his second crusade (1269–70), and then his death, burial, and the case for canonization in chapters 37–52. The quality of the *vita* shifts here, from "set piece" examples showing how Louis fulfilled this or that ideal ("penance" or "compassion") to a narrative structure, in part, perhaps, because this was the stage at which Geoffrey became Louis' confessor. The crusades, of course, were both utter disasters, and other sources reveal that there were criticisms of Louis' plans to launch a second one. Yet Louis' firm commitment to the crusading cause was the clearest mark of his sanctity, because it highlighted his devotion to the Cross, as well as his commitment to serve the Church, extend Christianity, and protect the Holy Land. The events of 1250—the landing in Egypt, the capture of Damietta, the king's own capture and then his release—are treated rapidly in chapter 25. Geoffrey is at pains to insist that everything that happened was the will of God, that Damietta was captured by a miracle of the Lord, and above all, that Louis' release (which was accomplished by ransom) "must be credited to divine miracle and His [i.e., God's] power and the merits of the holy king," beyond all hope and reasonable expectation. Geoffrey found better fodder in Louis' behavior while in Acre—his reinforcement of the defensive walls of key cities, his reception of local Muslims who converted to Christianity (ch. 27), his pious grief at the news of his mother's death (ch. 28). But Geoffrey seems to have understood that the subject of Louis' crusades was complicated, and thus repeatedly insisted that the disastrous failure of these crusades was owed not to Louis' own faults, but to the sins of others.

His description of Louis' second crusade followed much the same pattern, though it was richer in individual detail, probably because the events were more recent and Geoffrey had himself been more intimately involved. Geoffrey devoted a long chapter (41) to the reasons that Louis directed the crusade to Tunis, a short chapter to their Tunisian landing (42), another to the quick onset of widespread illness in the military camp (43), and then a long chapter (44) on his "pious and sorrowful death." In all, what Geoffrey highlighted was Louis' desire to aid the Holy Land, "avenge the injury to the Savior in the Holy Land" and recover the "rightful inheritance" of Christians (38) (drawing on classic crusading language), and his extraordinary hope of seeing the sultan of Tunis (al-Mustansir, d. 1277) convert to Christianity.

The discussion of the crusade of 1269–70 set the stage for the account of Louis' good death. Here, Geoffrey clearly had Philip's letter of 1270 at hand, reusing its language and following its account, although Geoffrey's narrative is longer and richer, with far more detail about the events of Louis' saintly death. It is entirely possible that Geoffrey, who had been there, was Philip III's "ghost" author for the original letter.[117] He highlighted Louis' especial devotion, the prayers, the taking of the sacraments, and so forth, reaffirming themes developed earlier on. And then Geoffrey recounted the return of Louis' bones (which he called relics in chapter 46) to France and their burial at Saint-Denis, and mentioned the occurrence of early miracles (though surprisingly he did not relate them) (46–50), before recalling the Josias comparison and ending with a direct appeal for Louis' canonization (51–52).

After Geoffrey's death, when William of Chartres took up his pen to further argue for Louis' sanctity, he too adopted the comparison to Josias in his opening paragraphs, offering a clear rhetorical indication of his desire to see his and Geoffrey's works considered together. William stated explicitly that Geoffrey's account was incomplete, and that he sought to fill in four important aspects of Louis' life that Geoffrey had neglected: "the good days of his rule," "the trials of his imprisonment," "the distress of his death," and the miracles that had begun to occur at his tomb and elsewhere (par. 2). His *vita* is shorter than Geoffrey's and is less clearly structured (unlike Geoffrey, William did not divide his text into titled subchapters), but is in some ways more interesting. Because of William's focus on the "good days of his rule," there is greater treatment of Louis'

---

[117] William of Chartres (par. 37) affirms that Geoffrey was present at Louis' death, as was William himself.

acts specifically as king, and William is more interested in some of the political events of Louis' lifetime than Geoffrey had been. William, a longtime royal clerk but never the royal confessor, would not have had access to the king's interior life in the way Geoffrey did. As a result, William's work is faster paced and touches more on notable incidents and anecdotes, with an interest in Louis' public and ritualized expressions of piety. For modern readers interested in the Capetian monarchy and the idea of medieval kingship, this may be a more exciting text.

William opens with an extended metaphor of Louis among princes of the time, shining as a sun among the stars (par. 1), a discussion of Geoffrey's *vita* and how it is wanting (par. 2), and the redeployment of the Josias metaphor (par. 3). The bulk of the text is in fact devoted to the four topics William claimed Geoffrey neglected. William's discussion of Louis' captivity and his time in the East runs from paragraphs 7 through 10; he treats Louis' governing and kingship from paragraphs 12 through 27; the account of his death runs from paragraphs 37 to 42 (wherein he returns to the sun metaphor with which he began); and Louis' early miracles run from paragraphs 43 to 60. But William also includes a fair amount of information that does not really fall into any of the four categories he sets out. So, for instance, William describes the annual processions that Louis established at the Sainte-Chapelle for the Crown of Thorns and the other Passion relics he had acquired in 1238 and 1241 (par. 4); and he speaks at length about the king's devotions, religious observations, alms, and abstinences. This is familiar territory from Geoffrey, but as if wanting to add more detail William devotes another long section later in the *vita* (pars. 28–36) to describing how Louis washed the feet of the poor and of lepers, how he fasted more than he needed too, how he gave extraordinary alms, how he built hospitals for the poor and convents for Dominicans, Franciscans, and other religious houses. Clearly there are also stories that William simply cannot resist telling, even if they do not fit his scheme. For instance, he recalls how Louis foretold that William himself would enter the Dominican Order (par. 11), and tells a story of Louis visiting a dying man in Egypt for whom William himself was caring (par. 10).

William's treatment of Louis' kingship opens with an explicit discussion of his royal duty (*regale officium*) in governing the realm (*regni regimine*). Where Geoffrey of Beaulieu had understood Louis' kingship to be found in the personal sanctity of his king who through ethical personal restraint might govern an alienated world, William's view of kingship was more contemporary, understood in terms of the use of Louis' own authority and power with respect to his subjects. Although William claimed that Louis "ruled peaceably" due not to "temporal power but to divine virtue" (par. 27), he was in fact interpreting the exercise of the rising Capetian authority against the classic tropes of good kingship. Drawing on the established notion of the king as the protector of the poor and weak, the defender of the Church, and the source of justice, William's vision of Louis' kingship was in a sense more modern than Geoffrey's, more in line with the priorities of Capetian kingship in the thirteenth century. In addition to these tropes, William touched on the king's relationship to his nobles; here we see Louis bringing the nobility to heel as a mark of his peacemaking.

Yet William also saw the whole of Louis' kingship as working toward the salvation of souls, "about which he was so actively concerned that he seemed to exercise equally a priestly rule (*sacerdotale regimen*) or a royal priesthood (*regale sacerdotium*)" (par. 12). Indeed, William went so far as to hint that by a kind of "pious usurpation" Louis was taking on the Church's role of caring for souls, above and beyond his royal duty to protect the bodily safety of his subjects. This is a striking formulation, and it is the closest we get anywhere in these texts to a claim of some kind of sacral kingship.

William argued that Louis fulfilled all the classic virtues of the good king, which included protecting the Church, doing justice, and keeping the peace. These were the ideals developed over centuries of writing about kingship, and enshrined in the coronation oaths that kings took. William described how Louis fulfilled these prescriptions through the power and authority of his royal office. He protected monasteries and churches and the religious poor—not through force (which was the original sense of the injunction, developed during the Peace of God movement), but by "settling disagreements, shielding them [i.e. the clergy] from the harm and vexation that so many cathedrals and convents of the Church endure" (pars. 16, 17). William probably also understood his discussion of charity and almsgiving as part of his portrait of Louis' good rule (pars.

33–36), and he detailed humanitarian aid that Louis sent to Normandy during a famine (par. 33), his emergency support and funding for the construction of the famous Hôtel-Dieu in Paris (par. 35), his construction of hospitals in other cities, and his sponsorship of Dominican and Franciscan building in Paris and Compiègne (par. 36). Finally, Louis collaborated in the business of the Church, which did not include, in William's formulation, the project of crusade. Rather, as a "true son of obedience," Louis fulfilled the decrees of the pope, aided papally empowered inquisitors of heretical depravity, and sought to constrain the Jews and their "usurious practices" (pars. 18, 21–22).

    Unlike Geoffrey, William exploits the ideals of the king's justice as the good exercise of power along with the legislative and judicial authority of the king. William explicitly praises Louis for rendering "due justice" yet "tempering the letter of the law with the mildness of mercy" (mercy is another classic royal virtue, usually paired with justice). Thus, following the advice of lawyers, Louis outlawed trial by combat (the judicial duel) (par. 24). And he would apply justice "no matter the rank of the offender," including to members of his own household (par. 25). When it came to egregious transgressions, Louis (seeming to test the idea that he tempered justice with mercy) was not lenient but rather held to the letter of the law. Here "justice" is understood specifically in terms of the king's judicial functions, rather than a vaguer notion of the king simply governing in a pious, ethical, and humble manner. In like vein, Louis hired only good men as *baillis* and *sénéchaux*, and as his personal advisors, swiftly firing anyone who engaged in graft or took bribes (par. 26).

    William was much less interested in Louis' crusading. The discussion of the king's captivity in Egypt and his "death narrative" necessarily required that William deal with events that occurred on the crusades. But nowhere does William discuss the crusading context for these events, and the crusades are nowhere singled out as cause for explicit praise. From reading William of Chartres one would not know that Louis had any commitment to the Holy Land (the term does not appear in his text), or even that he ever went on crusade (the term Geoffrey of Beaulieu uses, "pilgrimage," does not appear in William's text). The only introduction to the topic of the captivity of 1250 (par. 6) is the line "when he was made prisoner by the infidels in Egypt" with no explanation of how Louis got there. This is striking given the fact that William in fact accompanied Louis on *both* crusades.

Instead, the captivity and death narratives are set pieces that describe Louis' constancy of faith, and above all (as with Geoffrey) the miraculous nature of his release from captivity. So William explains how, while in captivity, the king rigorously maintained the recitation of the canonical hours, how during his negotiations over Damietta he withstood the torments of his captors, and finally how he was well treated and then released even as the "leading emirs of Babylon" (the Mamluks) planned a coup and assassinated the sultan (Turanshah). Unwilling to credit the Mamluks with anything resembling humane motivations, William interprets Louis' release after this event as nothing less than a miracle of God (par. 8). And later on, others are freed, but "not without the miracle of divine power" which is ascribed to "the king's own merits." Another story from the East (made famous by later iconography) of Louis picking up the bones of dead crusaders and giving them proper burial evinces his compassion and humility (par. 9).

Likewise, the narrative of Louis' death is wholly denuded of its crusading context, and an unaware reader would have no clues from William's account that he was anywhere but Paris. He does take up the scenario described by Geoffrey, but adds much more detail, emphasizing Louis' agony, his prayer and devotion, his supplication to the saints, and his beseeching of God (pars. 37–39). The night before he died, Louis exclaimed "We will go to Jerusalem!"—a reference, as William makes clear, to the heavenly Jerusalem, not the earthly goal of the crusades—and, having taken last rites, returned his spirit to the Creator (par. 39), dying, as Geoffrey had also said, at the very hour that Christ died on the Cross. William returns briefly to the metaphor of the sun that he has opened with (par. 42), thus marking the end of the *vita*, strictly speaking, before listing the seventeen miracles he credits to Louis (discussed above).

The Dominican letter to the College of Cardinals in September 1275, opened with the same scriptural text and deployed the same sun metaphor with which William of Chartres had opened and closed.[118] Yet it is

---

[118] Both texts begin with the words *Mirabilis in altis Dominus* (Ps. 92:4) and contain strong parallels. For example, compare William of Chartres: "Siquidem possumus per Solem istum

striking that the letter then makes different arguments for Louis' sanctity. It is squarely focused on Louis' crusading as the root cause of his sanctity, not as a "servant of the Church," but rather as a martyr in imitation of Christ on the Cross, willing to sacrifice everything he had for the propagation of the faith. It explains that Louis offered himself and his family and everything he had even unto death in the vigorous prosecution of Christ's cause. He was a standard bearer and a champion of the faith, who struggled against persecution. Working for the cause of Christ, whose sacrifice "on the altar of the Cross" the Dominican letter evokes directly, Louis "sacrificed" himself and his family," "followed the path of the True Sun [i.e., Christ], and died for Christ, indeed, in imitation of Christ on the Cross." The framework here is that of passion and sacrifice in the imitation of Christ, with no concern for self, family, or wealth. Sparing nothing for Christ was a biblical idea (see Luke 14:26–27, 33) and the claim—that dying on crusade was a sacrifice in imitation of Christ on the Cross—was another potent formulation that had gained currency in the thirteenth century as part of the development of crusading ideology.[119] Here, Jean of Châtillon and his Dominican brethren went a step further, claiming that Louis was a martyr. In this, the Dominicans were in lockstep with the other letters that the churchmen of northern France sent to the curia in 1275. Yet the claim was daring, and perhaps problematic, since the canonical definition of martyrdom required that a martyr passively

spiritualiter intelligere solem lucentem *inter seculi principes et rectores mundi velut solem inter sidera fulgentem:* illum scilicet recolendae ac praeclarae memoriae Regem Franciae Ludovicum, qui in Occidente exortus orbem terrae *luminosae vitae suae* illustrans radiis ..." with Jean of Châtillon: "Sane, sicut novit plenius vestrae Paternitatis discretio, *inter coeteros orbis terrae principes et potentes, velut inter sydera sol refulgens,* claruisse dignoscitur inclytae recordationis et clarae Dominus Rex Francorum, Clementissimus Ludovicus *luminosae vitae suae* per orbem diffundens radios ..."; emphases added.

[119] Christoph T. Maier, *Crusade Propaganda and Ideology: Model Sermons for the Preaching of the Cross* (Cambridge: Cambridge University Press, 2000); idem, "Crisis, Liturgy and the Crusade in the Twelfth and Thirteenth Centuries," *Journal of Ecclesiastical History* 48, no. 4 (1997): 628–57; idem, "Mass, the Eucharist and the Cross: Innocent III and the Relocation of the Crusade," in *Pope Innocent III and his World*, ed. John Moore (Brookfield, Vt.: Ashgate, 1999), 351–60; Penny Cole, David L. d'Avray, and Jonathan Riley-Smith, "Application of Theology to Current Affairs: Memorial Sermons on the Dead of Mansurah and on Innocent IV," *Historical Research* 63, no. 152 (1990), 227–47; Penny Cole, *The Preaching of the Crusades to the Holy Land, 1095–1270* (Cambridge, Mass.: Medieval Academy of America, 1991). See also M. Cecilia Gaposchkin, "The Place of the Crusades in the Sanctification of Saint Louis," in *Crusades: Medieval Worlds in Conflict*, ed. Madden, Naus, and Ryan, 195–209.

and voluntarily accept death from a persecutor of the faith.[120] Although the Dominican letter claimed that Louis had been persecuted, it was in reality Louis who had been the aggressor, dying of illness (rather than at the hands of a persecutor) while besieging the city of Tunis.

Jean's letter also nodded to the trope of Louis as a "patron and defender and a tireless consoler of the downcast, a sustainer of the needy," which again drew on the traditional image of the good king. And it pointed to the widespread belief in Louis' sanctity and the miracles attributed to him as further proof of his sainthood. Both the common people and the elites, Jean claimed, were talking of Louis' wondrous achievements. Jean probably insisted on this since one of the requirements of canonization was the *fama* of a candidate's saintly virtue—what we might call the "conventional wisdom" or "popular sentiment" regarding that virtue. The letter finished by strongly urging the cardinals to bring this to the pope and canonize Louis.

Boniface VIII's bull of canonization marks the official recognition of Louis' sanctity and represents the way in which, more than a quarter-century after Louis' death, he was now being remembered and modeled as saint. Issued on 11 August 1297 from the papal palace at Orvieto, the bull opens with a flowery exhortation in praise and celebration of the new saint before setting out the qualities of his sanctity. It then engages a discussion of Louis' just rule, which praises him for good kingship in the abstract language of the old kingship manuals: Louis governed his kingdom with prudence and care; he was zealous for peace and a lover of harmony; he ensured justice, never forsaking the path of equity while at the same time suppressing evil and punishing the wicked. Unlike the remainder of the bull, the praise of Louis' kingship is abstract, without narrative examples of Louis' actual reign (which we know made up part of the inquest report).

Although the bull then describes Louis' childhood and early piety, its core is the discussion of the crusade of 1248–54. Boniface narrates in some detail how Louis took the Cross (a new element), the preparations (also new), the initial successes, Louis' captivity, and the negotiations for

---

[120] Aquinas, *Summa Theologica* 2a 2ae qu. 124, pars 1 and 4.

his ransom. This includes the powerful story of his refusal, despite taunts and threats of crucifixion, to take an oath that he would renounce Christ if he failed to fulfill the terms. The bull also treats his good works in Acre. Geoffrey of Beaulieu and William of Chartres had also discussed the captivity—emphasizing Louis' continual prayer and his steadfastness, how the king impressed the Saracens by his demeanor, and claiming that his ransoming was a miracle. The story of Louis' captivity and his negotiation had also gotten a lot of play at the canonization proceedings. But in the canonization bull, the captivity becomes the core of Louis' wondrous sainthood. The function of the story, amidst descriptions of the crusade's failure and Louis' personal suffering, along with Louis' willingness to sacrifice himself for the army and die for the cause, was to construct a kind of Passion narrative—not of martyrdom, but of the patient endurance of suffering. The argument aligned with the claim the prelates had made in 1275 that Louis was a martyr, but emphasized more than his death on his second crusade his unwavering commitment to the cause in the face of torment on his first crusade, in ways consonant with the ideals of the genre of the Passion narrative and fully resonant with the larger priorities of late medieval sainthood. It was also a solution to the problem that Louis did not actually meet the canonical requirements of martyrdom. In any event, Boniface declined to treat Louis as a martyr, categorizing him instead along with the "confessors" of the Church in the catalogue of saints, a decision that Joinville would later criticize.[121]

The bull describes Louis' life after 1254 in terms of personal piety and devotion, including his personal ministration to a leprous monk at Royaumont, his various almsgivings, his asceticism and devotion, his crusade to Tunis, and his death. These were the attributes that placed Louis squarely within the scheme of lay piety and active charity which so strongly defined late medieval sanctity. Finally, Boniface briefly summarizes Louis' miracles, enjoins in particular the House of France (meaning, the Capetians) and the entire kingdom of France to rejoice at being honored with so "elect and virtuous" a ruler, instructs churches throughout

---

[121] Joinville, par. 5, in Joinville and Villehardouin, *Chronicles of the Crusades*, 142.

Christendom to add Louis' feast day to their calendar and venerate him appropriately, and offers an indulgence to those who make a pilgrimage to his tomb at Saint-Denis.

TRANSLATED TEXTS

Chapter One

Three Early Letters on the Sanctity of Louis IX

1. Philip III's Letter to French Prelates Announcing the Death of Louis IX (12 September 1270)

Philip, by the grace of God king of France, sends love and greetings to all his beloved and faithful archbishops, bishops and abbots, priors, deacons, priests, and other church leaders, and to all the regular and secular convents, colleges, and chapters established in the kingdom of France to whom the present letter may come.[1]

We are compelled to announce to you all, with much bitterness of heart, some cruel news—far too sad and sorrowful—for which all faithful Christians must weep and which must in particular be endured by each and every person within the boundaries of the kingdom of France, and especially lamented by us, with continual, repeated sighs. Not long ago, as was pleasing to God (who always directs the steps, the deeds, and the ends of his chosen people toward salvation in the fulfillment of His will), Louis—of famed and pious memory, most famous king of France, beloved of God and honored by men, and our late most dear lord and father, whose life is known to have been beneficial for the entire Church, whose memory is a blessing, and whose praise is preached in church—rendered his happy spirit to the most high Creator. After many praiseworthy acts of faith and charity; after many burdensome struggles which he faithfully and fervently undertook with a tireless spirit for the

---

[1] Philip was born in 1245, and became heir to the throne when his older brother Louis died in 1260. After his father's death he reigned 1270–85.

Christian faith and the propagation of the Church; after recently landing courageously in the port of Tunis without loss to his men, holding this well-known harbor, this gateway to the lands of Africa, which he proposed (should God so grant) to dedicate to the Christian faith once he had eradicated and banished the wicked filthiness of the barbaric Saracen people; after his victorious capture of Carthage, just as he was setting off, intent on a swift and powerful assault on Tunis by land and by sea to entirely eradicate the power and might of the infidel ruler and his army; in the midst of all this, God arranged to happily consummate and conclude his toil and struggle. Brought down by bodily weakness, he took to his bed, and after much suffering from this illness, at last he requested in most Christian fashion, and received with great devotion, all the sacraments of the Church. And in confession of the true faith, in fervent love and devotion to God, on the Monday following the feast of the blessed apostle Bartholomew,[2] at the very hour in which the Lord Jesus Christ, the son of God, breathed his last while dying on the cross *for the life of the world*,[3] he came to his final hour, lying on sackcloth and ashes.

With such a dire, gaping new wound, we are compelled to wail for such a sharply stinging bereavement and to mourn the deplorable loss and death of a pious father, in which we find and feel not only our own incurable injury and irreparable damage but an inestimable loss and lamentable harm to all of Christendom. Everyone grieves equally for the pious king, the peaceful king, the father of the poor, the refuge of the miserable, the consolation of the oppressed, the particular champion of all religion and innocence, the zealous supporter of justice, the defender of the faith and the Church. O, who might grant it to us, we who now occupy his place on earth, to follow in the footsteps of so praiseworthy a progenitor? To imitate his example, to fulfill his ideals, to live up to his sacred merits and evidence of salvation? We would rather justly glorify the virtuous merits and deeds of his life than mourn his death, if only the force of sorrow would allow us reason! Surely it is a great glory to have had such a parent, yet it is sadness without respite to have lost a father's consolation so great and so sweet, conversation so pleasant, such sound advice and aid. This,

[2] 25 August 1270.
[3] John 6:52.

indeed, would be thought a grief beyond solace were it not that those who had knowledge of his most saintly deeds have for him the certain hope that he is now carried off from the cares of this temporal kingdom into the eternal realm and glory without end.

So that we may turn away somewhat from our lamentation, let us change our groans and sorrows into the weapons of salvation, into the voice of prayer and the support of love. Let us devote to him now in death the gratitude that we had toward him when alive, so that we may receive the fruit of a blessing from the One who rewards all good things. Truly then, in accordance with the last will and judgment of our aforesaid most holy father, who humbly asked that after his death all religious people and institutions throughout the realm be requested to freely raise their voices to God in prayer and love for him, know that to this end we are now dispatching to the various parts of the realm our beloved men, the religious brothers Geoffrey of Beaulieu and William of Chartres, both of the Order of Preachers, and Brother Jean of Mons[4] of the Order of Brothers Minor, having once been dear members of our remembered lord father's household, as bearers of these directions, together with others of our own household and administration. Wherefore we ask and request of you one and all, with heartfelt emotion, that—mindful of that man's sincere love and devotion which he, our holy father and lord, always had and effectively displayed for the Church and its people, and mindful of that holy concern which he lavished to keep our realm blessed and flourishing, to keep it in quiet peace *as the apple of his eye*[5]—you may wish to offer to the highest King the gift of your prayers and masses and other loving support for his precious soul (though many believe it needs no outside intercession), also seeing to it that this same task is carried out in all places subject to your[6] control. May you pray continually and see that in the above mentioned places prayers are offered for us and for the whole Christian army.

Done in camp near Carthage, the Friday after the Nativity of the Blessed Virgin in the year of Our Lord 1270.[7]

---

[4] A Franciscan, confessor to queen Marguerite of Provence and perhaps to Louis IX as well.
[5] Deut. 32:10; Prov. 7:2.
[6] BnF ms. lat. 9376, fol. 65vb, here reads "nobis" where "vobis" is found in lat. 5526. This variant would indicate "under our control" and might perhaps make more sense.
[7] 12 September 1270.

2. *Clare Memorie Ludovici*: Gregory X's letter to Geoffrey of Beaulieu (4 March 1272)

Gregory, bishop elect, servant of the servants of God, sends greetings and apostolic blessing to our beloved son, Brother Geoffrey of Beaulieu of the Order of Preachers.

Recalling[8] the exceptional merits of Louis of illustrious memory, king of the Franks, concerning his life, which presented a model of blessed living to other orthodox rulers, the more we sense the fragrance of greater sweetness, the more we recall in memory one whom we loved with a pure heart when living, now called back home. Although it is true that we have some knowledge of his comportment, which he maintained by adhering to the will of his Redeemer, yet still we desire that this be made more fully known to us, especially concerning those things that were done more privately. Thus by this apostolic writing conveyed to you, we particularly ask and urge of your devotion that—fulfilling our wishes with dedication and diligence—you should not delay in writing about his aforementioned comportment, treating in order each and every one of the things he did and heeded, adding nothing beyond what actually happened, maintaining a foundation of absolute truth. And [send it] to us under your private seal, as quickly as you are able, by a sure messenger. Moreover, we wish you to say no word of this to anyone. And do not wonder that our name is not found on the seal appended to the present letter, which has been sent prior to the solemnity of our official consecration and benediction,[9] since those who before now have been elected Roman pontiffs have been accustomed to observe this practice in letters sealed before the rite of consecration.

Dated at Viterbo, four days before the Nones of March in the first year of our Apostolic office.

---

[8] The word "recolentes" is omitted from the version printed by Chapotin.
[9] Gregory had been elected on 1 September 1271, but was not crowned pope until 27 March 1272.

3. Letter to the Cardinals of the Church from Jean of Châtillon and the Dominican Provincial Chapter of France (September 1275)

To the reverend in Christ fathers and lord cardinals of the sacrosanct Roman Church and the Holy Venerable College, Brother Jean,[10] unworthy provincial prior of the Order of Preachers in France,[11] together with the diffinitors[12] of the Provincial Chapter as well as the priors and other brothers assembled at Le Mans in the name of God to conduct the Provincial Chapter, sends greetings and devout service in prayer with all reverence.

The wonderful Lord on high,[13] the highest Maker of all things and above all the praiseworthy author of our restoration and salvation, shows more laudably and marvelously to us the grace of his goodness by how much more brilliantly he pours down the light of his grace and power onto eminent and illustrious people, so that they might shine before all. And for this reason He is not only more devoutly and justly worshiped by the people and honored by the powerful, but also shown forth[14] by the examples of the greater and more honorable, and made known by their more excellent acts. Clearly, as the understanding of your fatherly spirit knows well, among all the princes and rulers on earth, *as the sun when it shines*[15] *among the stars*,[16] most merciful Louis, king

---

[10] According to Bernard Gui (a Dominican writing several decades later in the south of France) Jean of Châtillon served as provincial of France in 1267–69 and again from 1272 or 1273 until 1281. See Gillis Meersseman, ed., *Laurentii Pignon catalogi et chronica*, Monumenta Ordinis fratrum praedicatorum historica 18 (Rome: Institutum Historicum Fratrum Praedicatorum, 1936), 80–81 and 84–85 (we thank Dr. Simon Tugwell for this reference). It is worth noting that Jean had alternated in his office with Peter of Tarantaise (provincial 1263–67 and 1269–72) who at the time of this writing had been promoted to the cardinalate.
[11] "In Francia" is omitted by Chapotin.
[12] Dominican provincial chapters were attended not only by the priors of each house, but also by specially elected representatives called diffinitors.
[13] Ps. 92:4.
[14] Chapotin has the plural "illustrantur" where we follow de Rechac's more grammatically expected "illustratur."
[15] Ecclus. 50:7.
[16] Abdias 1:4.

of the Franks, of celebrated remembrance and illustrious memory,[17] is known to have brightly shone forth, pouring out through the world the rays of his illuminating life, energizing with the heat of love and beaming from the first inception of his faith, *as a shining light increasing to* a greater *perfection*.[18] The further he progressed in temporal age, the more fervently he seethed with love of God; and the higher he rose in dignity, the more humble and gentle was his spirit. He was always a pious father, a patron and defender, and even a tireless consoler of the downcast, a sustainer of the needy, outstandingly zealous for the faith, for the propagation of which he was prepared to expend everything he had. Twice he left his homeland for the journey of pilgrimage. He left his inheritance and, *like an alien*[19] *and stranger,*[20] sparing no efforts, no cost or expense, neither to himself nor to his people, he offered himself[21] and his brothers and sons to be sacrificed even unto death in the vigorous prosecution of the cause of Christ, all so that he might make recompense to that same One who, as the price for our salvation, offered Himself on the altar of the Cross, the standard bearer and champion of the faith. It is known that Louis, faithful in the struggle of this kind of persecution, following the path of the true Sun, finally set in the southern lands as though at the midday of fervent love. Hence it can easily be believed that though the sword of a persecutor did not take his holy life, he has not lost the martyr's crown.

It is our considered judgment, most reverend Fathers, that these various things that we have come to learn, because they were seen or heard by some of the brothers of our order who were close by his side in life and in death[22] or which come to us as common knowledge (*fama*), ought

---

[17] Chapotin has "recordationis et clarae Dominus Rex" where we follow de Rechac's "recordationis et clarae memoriae Rex."
[18] Prov. 4:18.
[19] Job 19:15.
[20] Num. 9:14.
[21] The verb "obtulit" is found only in Chapotin; in this case we have followed his reading since it makes grammatical sense of the passage, though it may have been his own silent emendation.
[22] Presumably Geoffrey of Beaulieu and William of Chartres were chief among those brothers alluded to here, though there is no reason to assume the reference is uniquely to them.

not be passed over in silence. Rather we have taken care[23] to submit them faithfully before your venerable College, since already both common people and magnates are relating this [common knowledge], or some of it, which the people are proclaiming, to such an extent that not only people in neighboring lands loudly acclaim these things, but even barbarous nations are able to marvel at them as well. And since, after his blessed death, the largess of heavenly gifts is believed to have made wondrous his sanctity *in signs and wonders*,[24] by miraculously effecting through him blessed wonders of healing both at his tomb and elsewhere, as is credibly related by many who are trustworthy, it is just and piously to be believed that he who, while living in the body kindly opened the *bowels of mercy*[25] to all, would now do so more powerfully while lying bodily in the bowels of the earth, having more intimately entered into the powers of his Lord.

Therefore, illuminated by the splendors of this light, and suffused with the sweetness of this renowned fragrance, contemplating his fuller glorification to the height of divine honor, in order to confound worldly pomp, to spurn secular glory, to crush the arrogance of unbelief, for the edification of all, low and high alike, with firm conviction and down on the bended knees of the heart, we beseech your fatherly spirit, speaking humbly and with one mind, that you may elect to lay before our lord the most holy highest Pontiff[26] all that we have presented in writing above, which we have been unable to present in person as we would have liked. And, if such will have pleased your goodness, may you urge him that *a bright lamp*[27] be no longer, as it were, left hidden *under a bushel*[28] at the cost of many good things, and that the faithful devotion of the people be not weakened, but rather that it be increased and out of its new joy the spirit may be carried to exaltation. Farewell to your sacrosanct College.

---

[23] The verb "curavimus" is omitted by Chapotin.
[24] 2 Cor. 12:12.
[25] Luke 1:78; Col. 3:12.
[26] The pope was still Gregory X, who however died shortly afterward, 10 January 1276.
[27] Luke 11:36.
[28] Matt. 5:15; Mark 4:21; Luke 11:33.

Given at Le Mans, in the year of the Lord 1275, in the month of September,[29] and jointly[30] sealed with the seals of the provincial prior and diffinitors, and of the priors and other brothers mentioned above.

Brother William of Tournai.[31] Brother Simon of Troyes.[32] The prior of Rouen. The prior of Poitiers. The prior of Angers. The prior of Bruges. The prior of La Rochelle.[33] The prior of Saint-Quentin. The prior of Le Mans. The prior of Troyes. The prior of Caen. The prior of Beauvais. The prior of Arras. The prior of Dijon. The prior of Auxerre. The prior of Amiens. The prior of Pons. The prior of Compiègne. The prior of Clermont. The prior of Chartres. The prior of Châlons.[34] The prior of Metz. The prior of Toul. The prior of Bourges. The prior of Constance. Brother Stephen of Gâtinais.[35] Brother Adam of Valle.[36] Brother Jean of Tournon.[37] Brother Richard of Peleyo.

---

[29] The French Provincial Chapter normally met on 8 September (the Nativity of the Virgin).
[30] We follow Chapotin's "communiter" here, where de Rechac has "muniter."
[31] William of Tournai was the author of *De instructione puerorum* (before 1264) and then (1272–74) master of theology at Paris. See Kaeppeli, *SoP*, 2:167–69; Palémon Glorieux, *Répertoire des maîtres en théologie de Paris au XIIIe siècle*, vol. 1 (Paris: Vrin, 1933) # 29; and *HLF* 20 (1895): 208–10. In the following notes we have attempted to identify only the named signatories.
[32] On Simon of Troyes or Du Val the best biographical summary is Carolus-Barré, *Le procès*, 249–51. Simon was an inquisitor for the kingdom of France from 1276, and prior of Provins by the time he testified for Louis' canonization hearings at Saint-Denis in 1282. Clearly a close associate of the royal family (see the reconstruction of his testimony on Louis in Louis Carolus-Barré, *Le procès de canonisation de Saint Louis (1272–1297): Essai de reconstitution*, ed. Henri Platelle, Collection de l'Ecole Française de Rome 195 [Rome: Ecole Française de Rome, 1994], 134), he was named an executor of the will of Peter of Alençon—son of Louis IX—in this same year. See also Kaeppeli, *SoP*, 3:348–50 (though repeating an incorrect reading of the present document that would suggest Simon was prior of Rouen at this time).
[33] "prior Rupellensis" omitted by Chapotin.
[34] "prior Carnotensis, prior Cathalaunensis" omitted by Chapotin.
[35] This may be Stephan of Gaigni/Gagny who has a brief entry in Kaeppeli, *SoP*, 3:356. See also a reference in Antoine Dondaine, "Le manuel de l'inquisitor (1230–1330)," *Archivum Fratrum Praedicatorum* 17 (1947): 110 n.79. We thank Dr. Simon Tugwell for the latter.
[36] Chapotin has "Adam Valle" where de Rechac reads "Adam de Valle." We have not been able to identify this man, or the last brother on the list, Richard de Peleyo.
[37] From Caen, later (1277–1279) master of theology at Paris and (ca. 1282) prior of Paris. See Kaeppeli, *SoP*, 3:23–24.

Chapter Two

Here Begins the Life and Saintly Comportment of Louis, Former King of the Franks, of Pious Memory

by Geoffrey of Beaulieu

For the honor and glory of the divine[1] name and the edification of the faithful, persuaded by the prayers of many great men and especially compelled[2] by obedience to the authority of my superiors, I have found it right and proper to present in writing the holy comportment and deeds of the most Christian Louis, former king of the Franks, so far as the divine mind shall see fit, through its grace, to inspire the memory of my own mind.

[1] How praise of King Josias befits King Louis.

To begin, therefore, I may adopt in commendation of the pious king that praise of King Josias, which we read in Ecclesiasticus, chapter 49: *The memory of Josias is like the composition of a sweet smell made by the art of a perfumer. His remembrance shall be sweet as honey in every mouth, and as music at a banquet of wine. He was directed by God to the repentance of the nation, and he took away the abominations of wickedness. And he directed his heart toward the Lord, and in the days of sinners he strengthened*

---
[1] *RHGF:* divi] divini *A B*
[2] *RHGF:* adstrictus] constrictus *A B*

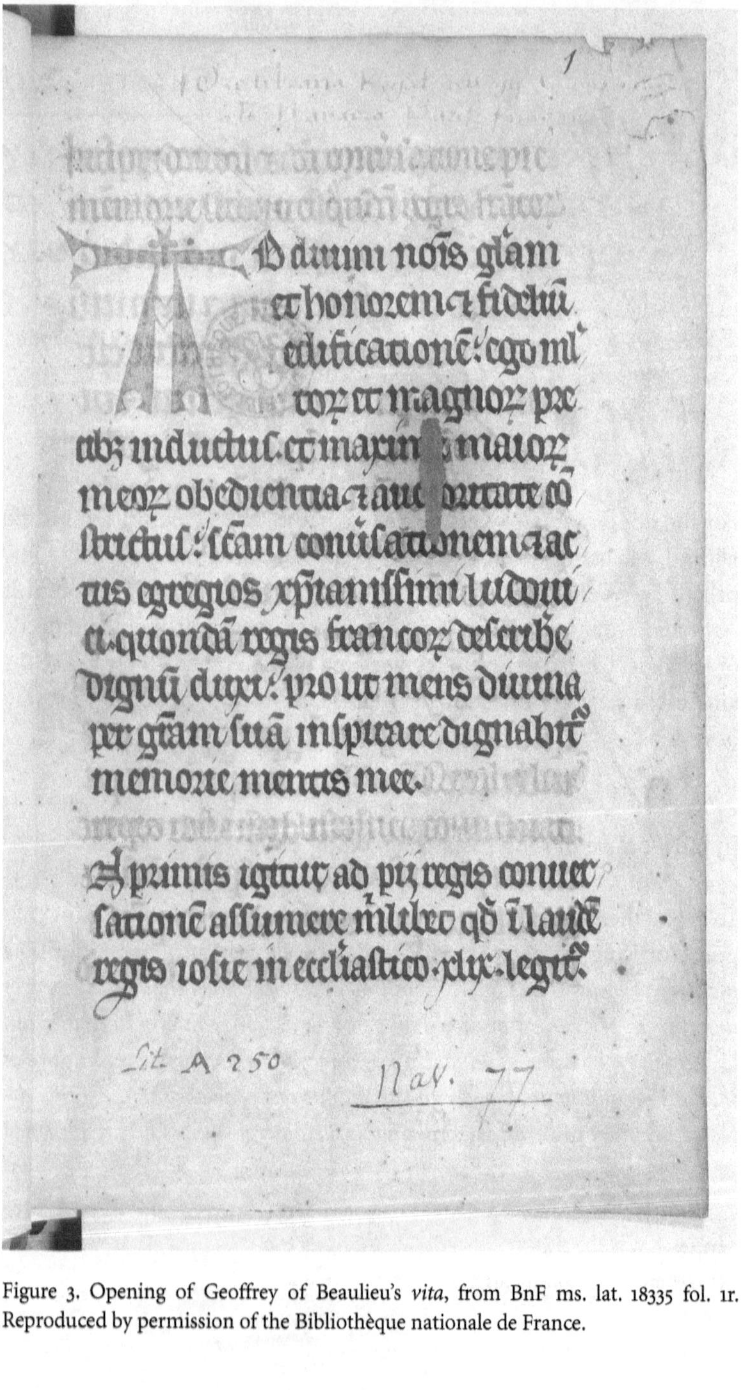

Figure 3. Opening of Geoffrey of Beaulieu's *vita*, from BnF ms. lat. 18335 fol. 1r. Reproduced by permission of the Bibliothèque nationale de France.

godliness.³ Moreover, many things are said in praise of this King Josias both in the fourth book of Kings,⁴ and in 2 Paralipomenon 34, that seem most properly to pertain to the praise of our king: *When he was yet a boy, Josias began to seek the Lord,⁵ and he did that which was right and pleasing in the sight of the Lord, and walked in all the ways of David his father. He turned not aside to the right hand, nor to the left.⁶ The name of his mother was Idida.⁷* He caused *the Temple* and House *of the Lord to be restored.⁸ There was no king before him like him, that returned to the Lord with all his heart, and with all his soul, and with all his strength; neither after him did there arise any like him.⁹* And he *kept Passover* which had not been kept before, and which no other kings had kept.¹⁰ I will be able to explain how all these many things specifically apply to our most glorious king, each in its proper place.

[2] That the name Josias is applicable to him

For the moment let it suffice for me to indicate just how the name befits our king. Josias, you see, is understood to mean "salvation of the Lord," or "elevation of the Lord" or "incense" or "sacrifice of the Lord." To whom would the meaning of this name better apply than to our pious king, in whom was truly the salvation of Our Lord? For truly he was one who devoted himself to his own salvation and to the salvation of those dear to him; who worked as hard as he could for the elevation and exaltation of the Christian faith; and who—in addition to the incense of mental devotion¹¹ which he continuously offered to

---

³ Ecclus. 49:1–4.
⁴ *RHGF* inserts "cap. xxii" but this is found only in the margin of A, added by a later hand.
⁵ 2 Par. 34:3.
⁶ 3 Kings 22:43; 4 Kings 22:2.
⁷ 4 Kings 22:1.
⁸ 4 Kings 23:6.
⁹ 4 Kings 23:25.
¹⁰ Cf 4 Kings 23:22–23.
¹¹ For the phrase "incensum mentalis devotionis," followed by "in odorem suavitatis," cf. Innocent III, *De sacro altaris mysterio. Libri sex*, *PL* 217, col. 833: "Moraliter autem incensum devotionis adolendum est in thuribulo cordis, igne charitatis, ut odorem suavitatis emittat." From chapter 57, "De oblatione et incenso, et quare sacerdos tertio circumducit et reducit

the Lord in his heart from childhood on, and the holy sacrifice of his physical penance which he openly displayed to the Lord in accordance with his station and the physical weakness of his body—*offered himself at last whole for a holocaust to the Lord*[12] *as a savor of sweetness*[13] with his double pilgrimages overseas. If *it was reputed to Abraham unto justice*,[14] in that at the Lord's bidding [Abraham] once offered upon the altar his only son, so much the more will the Lord *repute unto* eternal *justice* and never-ending reward[15] one so faithful that he not once but twice offered himself, and his brothers, as well as the chosen flower of his kingdom's army, unto death, in obedience to our Savior. And this was especially so in the final and pious and pitiable pilgrimage to Tunis where—departing with the counsel of everyone involved, with his own children and his whole army, out of zeal and exaltation of the Christian faith—then and there he was himself worthy of being a sacrifice to Christ. And in that place, like a martyr and tireless fighter of the Lord, he happily ended his life in the Lord. Moreover, on that journey there also died in the avowal of the true faith two of his own children, whom he loved with deep affection: the count of Nevers and the queen of Navarre.[16] Thus he may deservedly[17] be likened to King Josias. Let us now proceed, with the help of God, to an account of his praiseworthy life and comportment.

---

incensum, et quare totum undique incensatur altare," this reference would seem to lend Louis a quasi-priestly air.

[12] I Kings 7:9.

[13] Exod. 29:41 (and elsewhere; the phrase *in odorem suavitatis* is used repeatedly in the Vulgate in conjunction with sacrifice).

[14] Gen. 15:6.

[15] *RHGF:* pretium] premium *A B*

[16] Louis' son Jean Tristan had been born in Damietta 8 April 1250 during Louis' first crusade, and died 3 August 1270 outside Tunis. His bones (as with his father's) were brought back to Saint-Denis for burial. He was count of Nevers from the time of his marriage to Yolanda of Burgundy in 1265. Isabelle was the oldest child (of those who lived to maturity) of Louis and Marguerite of Provence. She was born in 1242, and became countess of Champagne and queen of Navarre upon her marriage to Thibaut V of Champagne in 1255. She accompanied her father, husband, and brother on the crusade of 1270, and died shortly after them in 1271.

[17] *RHGF:* merite] merito *A B*

[3] On the innocence of his life and his holy comportment.

Clearly it may be said of him, and quite truthfully, what we have said above about Josias: *When he was yet a boy, he began to seek the Lord, and he did that which was right and pleasing in the sight of the Lord. There was no king before him like him, that returned to the Lord with all*[18] *his heart, and with all his soul, and with all his strength; neither after him did there arise any like him. And he walked in all the ways of David his father. He turned not aside to the right hand, nor to the left.* He did, in fact, have a most Christian and most holy father; that is, King Louis [VIII], who himself, alight with zealous faith, took up the cross by the authority of the Church against the heretics who were greatly opposing the Roman Church and the Christian faith at that time in the Albigensian region. And having boldly pressed this expedition, and having for the most part powerfully suppressed the haughty pride of these enemies, while returning from this expedition, he happily died and passed on to the Lord.[19] The devoted successor of this pious father, and his earnest imitator, that Louis of whom we speak, did not turn aside from the holy footsteps of his father; not aside to the right, to fly off, swept away by prosperity, nor to the left, to be wrecked by trying circumstances. He was the kind who always stood firm, humble in good times and confident in bad times. Thus have we known him many times, in both conditions, as the Lord permitted.

[4] On the praise of the lady Blanche, his most pious mother.

Moreover we ought not to overlook *the name of Josias' mother*, who was called *Idida*, which is interpreted as "Beloved of the Lord" or "Dear to the Lord." This rightly fits the renowned mother of our king, that is the Queen lady Blanche—who was truly beloved of the Lord and dear to God,

---

[18] *RHGF:* toto] omni *A B*
[19] Louis VIII's short reign (1223–26) is notable for the newly direct royal intervention in the Albigensian Crusade, which greatly increased royal power in Languedoc by the time it ended in 1229. Louis died of dysentery at Montpensier on 8 November 1226 while returning from the crusade.

as well as useful and pleasing to mortals.[20] Guided by the holy nurture and sound doctrine of so pious a mother, our Louis began to develop as a boy of outstanding talent and promise, and to grow day by day to perfected manhood, and *to seek the Lord, and to do that which was right and pleasing in the sight of the Lord,* truly to *return to the Lord with all his heart, and with all his soul, and with all his strength,* like a good fruit from a good tree. And concerning the time when he began to reign and was no more than about twelve[21] years old, there are witnesses still here today who attended upon the king then and can say now with what force, hard work, justice, and power his mother guided, protected, and defended the rights of the realm; though, indeed, at that time the king faced many powerful foes as he began his reign. But, thanks to the merits of his innocence and the wise foresight of his mother, who always proved a manly woman (*virago*) combining her feminine spirit and sex with the heart of a man, those who would upset the kingdom went down in confusion while the justice of the king triumphed.

We must here mention that there was a certain member of the clergy who had heard some vicious gossip to the effect that before his marriage the king kept concubines with whom he sometimes sinned, and that his lady mother knew this but chose to turn a blind eye.[22] When this member of the clergy, much surprised, repeated this story to the queen reprovingly, she humbly defended herself and her son from this false gossip and added a most praiseworthy statement, that is: If this said king, her son, whom she loved above all other mortal creatures, lay sick to the point of death and she were told that he would be cured by sinning once with a woman who was not his wife, she would sooner see him die than that he even once would offend[23] his Creator through mortal sin. I myself heard this from the mouth of the king.

---

[20] Blanche of Castile married the future Louis VIII in 1200. After his death, she was in effect regent of France during Louis IX's minority and played a crucial role in suppressing challenges to royal authority. She would again fill the role of regent from the time of Louis' departure on crusade in 1248 until her death in November 1252.

[21] *RHGF, A:* duodecim] duo B

[22] *RHGF:* dissimulante matre sua] dissimulans dicta domina matre sua *A* dissimulante dicta domina matre sua *B*

[23] *RHGF:* offendere] offenderet *A B*

[5] Again,[24] on the purity and innocence of his life.

I, though unworthy, acted as confessor to the lord king for twenty years or thereabouts, and I heard his general confessions so often[25] that I would hardly know how to count them. To the honor of God, therefore, I state that in his whole life he himself never knowingly committed a single mortal sin—not one that I would dare to call mortal. There were some people who, from a superficial observation of his actions, worried that because of his accustomed[26] and natural kindness he would become too lax and negligent in his oversight of *baillis*[27] and other officials and close associates, and that he appeared slow in presenting justice. But anyone who paid attention to how careful and diligent he actually was in examining and reviewing good[28] and trustworthy officials and *baillis*, would perhaps have excused him for those things. For I truly believe that very few of the people who cast such doubts, were they given the responsibility he bore, would not have been found to have done many more things far worse than he.[29]

[6] On his position, concerning his direction of subordinates.

He wanted to have counselors and advisers, both clergy and laymen, who were as well chosen for their life as for their faith and wisdom,[30] and he would see that they were chosen from all places. In legal cases that appeared to turn against him, he would always stand against himself so far as he could do so in a good manner, and would present the case against

---

[24] *RHGF, A:* Item] *om. B*
[25] *RHGF:* toties] totiens *A B*
[26] *RHGF, A:* sollita] molita *B*
[27] *Baillis* were the royal officials charged with legal oversight, tax collecting, and enforcing royal rights within their areas of jurisdiction, known as *bailliages;* as such they oversaw *prévôts* in *prévôtés.*
[28] *RHGF, A:* bonis] bonus *B*
[29] We have chosen to keep Geoffrey's rather tortuous phrasing here, as he seems to have struggled to find polite language.
[30] *RHGF:* tam in fidelitate quam et sapientia] tam in fidelitate et sapientia *A* tam in vita quam in fidelitate et sapientia *B* [We have followed *B* in this passage]

his own interests, so that his counselors would not shy away from rendering a true judgment out of fear of offending him. He sent out through the kingdom many faithful, hardworking *enquêteurs*[31] to look into misdeeds, his own as well as those of his *prévôts* and *baillis*, and he saw to it that injuries were mended and restitution made. Many times he likewise instituted inquiries into the state of his household and punished proven offenders as they deserved.

[7] On the care and grace of his words.

He was most careful and gracious when he spoke. He avoided scurrilous and dissolute words, especially anything derogatory or false.[32] He rarely[33] or never uttered an insult or reproach against anyone, even[34] a petty miscreant, unless provoked by a great offense. In particular, he absolutely abstained from swearing of any kind, even in the conventional or mild way that can often occur in conversation. Sometimes,[35] to avoid other oaths, he would say instead, "By my name!" When he once heard even this criticized by a certain religious man, he gave it up altogether from then on. Rather, in accordance with the Gospel, *his speech was Yes, Yes: No, No*.[36] In complex dealings, serious deliberations, or legal cases, few or none judged more attentively or truly than he. And what he worked out in his mind he knew how to convey with prudence and grace. Thus grace would flow from his lips, like a truly wise man, and he made himself worthy of love with his words. As much as possible, *his speech was always in grace seasoned with salt*.[37] Moreover he was most gracious,[38] and

---

[31] The Latin word here is *inquisitores*, but we have used the French *enquêteurs*, to avoid confusion with papal "inquisitors of heretical depravity." It should be noted, however, that the same Latin word was used for both offices.
[32] *RHGF, A:* mendacibus] mendaciis *B*
[33] *RHGF:* et rarissime] rarissime *A B*
[34] *RHGF:* quantumlibet] quantumcumque *A B*
[35] *RHGF:* Aliunde] Aliquando *A B*
[36] Matt. 5:37; James 5:12.
[37] Col. 4:6.
[38] *RHGF* indicates that *A* reads "grossimimus" but the abbreviation is actually for "gratiosissimus." Same abbreviation appears in *B*.

even[39] just to see his face was enough to move the affections of everyone to love him.

[8] On his humility, particularly in his demeanor and dress.[40]

From the time that he returned from overseas he never dressed in scarlet or green or brown cloth, or various furs, but only in clothing of dark color, either camel-colored or dark blue. And, since such clothing seemed to be of less worth[41] for charitable donation to the poor than did the more costly clothes he wore when young, he made up for this by ensuring that each year his almoner would have sixty Parisian[42] livres to give for the sake of God, in addition to what he usually received; for our pious king did not want his more public show of humility to come at the expense of the poor. In a similar way he chose to use only plain white iron spurs and bridles, nothing gilded; and plain white riding saddles without any decoration.

[9] On washing the feet of the poor.

It was his practice on any given Saturday to wash the feet of three of the poorer and older men who could be found, which he did on bended knee, humbly, piously, and in a most secret place. After washing, he dried their feet and humbly kissed them. In similar fashion he brought water to wash their hands, which he kissed in the same way. He then provided a certain sum of money to each, and he himself waited upon them as they ate.[43] If it happened that he could not perform these devout duties due to poor health,[44] it was his wish that his confessor, in the presence of his almoner,

---

[39] *RHGF* et] etiam *A B*
[40] This rubric is given twice in *A;* first at the bottom of fol. 5r and then at the top of 5v: Both times it reads "De humilitate eius et primo de habitu et veste" [*RHGF* omits "eius"].
[41] *RHGF, A:* huius minoris valoris esse] huiusmodi esse *B*
[42] *RHGF:* paratas] parisienses *A B*
[43] *RHGF, A:* et ad comendendum ipsemet eis ministrabat] *om. B*
[44] *RHGF, A:* infirmitatem] *om. B*

should do these same things in the same way on his behalf.[45] A further praiseworthy example of such pious humility is this: once on a certain Sabbath, when he was at the Abbey of Clairvaux,[46] he desired to take part in the washing of the feet of the monks, which they call the "mandate."[47] That is, according to the custom of their order, after Vespers, the monks wash each other's feet with solemn devotion. The king himself, out of humility, many times wished to lay aside his cloak and humbly wash the feet of the servants of God with his own hands, on bended knees. But, seeing that many powerful dignitaries were present who did not know him well, he thought it wiser to refrain from this duty of humility.[48] Many instances and edifying examples[49] of his outstanding humility, kindness, mildness, and patience could be given, but our present work might then exceed its limit. In these aforementioned virtues, however, I do not know if there was another person of his station who was his equal in all the world.

[10] **Again, on his humility.**

Another instance that demonstrates his humility is that he stated in his final desire and ordered to be written into his testament that no great pains and no unnecessary expenses should be incurred with his burial, so that in death, just as in life, he would be an example of humility.[50] He always showed the greatest respect to his confessors, so much so that sometimes when he had taken his seat for confession before his confessor, if he then wanted some door or window shut or opened, he would hastily get up from his place of confession and go humbly to shut it or do something of this sort,[51] all to spare his confessor from having to do

---

[45] *RHGF, A:* vice] *om. B*
[46] One of the oldest and most important Cistercian monasteries, founded in 1115 by Saint Bernard, and now in the modern department of Aube.
[47] *Mandatum*, referring to the "mandate" of Jesus to the apostles to imitate his washing of their feet on the Thursday before Easter (Maundy Thursday).
[48] *RHGF, A:* De consilio ab hoc humilitatis officio supersedit] de consilio ab hoc humilitatis exemplum semper exhibuerat vivus ostenderet et defunctus *B*
[49] *RHGF, A:* exempla] *om. B*
[50] This sentence *om. B*
[51] *RHGF, A:* aliquid] ad aliquid aliud *B*

it. When his confessor opposed this action, he would humbly answer, "Dear friend,[52] you are the father and I am the son."[53] Again, it testifies to the commendation of his humility, that often, freely and without shame, indeed in a most pleasant fashion, he would relate to us how he had been taken prisoner at Mansura by the Saracens, and what he did with them at that time, and how he came to be set free. If there was something said or done that was not to his liking, if he needed at the time to pretend otherwise, he knew how to do so very carefully and well. He would pick one or more people whom,[54] in addition to his confessors, he would earnestly ask to let him know faithfully and not spare him in any fashion if they should ever observe or hear from others anything about him that was worthy of reproach. In this way, moreover,[55] he kindly and patiently received personal correction.

[11] How he was chaste[56] and self-controlled in his marriage.

With the consent of his wife the queen, the couple refrained from carnal relations through all of Advent and all of Lent, and also on certain days of the week and similarly during vigils and major feast days. Moreover, he refrained on solemn days when he was to take communion, out of respect for the holy mystery, and for many days both before and after. If, however, for some reason it happened that he visited his wife the queen during these days of abstinence and spent time with her, and—due to the nearness of his wife and human weakness—he should feel an inordinate movement of the flesh, he would rise from the bed and stride about the room until his rebellious body had calmed down.

---

[52] *RHGF:* amen] karissime *A B*
[53] *B* inserts a section break here (before the word "item") with a new rubric: "De huius sepulture." Because this rubric does not seem to reflect accurately the content of the following passage, we have not included a new section break here.
[54] *RHGF:* aliquos etiam sibi] aliquos sibi *A* aliquos sibi karissimos *B*
[55] *RHGF:* ipse vero] ipse autem *A B*
[56] *RHGF, A:* caste] sobrie *B*

[12] That he wished to abdicate his royal power and enter a religious order.

The fact should not be passed over in silence that many years before his death, seeking the height of all perfection, he resolutely planned from heartfelt devotion that when his eldest son should come of age he would give up his kingdom, obtain his wife's consent, and enter a religious order—specifically one of two orders; that is, the Brothers Minor or the Preaching Brothers. He was particularly fond of these two, for he used to say that if he could divide himself in two, he would give half to one and the remainder to the other. And so he used to remark in private that it was no small source of pride to him that the members of his household, who were constantly in his presence, could not decide which of these two orders he loved the most. But when he got the opportunity, and had secretly divulged this plan to his wife the queen (insisting she not reveal it to a single soul), she had absolutely no desire to accede to his request, his heartfelt longing, for any reason. Rather, refuting the king's proposal, she pointed out sound reasons against it: divine providence had placed him more usefully in his original state so that he might safeguard the realm and advance the interests of the entire Church. Thus, frustrated in his pious proposal, he remained in this world, though from then on with less love of the world and with greater humility and fear.

[13] On the religious education and instruction of his children.

Since holy and highborn offspring ought to result from such a sacred marital union, and since by the grace of God such offspring did come forth in plenty, it follows that we should observe how catholic this pious father was in the instruction and discipline of his children. He wanted his sons, as they grew to manhood, not only to hear Mass every day but also Matins and the singing of the canonical hours. And he wanted them to listen to sermons with him, and each one of them to learn their letters, recite the Hours of the Blessed Virgin, and always attend Compline with him—which he would have recited solemnly in church each day after supper with a final special antiphon for the Blessed Virgin sung very loudly and devoutly. When this was done he would return with his sons to his bedroom where a priest[57] had sprinkled holy water about the bed and throughout the chamber, and the boys would sit down around him. And it was then his custom to speak edifying words to them for their instruction[58] before they retired.[59] On Good Friday he did not want them to wear caps of roses, or any caps at all,[60] out of respectful memory of the holy Crown of Thorns, with which the head of the Savior was cruelly crowned on that very day, and with which Crown the King of Kings had so magnificently honored [Louis'] kingdom.

[14] That two of his sons would be raised for a religious life.

In praise of our king we must not pass over this fact: when he was first overseas as a pilgrim to the Holy Land, and even afterward[61] when he had returned to France, he arranged and wished it written into his testament—led, in our opinion, by the spirit of God—that when the two sons who had been born to him overseas, that is lord Jean and lord Peter,[62] reached the age of reason, they should be educated[63] within a religious enclosure; that is, one in the house of the Preaching Brothers of Paris and the other in the house of the Brothers Minor. And these places received adequate provision for this purpose at the king's own expense. It was his intent that they would there[64] be instructed in holy principles and writings, and be brought to a beneficial love of religion. With all his heart he

---

[57] *RHGF*, A: a sacerdote] *om.* B
[58] *RHGF*, A: institutionem] instructionem B
[59] *RHGF*, A: recederent] descenderent B
[60] This passage seems to refer to a festive practice of wearing a wreath or crown of roses on holidays, deemed inappropriate by Louis in this case. The phrasing here refers explicitly to a cap or hat ("capellos de rosis") but in later liturgical reworkings of this passage it became a wreath ("serta"); for instance in the office *Ludovicus decus regnantium*, in *Blessed Louis, the Most Glorious of Kings: Texts Relating to the Cult of Saint Louis of France*, ed. M. Cecilia Gaposchkin (Notre Dame, Ind.: University of Notre Dame Press, 2012), 173.
[61] *RHGF*: et etiam inde postquam] et etiam postquam A B
[62] On Jean Tristan see note 16 above. Peter of Alençon was born in 1251 during Louis' first crusade, survived Louis' second crusade, and married Jeanne of Châtillon, before dying in Salerno in 1284 fighting for his uncle Charles of Anjou.
[63] *RHGF*: nutrirentur] educarentur A B
[64] *RHGF*: illic] illuc A B

longed that they—influenced by the evidence of salvation, inspired by God—would enter those orders at some time and place. Likewise, to his first born daughter, who would later become queen of Navarre, when still overseas, he wrote with his own hand and sent a special letter in which he urged her most effectively and piously toward contempt of this world and toward love of and entry into religion.[65] Moreover, out of his piety, he offered to God, so far as he could, his daughter, lady Blanche, at the abbey of the nuns near Pontoise (where the body of his holy mother is buried), so that his daughter might there be religiously raised and formed in the love of religion, through the words of salvation and the example of the holy nuns.[66] Although the One whose providence in arranging matters is never wrong, has seen fit to order things differently for these same children—since, perhaps, it better served their own good and the practical needs of the Church of God for them to pursue marriages in this world rather than to enter an order—we still mention these matters so that we may lay before you the pious king's devotion to faith[67] and the fervor of his holy longing, with which he aspired to every pinnacle of perfection, as much for himself as for his children. And I do not believe that his pious aspiration would go without its crowning reward, even though his pious wish was not fated to have the desired result.

Moreover, as the conclusion of this particular chapter, I have thought it well worth showing also how the king, as a truly catholic father, as if by divine revelation, aware of his own death, before his final illness, wrote down with his own hand, in French, salutary instructions and catholic teaching that he has left to his firstborn son and through him to his other

---

[65] See note 16 on Isabelle above. A letter of advice that Louis wrote for Isabelle does survive. See David O'Connell, *The Instructions of Saint Louis: A Critical Text* (Chapel Hill: University of North Carolina Press, 1979). As O'Connell shows, however, this text cannot be the one that Geoffrey refers to (unless Geoffrey is confused), because Geoffrey mentions a text written during Louis' first crusade urging Isabelle to enter religion and thus before her marriage, whereas the "Instructions" that survive seem to have been written later (probably about the same time as the *Enseignements* to Philip) when Isabelle was a married woman, and in any case do not advise her to leave the world for a convent.

[66] Blanche was born at Jaffa during Louis' first crusade. Although he apparently wished her to become a nun at the royal Cistercian abbey of Maubuisson, she married the infante of Castile in 1268. After his death she returned to France and spent much of her widowhood at the Franciscan abbey of Saint-Marcel outside Paris, where she died in 1323.

[67] *RHGF, A:* Devotione fidei] devotione *B*

children as a kind of testament. I have had in my possession since his death a copy of these instructions written in his own hand. As briefly and finely as I could I have translated from French into Latin these instructions, which are the following:

[15] The instructions which the pious king wrote for his firstborn son before his death and left as if it were a testament.[68]

My dearest son:

First, I instruct you that *you shall love the Lord your God with your whole heart and with your whole strength*,[69] for without this there is no salvation.

Next, you ought to protect yourself from all things that you know will displease God—that is, from all mortal sin—so that[70] you might allow yourself to be crucified by every form of martyrdom rather than to commit a mortal sin of any kind. Moreover, if the Lord has permitted some tribulation to befall you, you ought to bear it kindly and give thanks for it, knowing that God is providing for your own good and that you may indeed deserve it. Even more, if the Lord has brought you prosperity of whatever sort, you ought to humbly return thanks, and beware lest you thereby degenerate into wickedness, either by a vain glory,[71] or by some other way, because you should not fight against or offend God for his gifts.

Next, I advise you to make confession often and to choose upright and wise men as confessors, who have the knowledge to instruct you in those things you must beware of[72] and in those you must do. Be so modest

---

[68] For the relationship of Geoffrey's Latin version of the *Enseignements de saint Louis* (in fact the source of all the "short" versions of this text, in both the Latin and the French traditions) to other surviving versions, see O'Connell, *The Teachings of Saint Louis*. It should be noted that A gives a French version of the *Enseignements* immediately following the text of Geoffrey's Latin *vita*.
[69] Deut. 6:5.
[70] *RHGF*: ita quod] itaque *A B*
[71] *RHGF, A*: per unam vanam gloriam] per vanam gloriam *B*
[72] *RHGF, A*: tibi sit cavendum] tibi cavendum *B*

toward your confessors that they, as well as your other friends, may dare to criticize you without fear.

Next, willingly and devoutly listen to the Divine Office. And when you are in church, beware of gazing idly about you or of chattering on about empty things, but pray earnestly to God,[73] either with your mouth or in heartfelt meditation. And attend with special devotion to the secret of the Mass, at the moment of the consecration of the body and blood of the Lord Jesus Christ.[74]

Next, have a pious heart toward the poor, the suffering, and the downtrodden; and come to their aid so far as you can, and be of solace to them.

Next, if you are sick of heart, tell this to your confessor or to some other worthy man, for then you will bear it more easily.

Next, you should like to have around you[75] the company of worthy men, whether they be secular or religious; converse with them often and shun the company of the depraved.

Next, hear sermons willingly, both in public and in private, and be willingly attentive to securing the pardon of sins from our mother the Church.

Next, you should favor the good and reject the bad in those around you.

Next, let no sinful suggestion be heard in your presence, nor any word that deprecates another. Especially see that you allow no word of blasphemy against God or his saints to be spoken by anyone, but that you correct them on the spot.

Next, for all the blessings heaped upon you by God, may you render thanks to Him so that you may be[76] worthy to receive even greater ones.

Next, be just to those placed under you, keeping to the line of justice, *and turn not aside, neither to the right hand nor to the left.*[77] And always give the benefit of the doubt to the poor over the rich, until you are sure of the truth. If someone should have a complaint against you, side with

---

[73] *RHGF:* Dominum] Deum *A B*
[74] *RHGF:* domini nostri Jesu Christi] domini Jesu Christi *A* Jesu Christi *B*
[75] *RHGF, A:* tecum] totum *B*
[76] *RHGF, A:* sis] sic *B*
[77] 2 Par. 34:2; Isa. 30:21.

the cause of your adversary, until the truth is clear to you. In this way those of your counsel[78] will more readily stand on the side of justice.

Next, if you know for certain that you hold property belonging to another, either from your own reign or from that of your predecessors, return it at once. If the matter is unclear, have it inquired into by wise men.

Next, work hard to see that all those placed under you are preserved in *justice and peace*,[79] and especially people of the Church and religious orders. It is said of my grandfather, King Philip [II], that when one of his councillors told him that the clergy caused him many losses by usurping his rights, and that many people wondered that he tolerated it, the king replied to him, "I well believe what you say, but when I ponder the many benefits that the Lord has brought me, I would much rather suffer in this way than raise a scandal between the Church and me." Love then, my son, such people of the Church, and[80] keep the peace with them so far as you are able.

Next, freely come to the aid of the religious poor in their requirements, and especially for those through whom God is more honored on earth.

Next, honor your parents and reverently keep their commands.

Next, bestow ecclesiastical benefices upon worthy individuals following the counsel of holy men, and upon those who possess no other benefices.

Be on your guard never to initiate a war against another Christian without very good reason; and, if it must be done, see to it that innocent people, churches, and their property do not suffer undeservedly. As swiftly as you can, turn from wars and strife to peace, even from the wars among those placed under you, as did the blessed Martin,[81] who judged that he had achieved the pinnacle of virtue when he had restored peace among combatants.

---

[78] *RHGF:* illi qui sunt de consilio tuo] illi de consilio tuo *A B*
[79] Cf. Ps. 84:11.
[80] *RHGF:* serva] et serva *A B*
[81] Saint Martin of Tours (AD 316–97).

Next, let it be your concern to have faithful *baillis* and *prevôts* and to inquire diligently into how they act; similarly with those who see to your hospitality.

Next, be piously obedient to our mother, the Roman Church, and to the pope, as to your spiritual father.

Next, work to remove all sin from your realm, especially blasphemy and heresy.

Next, be ever mindful to acknowledge and give thanks to God for all his benefits.

Next, watch that the costs of your household be moderate.

Lastly, my son, I beseech you that if I die before you, you will faithfully aid my soul with masses and with prayers, and that you will invoke the holy congregations of our realm that they may pray for me, and that you will associate me with all the good you are going to do.

My dearest son, finally I give you every blessing that a pious father may give his son. May the whole Trinity and all the saints *keep you from all evil*,[82] and may God's grace so shape your will that He may be served and honored through you, so that after this life we will come, together, to see and love and praise Him without end. Amen.[83]

Behold the testament of a pious father to his sons! Oh, testament of life and peace! Testament from which nothing should be deleted through forgetfulness, nothing changed through addition![84] Testament confirmed not at the death of the testator, but at the attainment of life everlasting![85] It is as if this pious father compiled his testament from those possessions which were truly his own; and what he had, he then gave to others. These virtues, which he has bequeathed to his sons, he possessed wholly within himself; just as one first learns to do something oneself, and then teaches others. And we,[86] my dear ones—especially princes and prelates—are the

---

[82] Ps. 120:7.
[83] *RHGF, A:* amen] amen amen *B*
[84] *RHGF:* nulla similiter ordinatione mutandum] nulla superordinatione mutandum *A B*
[85] This sentence *om. B*
[86] *RHGF:* Hujus nos] huius et nos *A B*

legatees and heirs, in our own way, of this sacred general testament of this father, our king.

Let these words now suffice concerning the teaching and instruction of his children. Let us now set out some things[87] concerning his manner of penance.

[16] On his manner of penance. And, first, on his[88] confession.

Just as we have already related how it was written in praise of King Josias that *he was directed by God to the repentance of the nation,* in the same way [King Louis] was divinely held up and shown by God as a model and example of penance for people of all stations. His approach to penance took many forms.[89] It was his practice throughout the entire year to confess in humble piety each Friday, always in some very secret place chosen for this purpose, always, as it were, providing in advance a suitable spot no matter which of his manors he happened to be inhabiting. And this should not be passed over below.[90]

[16*bis*] On his discipline.[91]

Now, after he had made confession he would always receive discipline[92] from his confessor with five identical slender iron chains, the heads of

---

[87] *RHGF:* aliquid] aliqua *A B*
[88] *RHGF, A:* eius] ipsius *B*
[89] *B* here inserts a separate rubric: "De confessione ipsius." *A* has a paragraph marker here. Since the new chapter topic seems redundant (already announced in the heading to ch. 16) we do not insert a new chapter here.
[90] The passage as it actually reads in both *A* and *B* makes little sense: "Et licet consuevisset infra nec omittendum infra." *A* was silently emended in *RHGF* to read "Et licet consuevisset intra, tamen non omittebat extra." Our guess is that Geoffrey initially wrote "Et licet consuevisset infra" but intended to cancel that phrase and replace it with "nec omittendum infra"; a later scribe might then have missed the cancellation marks and copied out both phrases.
[91] The rubric "De disciplinis eius" is found only in *B*. We include it in the text, but label the chapter "16*bis*" in order to continue to allow easy reference to the chapter numbers established in the *RHGF* edition.
[92] In this context "discipline" refers to penitential whipping or flagellation.

which were well bound to a small ivory case; when the disciplines were finished, these little switches[93] would be folded up and stored away. He would carry this case secretly in a purse that hung from his belt. He used to bestow similar boxes with similar iron switches upon certain of his children or personal friends for the time and place of receiving disciplines, as a form of secret gift. If his confessor was sometimes lenient with his blows, and the king thought he was sparing him this way, he would nod to him as a sign to strike harder. No church celebration, no matter how solemn, interfered with these disciplines.

I do not believe I should neglect to mention that he once had a certain confessor accustomed to bestow strong and harsh disciplines, from which his delicate flesh suffered greatly. He did not wish to reveal this to this confessor while he was alive. But after this confessor died, he did humbly mention it to his other confessor, as though joking and laughing. And although, as mentioned, it was his custom to confess every Friday, yet if something that required confession confronted him on another day, he would go straightaway to confession without hesitation. When this occurred during the night, as was often the case, if he happened to have his confessor at hand he would summon him before he began Matins. If he were unable to get him right away, in the meantime he would confess to his chaplain who assisted him in reciting the Hours.

I must not fail to note that, after his return from overseas, it was his wish to have[94] two confessors—one from the Order of Brothers Minor, the other from the Order of Preachers. This was so that if one was not readily at hand, he would have the other right there; and so that he might show his love and support for each order; and, above all, because his conscience could thereby remain freer from anxiety—because[95] *in the mouth of two witnesses every word stands*,[96] and, according to the saying of Solomon, *where there is much counsel, there is safety.*[97]

---

[93] The word *virgule* comes at this point in B, whereas RHGF and A have it in the previous clause, where it makes little grammatical sense.
[94] *RHGF:* Semper duos voluit confessores] semper duos habere voluit confessors A B [habere *add. in marg* by a later hand in A]
[95] *RHGF:* quod] quia A B
[96] Deut. 19:15.
[97] Prov. 11:14.

[17] That he sometimes[98] wore a hair shirt.

Moreover, on Fridays during Advent and Lent, he would wear a hair shirt right next to his skin. He would do the same thing on the four vigils of the Blessed Mary, even though his confessor told him many times that such penance was hardly suitable to his station, but[99] that rather he should bestow great alms on the poor and display timely justice to his subjects.[100] Finally, he humbly admitted to his confessor that a hair shirt of this sort was extremely painful to his[101] delicate skin. So, upon [the confessor's][102] advice, he humbly gave up the use of the hair shirt. From time to time during Lent, however, in lieu of a hair shirt he might wear a wide belt or band of hair. And in place of this hair shirt, as a kind of compensation, it was his wish that every Friday in Advent and Lent his confessor be given on his order forty Parisian sous for secret distribution to the poor.

[18] On his abstinence.

It was his habit to fast every Friday throughout the year, and to abstain from meat or fat each Wednesday. Sometimes he even used to abstain from meat on Mondays in the same way,[103] but because of his bodily weakness he gave up this day[104] upon the advice of wise men. Moreover, he fasted on bread and water on the four vigils of the principal feasts of the Blessed Virgin. Indeed, he wished to fast on bread and water on Good Friday and when observing the Vigil of All Saints and some other solemn fasts throughout the year. On Fridays in Lent and Advent he abstained from fish and fruit. Sometimes, however, as allowed by his[105] confessor, he

---

[98] *RHGF:* quoque] quandoque *A B*
[99] *RHGF:* debebat] solebat (added above line by later hand) *A om. B*
[100] *RHGF, A:* et subditis festinam iusticiam exhibere] *om. B*
[101] *RHGF, A:* ejus] sue *B*
[102] *RHGF:* ejus] *om. A B*
[103] *RHGF:* Aliquando etiam diebus Lunae a carnibus similiter abstinebat] Aliquandiu et diebus lune similiter abstinebat *add. in marg. A* (probably by original scribal hand) Aliquandiu eciam diebus lune similiter a carnibus abstinebat *B*
[104] *RHGF, A:* diem] *om. B*
[105] *RHGF, A:* sui] *om. B*

enjoyed a single kind of fish and a single kind of fruit on this day. He heard that a certain member of a religious order abstained completely from eating any kind of fruit whatsoever, except when new fruits were first offered to him; then he would only taste them once, as though as an act of grace, and then abstain from them[106] for the whole year. While the holy king related this to his confessor—as though sighing that he himself did not dare to attempt such perfection—he formed a plan that started from the opposite end of things; that is, from then on, when new fruits would be first offered to him he would not eat them, as though sacrificing *firstfruits to the Lord*,[107] and afterward he would eat with a good conscience. I believe he always thereafter observed this practice, just as he had proposed. To the best of my recollection I have seen no one,[108] or few people indeed, who diluted his wine with as much water as he did.

[19] On his works of compassion and dispensing of alms to the poor.

From childhood his sense of compassion grew with him, and he always bore the pious bowels of charity[109] for the afflicted and the poor. I should not be silent about—and yet I am not able to explain in full—*his alms, which all the Church of the saints declares.*[110] For instance, every day, wherever he was, more than 120 of the poor dined at his house on bread and wine and meat or fish. During Lent[111] and Advent and on other sacred days the number of poor was increased. Often the pious king served the poor and passed around dishes and sliced the bread himself, and distributed many coins with his own hand, and he would pick the poorer

---

[106] *RHGF*: erat] eo *A B*
[107] Cf. Exod. 35:5 and I Kings 15:21 (among other Biblical appearances of *primitias Domino*). "Firstfruits" in general refers to the religious offering of the first produce of a harvest.
[108] *RHGF*, A: Nullum] neminem *B*
[109] The words "pia viscera caritatis" are found only in the margin of *A*, but probably in the original scribal hand. "Viscera caritatis" is not a Biblical phrase, but was frequently employed by Church Fathers such as Saint Augustine; we have preserved the time-honored English translation "bowels of charity" in spite of its rather archaic tone.
[110] Ecclus. 31:11.
[111] *RHGF*: vero] *om. A B*

among them and give them more. Especially, however, on certain days of fasting and solemn vigil, before he would himself sit down to eat, he would serve all the things that I have just mentioned, with his own hands, to two hundred poor. Beyond these things, every day at lunch and dinner he would have three poor and aged men seated right next to him to eat, sending them some food from his own dishes out of charity. And at the end[112] he would give each a certain sum of money.

Again, *who is able to declare*[113] such generous and frequent alms as this pious king lavished upon numerous poor and many convents of nuns as well as monks, hospitals of the poor, leper houses, and other institutions for the poor, just as though he were their very own father? Indeed, among his other works of piety, each year, at the beginning of the winter, it was his practice to lavish a sum of money on the convents of the Brothers Minor and the Preachers of Paris, to provide for their necessities.[114] And when they were in greater want, he would increase his gift. When he had completed his granting of alms, born from the overflow of piety he bore in his heart, he would remark, with a most cheerful countenance and pious heart,[115] to those of his household who were with him, "Dear God, I think how well these alms are spent upon such and so many brothers, who flow from all over the world to these convents in Paris to study sacred doctrine, and then take what they have absorbed from divine Scripture and pour it forth across the world for the salvation of souls and the honor of God!"

Moreover, from the time of his youth he undertook to build so many religious houses and monasteries, and in particular that famous Cistercian monastery of the Blessed Mary of Royaumont, with the strikingly beautiful church that he built from his own funds and endowed with abundant income, where a large and holy congregation of monks serves the Lord. He also built numerous houses in various parts of his kingdom for the Preaching Brothers and Brothers Minor, and completed others that had not yet been finished. He expanded the *Maison-Dieu*[116] at

---

[112] *RHGF:* in fine prandii] in fine *A B*
[113] Cf. Ecclus. 18:2.
[114] *RHGF:* necessitatibus] necessariis *A B*
[115] *RHGF, A:* ac corde devoto] *om.* B
[116] *RHGF:* domum] domum Dei *A B*. *Maisons-Dieu* were charitable lodgings for travelers and the sick.

Paris at great expense and augmented its income. Moreover at Pontoise, Compiègne, and Vernon he put up large, expensive houses for the poor, and richly endowed them. He personally acquired the monastery of Saint-Matthew near Rouen and located there some fifty holy sisters of the order of the blessed Dominic, piously serving the Lord, and endowed them with adequate income.[117] He saw to the construction of a large home for blind paupers in Paris, where more than 350 poor blind people now stay and hear the Divine Office[118] in a chapel built there.[119] Furthermore, he gathered in the house of the *Filles-Dieu* at Paris a great crowd of pitiful women who for want of food were living, or ready to live, in sin, who sought only bread and water from him[120] so that they might avoid sin.[121] And for their support he provided to them four hundred Parisian livres every year, and free clothing for those who came to stay. In addition, for the Carthusian brothers he supplied a suitable location in a place near Paris called Vauvert and gave them income adequate to live on.[122] Also he bought at his own expense a house in Paris for the honest women known as beguines and turned it over to them, wherein some four hundred live in honest devotion.[123] And he provided daily support to many of them[124] for as long as they might live, especially impoverished noblewomen. Likewise, in many other cities and towns of his kingdom he provided residences for these beguines, and to many he provided food.[125] Moreover, according to the wish of King Philip [II] of pious memory, every year around the start of Lent it was customary to spend about three thousand livres on needy members of the Church, but no formal confirmation of this existed; so his successor, that most devout king [Louis IX], confirmed

---

[117] This community was founded between 1258 and 1264.
[118] *RHGF:* divinum servitium] divinum officium *B*
[119] Louis founded a hospital for the blind, known as the *Quinze-Vingts*, around 1260.
[120] *RHGF, B:* ab ipso] *om. A*
[121] The *Filles-Dieu* was a house for reformed prostitutes founded in 1226 by the bishop of Paris; Louis subsequently offered generous support.
[122] Louis first asked the Carthusian Order to establish a house in Paris in 1257; after a temporary stay at Gentilly, the Carthusians eventually received from him the site of Vauvert (south of the city walls) in 1259.
[123] The Grand Béguinage was founded by Louis by 1264, on the Right Bank in the parish of Saint-Paul.
[124] *RHGF:* et pluribus exceptis] et pluribus ex ipsis *A B*
[125] Pluribus ex eis victo providit *add. B*

this holy almsgiving in perpetuity by his written charter, so that it could [not][126] fall into disuse.

Likewise,[127] our most pious king, father and consoler of the poor, who in his very heart had established a spiritual hospital welcoming to the Lord, charitably embraced all religious members of whatever poor order—as long as it had been recognized by the Apostolic See—who came to him; and he provided suitable accommodation for them in Paris at his own cost. When he became aware that some in his household grumbled among themselves about the scope of his almsgiving, he would tell them that since it was sometimes necessary for him to be excessive in his expenses, he preferred such excess in the name of alms for the sake of God,[128] rather than for mere things of this world; so that his excess for matters of faith might atone and redeem the excesses he often had to make for worldly matters. Nevertheless,[129] he was generous and liberal in all royal solemnities, just as much in his daily household expenditures as in *parlements* and councils of knights and barons, as was befitting his royal state. And he was served in a very courtly and appropriate way in his[130] household, more so than in the times of earlier kings.[131] He always wanted the leftovers from the royal table to be kept diligently and faithfully, and[132] no one to be allowed to carry any of these leftovers away from the house without permission for special almsgiving. The poor received great advantage from this.

[20] On awarding of benefices.[133]

In dispensing Church benefices that were in his direct gift and patronage, he always kept God before his eyes; and to the extent he could, he

---

[126] *RHGF* justifiably suggests in a note that "non" must be inserted here.
[127] *RHGF:* igitur] item *A B*
[128] *RHGF:* Dominum] Deum *A B*
[129] *RHGF:* Nihilominus tamen] nichilominus *A B*
[130] *RHGF:* domo sua] domo *A B*
[131] *RHGF:* plus quam in praedecessorum suorum regum curiis] plusquam aliorum regum temporibus retroactis *A B*
[132] *RHGF:* ita] iterum *A B*
[133] *B* does not place a chapter break here, or insert any kind of rubric. Our translation follows *A*.

bestowed these on well-chosen and proven people. This was especially true of cathedral churches, by reason of the royal control over these church temporalities, where the awarding of prebends customarily pertained to him when a see was vacant.[134] He had these people inquired into and chosen by the chancellor of Paris[135] and other good men, especially Preaching Brothers and Brothers Minor. And he wanted the men who were chosen[136] to be remembered in writing, so that he might provide for them at the right time and place. I should not neglect to mention that he always observed this custom, that he would not give another church benefice to anyone, no matter how learned or famous, who already possessed one, unless that person simply resigned the first benefice.[137] And he did not want to concede to anyone a benefice that was not vacant, until he had clear evidence[138] that it had become vacant. His heart greatly rejoiced in the Lord[139] when he would bestow some fine church benefice on a man of great and proven reputation.

Now, let us briefly conclude these matters which pertain to the praise of his piety and compassion. He held that whatever was expended for works of piety, or for the benefit of the poor, or conferred on people of proven worth, was best spent. What was being spent on excess building of his houses, or other vanities of this world, he seemed to consider a waste. It is crucial to grasp this fact, which clearly appears as a work of divine might and a statement of the merits of this holy king: Although he was not extravagant in giving generous gifts to the barons and knights of his kingdom, and seemingly restrained in such public praise and commendation as would inspire their hearts to love him, yet, nevertheless, *all people both great and small held him in great reverence and fear* because of his faith, his holiness, and his justice. For *knowing him to be a just and holy man*, they *feared* him.[140] So it was that after his earliest youth no one dared rebel or move in any

---

[134] *RHGF, A:* regalis] regalium *B*
[135] This is the chancellor of the Cathedral of Notre Dame, who by virtue of this office was also chancellor of the University of Paris.
[136] *RHGF:* clericos] electos *A B*
[137] *RHGF, A:* prius beneficium] primo beneficio *B*
[138] *RHGF:* certitudinem] certitudinis *A B*
[139] *RHGF, A:* a Domino] in Domino *B*
[140] Cf. Mark 6:20.

way against him. Or, if someone rebelled, he was laid low under his command. And so, as we read of the peaceful King Solomon, he kept *peace on every side round about* his kingdom.[141] And as is said of *Asa, king of Judah*[142] he *reigned in peace, there had no wars risen in his time, the Lord giving peace* on every side.[143] In all truth, if there were people who were secretly hostile or jealous,[144] with loving understanding he would win them over to peaceful good will through courtly manners and timely assistance. And since his ways were pleasing to the Lord, he turned his personal enemies, were it even possible for him to have any, toward peace. His behavior was forgiving and gentle not only to his own subjects but also to others nearby and to neighbors living on his borders, both princes and local leaders. To keep and maintain peace among them he often appointed wise and discreet[145] legates with ample resources; and prompting[146] them thus to keep the peace, he kept the poor common people safe from the grievous woe they usually suffer in wars. In this kind manner he[147] bore himself so faithfully, mercifully, and mildly in all things, not only for his subjects but also for neighbors and those who were far away, that he deserved the love and respect of all, and to preserve his kingdom in peace as though in the protection and tranquility of his heart. For it is written, *Mercy and truth preserve the king, and his throne is strengthened by clemency.*[148] Indeed *his throne sparkled as the sun before all*[149] and in the regard of others. For just as the sun pours down its rays everywhere, so from him the blessings of his light and warmth come down everywhere, as it were, in the glowing examples of his praiseworthy life, and the good works born of his unquenchable charity and love.

---

[141] Cf. 3 Kings 4:24.
[142] *RHGF, A:* Juda dicere] videre *B*
[143] Cf. 3 Kings 9; 2 Par. 15:5–6.
[144] *RHGF:* hostes et aemulos lateter] hostes aut emulos latentes *A B*
[145] *RHGF, A:* discretos] *om. B*
[146] *RHGF:* inclinabat] inclinans *A B*
[147] *RHGF:* Sic autem gratiose erga] Sic autem graciose *A* Sic autem erga *B*
[148] Prov. 20:28.
[149] Cf. Ps. 88:38.

[21] On his devotion to the Divine Office, and on his manner of prayer.

He wanted to hear the singing of all the canonical hours and[150] the Hours of the Blessed Virgin every day. Even if he was journeying on horseback, he would still softly recite them with his chaplain, both the offices for the day and for the Blessed Virgin. Moreover, he recited the Office of the Dead, with the nine readings, every day with his chaplain, even on solemn feast days. It was a rare day indeed that he did not attend two masses, and often he would hear three or four. When he once heard, however, that certain nobles were grumbling about how he would hear so many masses and so many sermons, he answered that no one would ever say a thing if he spent twice the time playing dice or riding in the woods hunting and hawking! At one time he would get up around midnight to attend Matins sung by his chaplains and clergy in the chapel, so that after Matins he would have a quiet time for prayer before returning to bed. That way, as he frankly confided, he did not have to fear any interruptions breaking in if the Lord was inspiring his devotion. At that time it was his wish to remain at prayer for the length of Matins in church. But, since he had to rise early at Prime for pressing business, and his head and body would get worn down and afflicted by such vigils, he gave in to the prayerful advice of his counselors; that is, that he should get up for Matins at such an hour that after a brief interval he could hear Prime and masses and other Hours all together. He did not want any sort of conversation to interrupt while the Hours were being sung, unless some clear necessity was pressing; and even then just a brief and succinct word. Just as we have noted above praising King Josias, that he *kept Passover, there was none before him like him*,[151] *neither did any of all the kings keep such as this*,[152] in the same way this one [Louis] saw to it that the important sacred feast days of the year, not only Easter but the other feasts as well, were devoutly and earnestly celebrated. He assembled for this purpose many times in the course of the year select clergy with beautiful voices, especially from the

---

[150] *RHGF*: et etiam] et *A B*
[151] Cf. 4 Kings 23:22–25.
[152] Cf. 2 Par. 36:18.

Bons enfants[153] who lived in holy congregation at Paris, for whose retreat from the world he dispensed funds on which they lived much of the year in their studies.

He greatly longed for the grace of tears, and he would piously and humbly lament this shortcoming to his confessor, saying to him in confidence that, when in the Litany it was said "that you may bestow upon us a fountain of tears,"[154] he would earnestly say, "O Lord, I dare not ask of you a fountain of tears, but a few scant drops of tears would do to water the parched hardness of my heart." Once,[155] in private, he revealed to his confessor that when the Lord had given him some tears in prayer, which he felt pleasantly flowing down his cheeks into his mouth, their flavor was most sweet, not just to his heart, but to his taste also.

He often went to visit religious houses and, humbly on bended knees, would ask in chapter for the support of their masses and holy prayers for himself and for his family, living and dead. And he did this with such humility that the monks were often brought to tears. He was most faithful in his own prayer and in seeing that others prayed for those of his household, those living in his service, and those dear to him who had passed on.

[22] On his pilgrimage to Nazareth.

It seems to me that I must not pass over in silence how humbly and in what a catholic manner the devout king behaved while overseas, during the pilgrimage he made from Acre to the holy and devout city of Nazareth. During the Vigil of the Annunciation,[156] wearing a hair shirt next to his skin, he went from Sepphoris (where he had spent the night) into Cana of Galilee and then to Mount Tabor. And then, during the same vigil, he went down into Nazareth. When he saw the holy place from afar,

---

[153] *Bons enfants* or *boni pueri* were communities of poor university students, founded in northern French towns including Paris in the 1240s and 1250s.
[154] "Ut fontem lacrymarum nobis dones." Cf. *PL* 151, col. 867B ("Litaniae cum VII Psalmis").
[155] *RHGF*: Aliquando etiam] aliquando *A B*
[156] 25 March. Since Louis was in Acre from May 1250 to March 1251, this must have been March 1251.

he dismounted from his horse and most devoutly worshiped on bended knees, and proceeded from there on foot until he entered the sacred city and pious site of the Incarnation. Despite his great exertions, he piously fasted that day on only bread and water. Indeed, those who were there can now bear witness to just how devoutly he behaved, and how solemnly and gloriously he caused Vespers and Matins and the Mass and the other offices fit for such a high and solemn occasion to be performed. And some of these witnesses were able to believe and truthfully attest that from the moment the Son of God took on the flesh of the glorious Virgin at that spot, never had the Divine Office been performed with such devout solemnity there. And following the celebration of Mass there at the altar of the Annunciation by his confessor, the devout king received Holy Communion. Then lord Eudes of Tusculum,[157] legate of the Apostolic See, celebrated solemn Mass at the great altar of the church, and delivered a devout sermon. The king, catholic[158] in all matters, desired to have the most precious and devout ornaments for the church, and he had with him paraphernalia and ornaments of various colors, all as was fitting for various solemn celebrations, and he personally attended with care and particular attention to this matter. Moreover, he earnestly solicited the pardon of sins from our lord the pope and other church prelates, and made frequent pious and humble visits [to this church] when they had been granted.

[23] That he devoutly listened to sermons and studied sacred Scripture.

He wanted to hear sermons very often, and when they really pleased him he could recall them accurately and knew how to repeat them to others quite magnificently.[159] When returning from his pilgrimage overseas, which took ten weeks or so, while he was making some delay at sea,[160] he

---

[157] Eudes of Châteauroux was a theologian at Paris, papal legate, and cardinal. He accompanied Louis on his first crusade, and died in 1273.
[158] *RHGF, A:* catholicus] *om. B*
[159] *RHGF:* gloriose] graciose *A B*
[160] *RHGF, A:* in mari] in navi *B*

ordered that three sermons be given every week aboard ship. In addition, when the sea was calm and the ship hardly needed the labor or[161] effort of the sailors, the pious king wanted these same sailors to hear a special sermon intended just for them; that is, on the articles of the faith, and morals, and sins; for he understood that such people rarely heard the word of God. He also desired that these same sailors each confess to priests chosen for this purpose. And with his own mouth he gave them very beneficial and effective encouragement, persuasively pointing out to them how often they risked death due to the sudden dangers of the sea. Among other things that he said, one is outstanding and memorable; that is, that if any sailor wanted to confess his sins, but the ship could not spare him at that moment, "I," said the king, "will put my hand in place of his[162] and hold the line or do whatever needs doing." Nor was this an empty, pious encouragement. For some[163] sailors confessed then who had not confessed at all for many years.

Our faithful king, while he was still overseas, heard about a great Saracen sultan who (they said) searched diligently for all manner of books that could be essential for Saracen philosophers, and had them copied at his expense and stored in his book cupboard, so that learned men could have a supply of these books as often as they needed them. The pious king—considering that the children of darkness seemed to be more prudent than the children of light and more zealous in their error than the children of the true Church were in the Christian faith—therefore decided[164] that upon his return to France he would have copied at his own expense all the useful and authentic books of sacred Scripture which he could locate in the various monasteries' book cupboards, so that not only he, but other learned men and the religious of his household could study them for the use and edification of themselves and their neighbors. This is what he thought, and upon his return he had a good, strong place built; that is, at Paris in the treasury of his chapel, where he dutifully amassed

---

[161] *RHGF:* et] vel *A B*
[162] *RHGF, A:* libenter manum meam apponam] loco ipsius libenter manum meam apponam *B*
[163] *RHGF:* nonnulli] nulli *corr. to* nonnulli *by later hand A* multi *B*
[164] *RHGF, A:* concepit] concepit in corde *B*

many original works of Augustine, Ambrose, Jerome, and Gregory[165] and also books of other orthodox teachers, all of which he willingly and earnestly studied as time allowed, and freely[166] permitted others to study. He especially tried to do some studying, as time allowed, after[167] his daily nap and before he would appear in public to speak with visitors or listen to Vespers.[168] In general he wanted to have new copies made rather than purchase books that were already copied, saying that this way the total number of holy books was increased and so their utility was more abundantly augmented. He disposed of these books—which, as we have said, he had made and which he left in his book cupboard in Paris—in his testament, by leaving one part to the Brothers Minor, another to the Preaching Brothers, and the rest to the monks of Royaumont, a house of the Cistercian Order[169] that he had founded at his own expense. When he was studying his books and other persons of his household were present who were not versed in Latin, he would translate from the Latin into French[170] before them, properly and correctly, what he understood as he read.[171] He was not given to reading the writings of the schoolmasters, but rather authentic and proven holy books.

[24] How great was his devotion to things pertaining to the faith; and first on the Sacred Crown[172] and other holy relics.

How great was his faithful devotion and effort, how great was the expense, how great the danger to his agents, when he obtained from the emperor in Constantinople the sacrosanct Crown of Thorns of our Savior, as well as a large piece of the Holy Cross and numerous other precious, sacred

---

[165] These saints are the four Church Fathers Augustine (354–430), bishop of Hippo; Ambrose (c. 340–97), bishop of Milan; Jerome (c. 347–420); and Pope Gregory the Great (540–604).
[166] *RHGF, A:* libenter] liberaliter *B*
[167] *RHGF:* propter] post *A B*
[168] *RHGF:* vesperas audiendum] vesperas audientas *A B*
[169] *RHGF, A:* ordinis] *om. B*
[170] *RHGF, A:* in gallicum de latino] de gallicum in latino *B*
[171] *RHGF, A:* intelligebat legendo] intelligendo *B*
[172] *RHGF, A:* de sacra corona] de sacra corona domini *B*

relics![173] And with what joy did our devout king journey out to reverently take possession of these said relics! And again, with what solemn devotion did all the clergy and populace receive[174] in procession at Paris these valuable relics, when the king himself, barefoot, bore on his own shoulders for some way this sacred treasure![175] The little book that was diligently compiled about these matters bears witness to all these things,[176] from which is now read at Matins the solemn rites for the said Crown and the other relics.[177] The devout king established the celebration of these rites twice each year, that is on the anniversary of the days that they were received in Paris.[178]

Moreover, those who have been to Paris and seen for themselves can bear witness to how marvelous, how beautiful and remarkable is the chapel he built in Paris, and how costly and astonishing is the reliquary,

---

[173] Geoffrey here (and elsewhere) uses indirect questions (e.g. "How great was his effort?") in a lengthy sentence to suggest that something happened though he was not a witness himself. This presents a challenge for translation into English; we have rendered this passage as a series of shorter exclamations, though they should more literally be understood as rhetorical questions.

[174] *RHGF*, B: sint receptae] sunt recepte A

[175] Geoffrey here collapses two separate events. Louis actually received two principal installments of Passion relics that were housed in the Saint-Chapelle: the Crown of Thorns in 1239, and then a collection of other relics including a fragment of the True Cross in 1241. A third installment, including the Holy Lance, arrived in 1242.

[176] *RHGF*: testis est is] testis est de hiis omnibus A B

[177] The "little book" referred to here is probably the account of Louis' reception of the Crown of Thorns and other relics by Walter Cornut, archbishop of Sens. His text "De susceptione coronae spineae Jesu Christi" is printed in André Duchesne, *Historiae Francorum scriptores...*, vol. 5 (Paris: Cramoisy, 1649), 407–11; in *RHGF* 22:26–31; and in Paul Edouard Didier Riant, *Exuviae Sacrae Constantinopolitanae: Fasciculus Documentorum Minorum, Ad Byzantina Lipsana in Occidentem Saeculo XIII Translata, Spectantium, et Historiam Quarti Belli Sacri Imperii Gallo-Graeci Illustrantium* vol. 1 (Geneva, 1876; reprint, Paris: Editions du CTHS, 2004), 45–56. The other principal account of these events was written by Walter of Saint-Quentin, and can be found in E. Miller, "Review of *Exuviae Sacrae Constantinopolitanae*," *Journal des Savants* (1878): 292–309, 389–403.

[178] The Feast of the Crown of Thorns was celebrated at the Sainte-Chapelle on 11 August, and the Feast of the Reception of the Relics at the Sainte-Chapelle on 30 September. In fact, the Crown of Thorns arrived at Villeneuve-l'Archevêque (near Sens), where Louis met it, on 10 August 1239. On 11 August, the king bore it back in procession to Sens, and this became the feast day. The next day it was embarked by boat for Paris, arriving at Vincennes on 18 August and in Paris on 19 August; it was taken first to Notre Dame and then after a service to the chapel of Saint-Nicholas in the Palace, since the Sainte-Chapelle had not yet been built. Here B inserts a new chapter heading: "De festo corone." Again, this seems not to reflect the content of the following passage so we have not included it in the main text.

all ornamented with gold and silver and precious stones, that he commissioned,[179] to receive and fittingly house the aforesaid holy relics. He instituted canons and chaplains for this chapel, and assigned ample income as befitted the royal dignity, so that the Divine Office would there be rendered to the Lord in perpetuity.[180] All of these things testify to the king's zeal for the Christian faith.

[25] On his first pilgrimage overseas, how he captured Damietta, and how he was made a prisoner and then freed.[181]

Just about the whole world knows the fervor of faith with which he twice undertook a pilgrimage overseas, and what expense, labor, and peril he endured. Those who were there with him are witness to how miraculously the Lord delivered Damietta to him on his first pilgrimage, after much effort on his first arrival in Egypt; and to the great constancy and wisdom with which he behaved in word and deed after he was captured (with divine consent) by the Saracens and while he was in their power;[182] and also that the Saracens themselves esteemed him to be a very holy, truthful, and wise person. One must consider, too, that although it is no great wonder that he was captured by the Saracens, the fact that he, his brothers, and the Christian army were all freed safe and sound from these impious hands—against almost everyone's hope,[183] with ease and for a paltry ransom—must be credited to divine miracle and His power and the merits of the holy king.

Moreover, I cannot silently omit[184] the fact that when the king was taken captive he was gravely ill from the deadly and widespread sickness with which the greater part of the army was at that time laid low, so much so that there was then small hope of his survival. But when he was captured, through the providence of the One who ensures that *to them*

---

[179] *RHGF*: fieri fecit] fieri fecerit *A B*
[180] The Sainte-Chapelle was consecrated on 25 April 1248 by Eudes of Châteauroux.
[181] *RHGF, A*: deliberatus] liberatus *B*
[182] Louis arrived at and captured Damietta on 5 June 1249. He was in captivity from 6 April to 6 May 1250.
[183] *RHGF*: contra spem fere omnem] contra spem fere omnium *A B*
[184] *RHGF*: silendum est] silendum *A B*

that love Him, *all things work together unto good,*[185] the sultan put him in the special care and cure of his own doctors—who knew the art of curing this disease better than our own—and saw to it that all necessary things that the king requested were courteously and abundantly provided. Thus could it be truly said of him and his: *And he gave them unto mercies, in the sight of all those that had made them captives.*[186]

[26] How he behaved in Acre, and on his stay in the Holy Land.

After he had been freed through divine power, and peace or a truce had been established with the Saracens, and prisoners[187] had been returned when possible, the pious king went to Acre. Here they held a great council of knights and church prelates—including both his own men and those from these lands—with many wise men expressing the view that if, after such misfortune, he were now to return to France, he would place the Holy Land in the greatest danger of utter ruin, and it would mean the loss of all prisoners whose freedom had not yet been obtained. The king, prompted by piety and strength of faith, agreed to stay in Syria for as long as it pleased the Lord, even though some of his own people recommended another course.[188] And so it was that he remained in the Holy Land for five years or thereabouts, and his stay was not *void and empty.*[189] It was during that time that, at great expense, he fortified Caesarea with the strongest of walls all around the city; and likewise Jaffa and Sidon. Moreover, he did much to strengthen and extend the walls of Acre. Although his efforts, while enormously expensive, might seem[190] to have produced little benefit to Christianity, we believe that he should not be blamed for this; rather this proceeded from the secret judgment of God which is hidden from us, stemming not from his own sins, but the sins of others.

---

[185] Cf. Rom. 8:28.
[186] Ps. 105:46. "in misericordias" from the Vulgate passage *om. A* and *RHGF,* found only in *B.*
[187] *RHGF, A:* firmatis necnon captivis] *om. B*
[188] *RHGF:* aliter suaderent] aliud suaderent *A B*
[189] Gen. 1:2.
[190] The word "visi" included in *RHGF* is added only by a later hand above the line in *A.*

[27] How piously he received Saracens who came to the faith.

Moreover, during this time many Saracens came to him to adopt Christianity, whom he welcomed happily and had baptized and carefully instructed in the faith of Christ. He supported them at his own expense, brought them back to France with him, and assigned provisions to them and to their wives and children for as long as they lived. From his own funds he also saw to the purchase of slaves, many Saracens and pagans, and had them baptized, and assigned provisions to them as well.[191]

[28] How[192] he behaved when he heard of the death of his pious mother.

While *he stayed at Jaffa*[193] to erect the walls there, reports of the pious death of his most renowned mother, lady Blanche, arrived.[194] When the lord papal legate[195] first heard these reports, he summoned the archbishop of Tyre,[196] who was then the keeper of the lord king's seal, and he wished me to be the third member of their group. The legate, with the two of us, then went to the king and said that he wanted to speak with him privately in his chamber, with the two of us still present. Seeing the solemn face of the legate, the king understood[197] that he wished to convey sad news. Therefore this man, filled with God, led the legate and us from his chamber into the adjoining chapel,[198] closed the doors, and sat with us before the altar. Then the legate sensibly reviewed for the king the many great blessings that divine goodness had bestowed upon him since his childhood, mentioning among others that through His grace He had

---

[191] This sentence *om. B.*
[192] *RHGF, A:* quomodo] qualiter *B*
[193] Acts 9:43. The biblical reference is to the apostle Peter.
[194] Blanche died in late November 1252. Louis was in Jaffa from May 1252 until June 1253.
[195] See note 157 on Eudes of Châteauroux above.
[196] Giles of Saumor (d. 1266).
[197] *RHGF:* cognovit] cogitavit *A B*
[198] *RHGF, A:* in capellam suam] in capellam *B*

granted him such a mother who had reared him so piously,[199] brought him up in such a catholic fashion, and had so faithfully and prudently managed and administered the business of his realm. After a brief pause, the legate, with sobs and tears, revealed the ruinous, lamentable death of the said queen. The catholic king—wailing aloud, dissolving in tears on his knees before the altar, weeping with hands clasped in most pious prayer—said, "I thank you, Lord God, that it has pleased your goodness to grant to me my most beloved lady mother for so long. And now, Lord, you have taken her to you through the death of her body, according to your will. It is true, Lord, that I loved her above all other living creatures, as she well deserved; but in so far as this is what pleases you, blessed be your name forever. Amen." Having said this, and after a brief prayer from the legate on behalf of the soul of the departed lady, the king wished to remain alone in the chapel. Then the legate and archbishop left, and he kept me alone with him. And for a while he remained in pious meditation sighing before the altar. But, not wanting him to be weighed down by immoderate grief, I sought to console him as best I could, humbly telling him that he had rendered to nature[200] what was owed to nature; but now it was fitting that he render to the grace of God, which was in him, what pertained to reason enlightened by grace.[201] He sensibly accepted this counsel and carried it out. For soon he arose from that place and went to his oratory where he was accustomed to say his Hours. He called me there with him alone and, as was his wish, together we recited the whole of the Office of the Dead; that is, Vespers and Vigils with the nine readings. I was not a little surprised in that,[202] though his heart was deeply wounded and shaken by such a fresh and terrible wound, I do not recall that I noticed him falter or err in any verse of a psalm or any reading that he recited, as is often the case when the human heart is upset by sad and sudden news. This I[203] ascribed to the virtue of divine grace

---

[199] tam pie nutrierat *add. B*
[200] *RHGF, A:* nature] *om. B*
[201] Geoffrey ("redderet quod ad rationem illuminatam per gratiam pertinebat") is here echoing Peter Lombard's commentary on Paul's Letter to the Romans. Compare *PL* 191, col. 1345 ("naturali ratione illuminata per gratiam").
[202] ex hoc *add. B*
[203] *RHGF:* ergo] ego *A B*

and the steadiness of his heart. He proved to be a most faithful son to his holy mother's soul. For he procured innumerable masses from many[204] religious communities, and their offering of prayers for her soul. From that day forth he wanted a special Mass said before him every day, except on Sundays and the principal feast days.

He still remained in the Holy Land for more than a year after this. For when he was done restoring the walls of Jaffa, he went on to build strong ones around the city of Sidon. When this was done, he learned from numerous letters and messengers from France that following the death of his mother great danger was looming for his kingdom,[205] as much from England as from Germany. Taking counsel with wise men, he agreed to return to his own realm, though he left many knights with the papal legate, and funds for the support and maintenance of the Holy Land. I can hardly express the tears and devotion, the blessings and good will of the entire populace of Acre including both the knights and clergy, which followed him all the way to his ship.[206]

[29] **On his return to France, and how he acted at sea.**

Out of devotion he saw to it that before boarding ship the Body of Our Lord Jesus Christ was placed on board so that the sick could take communion, as well as himself and his family when it might seem useful. And since other pilgrims—no matter how illustrious—were not accustomed to doing this, he obtained a special privilege for this from the papal legate. He arranged for this sacred treasure to be placed on board the ship in a most worthy and appropriate place, and there he put up a costly tabernacle covered with a cloth[207] of gold and silk. He had an altar set up there,[208] decorated appropriately,[209] where every day he would hear the Divine Office—that is the canonical Hours and all that pertains to

---

[204] Plurimis *add.* B
[205] *RHGF:* matris suae regno suo] matris regno *A B*
[206] *RHGF:* navim] navem *A B.* Louis departed from Acre on 24 or 25 April 1254.
[207] *RHGF:* pannisque] pannis *A* et pannis *B*
[208] *RHGF, A:* ibidem] *om.* B
[209] *RHGF, A:* et decenter ornari] *om.* B

the Mass except the Canon[210]—with the priest and ministers dressed in sacred robes as appropriate to each day. He was very attentive to the sick on board,[211] that they should have what they needed according to the affliction of each; and especially that, following confession, they should receive all the sacraments, especially Holy Communion and Extreme Unction. He saw to it that the dead received their due last rites from his own chaplains.

[30] How he acted when in danger of shipwreck.

It must not be passed over that on the third night out from the port of Acre, a little before dawn, while we were near Cyprus, the ship suddenly ran upon a rock—either a spit of land or a sandbar as hard as stone. This rock[212] or spit extended some distance into the sea. Thereupon the ship was strongly driven with double force with all on board shouting and screaming, rightly figuring that the ship was shaken down to the hold. Even the sailors, as though all was lost, did not know what to do or how to react. The catholic king, however, maintained faith and hope in God. Grasping the nature of the danger, with no regard for the safety of his own body—or indeed for that of his wife, the queen, or for that of his children, who lay beside him in dismay—he roused himself into prayer before the altar, devoutly prostrate before the holy Body of Christ and the holy relics, humbly praying that almighty God might grant his aid in the present danger. And I believe[213] that divine piety saved the ship and all within it from shipwreck because of the prayers and merits of the king, since hardly two or three in a hundred ships would have survived a similar peril. For the ship by its strength, or rather by divine power, broke through the spit or rock and made a path for itself through the middle of it. The sailors, striking a light and examining the hold of the ship and finding no damage, dropped anchor free of danger and waited for dawn.

---

[210] *RHGF, B:* canonem] canonicas *A*
[211] in navem *add. B*
[212] *RHGF:* rupes] rupis *A B* (the silent emendation in *RHGF* seems necessary)
[213] *RHGF:* credere debemus] credo *A B*

When day came, the king, filled with the faith of God,[214] returned to the altar in secret and lay prostrate, giving devout thanks for such a great and miraculous blessing shown to him and to his family by the Savior of us all. The priests, however, who were sleeping in beds around the altar, rose up and were amazed to see the king devoutly prostrate in prayer. But he himself humbly explained the truth to them.

[30*bis*] On the joyous return of the king to France.[215]

Therefore, returning to France after various dangers of sea and land, the glorious pilgrim was received with immense joy and solemn processions wherever he went, as was fitting. But this true lover of humility declined all these things as far as he could. Thus when he was received with such honorific rituals on the day he entered Paris, he was displeased by the many honors of immense and superfluous expense which he saw. And for this reason, in order to flee and diminish the follies of dances and sumptuous splendors and vanities of this sort that he knew were being prepared for that evening throughout the streets of Paris, to the wonder of many, after he had dined he left the city and spent that night at his manor in Vincennes which stood a full league apart from the city.[216]

---

[214] *RHGF, A:* fidei] fide dei *B*

[215] This chapter is not found in *A*, and consequently has not been included in any edition. To preserve ease of comparison with the *RHGF* edition, we have not renumbered the paragraphs. *A* has a slightly different chapter heading "De iocunditate eius in Francia" (which in fact was crossed out in the manuscript by a later hand) and then jumps immediately to the next chapter. *B* (fol. 41r–v) has the rubric "De iocundo regressu regis in Franciam" and then the following chapter: "[I]gitur post varia maris terrarumque pericula, gloriosus peregrinus revertans in Franciam cum immenso gaudio et sollempnibus processionibus prout dignum erat excipiebatur ubicumque transiebat, sed verus humilitatis amator hec omnia prout poterat declinabat. Unde cum primo die quo intraverit Parisius cum tanta sollempnitatis // (41v) honorificentia fuisset receptus, displicuerunt sibi plurimum honores tam inmensi et expense superflue quas videbat. Et ob hoc ad fugiendum et eciam ad minuendum inepcias chorearum et sumptuosorum luminarium et huiusmodi vanitatum quas in sero illius diei per omnes vicos Parisius intellexerat preparari, post comestionem mirantibus multis civitatem exivit, mansitque nocte illa in suo manerio de Vicenis quod per magnam luecam [*sic*, for leucam?] a civitate distabat."

[216] The king arrived back in Paris 4 September 1254. Vincennes was the royal castle just east of the city, on the edge of the modern Bois de Vincennes.

[31] How he acted upon returning to France.[217]

After his return[218] to France, those who observed his comportment and especially those who knew the sincere truth of his heart bear witness to how devoutly he acted toward God, how justly toward his subjects, how mercifully toward those in need, how humbly toward himself, and, finally, how he strove with all his might to perfect each virtue. And so, in the opinion of those of sound judgment, in much the same way that gold is even more precious than silver, the saintly and new comportment with which he returned from the Holy Land outshone his previous comportment even though his behavior as a younger man had always been good and pure and very commendable.

[32] On his zeal in stamping out foul swearing[219] and blasphemy.

His efforts were especially directed toward the worship of God and the exaltation of the Christian faith. Now he was most upset and anxious in his heart about that widespread plague which from times long past had particularly afflicted his realm; that is, the vice of foul swearing and blaspheming against God[220] and his saints. Moved by divine zeal and thinking deeply as to how, to the honor of God, this hateful crime might be ripped out by the roots from his realm, he carefully took counsel with lord Simon, who was cardinal priest of Saint Cecilia and then papal legate in France.[221] On the papal legate's authority as well as his own, he brought together in Paris the great men of the realm, both princes and prelates, so that a plan and wholesome remedy for curbing or rather wiping out this

---

[217] This is the rubric from *B*: "Qualiter se habuit reversus in Francia."
[218] *RHGF, A:* est reversus] reversus *B*
[219] *RHGF, A:* turpes zelationes] turpes iurationes *B* [we follow the more logical reading in *B*]
[220] *RHGF:* Dominum] Deum *A B*
[221] *B* has "tunc" before both clauses. *A* does as well, but it is crossed out in the first clause. Simon of Brie was well known to Louis IX as treasurer of the Church of Saint-Martin of Tours and then keeper of the royal seal, before being named cardinal priest of Saint Cecilia in 1261 and departing for Rome. He returned as papal legate to France in 1264, and eventually reigned as Pope Martin IV (1281–85).

despicable vice could be set before them.[222] Therefore, after the lord legate had given a solemn sermon on this subject to great effect, our catholic king, inspired by holy zeal, delivered with his own voice a devout exhortation based on plain and powerful reasons. With common counsel and consent, the king thus promulgated a general edict which he desired to be published and observed throughout his entire kingdom, which was in these words:

[32*bis*] The edict he[223] published against swearers and blasphemies.

[Neither existing manuscript of Geoffrey's *vita* actually includes the text of this edict].[224]

[33] On the branding of the lips he had inflicted on a blasphemer.[225]

Then, after the publication of this sort of edict, a certain citizen of Paris of middling status blasphemed against God by swearing a truly shameful

---

[222] *RHGF, A:* vitio] ultio *B*
[223] "Ab eo" only in *B* [we follow this reading]
[224] It is not entirely clear what text Geoffrey intended to include here, mainly because his chronological indications are contradictory. On one hand, the placement of this episode immediately after Louis' return from crusade suggests that Geoffrey had in mind the issuing of the Grand Ordinance of December 1254. These reform statutes were aimed at royal officials and were issued in several versions, and did include the simple and geographically limited clause: "We wish and we order that our above-mentioned seneschals and all others who hold their offices from us, and not least all who receive our wages in these two *bailliages* should abstain from all speech that verges on abuse of or contempt for God, his Mother, and his saints …." See Eusèbe Laurière et al., eds., *Ordonnances des roys de France de la troisième race, recueillies par ordre chronologique*, vol. 1 (Paris: Imprimerie royale, 1723), 70. This short sentence, however, hardly seems to match Geoffrey's description of a major council and an edict focused on the problem of blasphemy. More specifically, the reference to Simon of Brie as papal legate should indicate a date after 1264, and Louis is indeed known to have issued fuller statutes on blasphemy, perhaps around 1268–69. See ibid., 99–102 for one version of a French text. Since it is not certain, however, that this is the exact text that Geoffrey intended to copy, we have not wished to give a false impression by including it in translation here. Quite possibly Geoffrey combined events in hindsight, remembering Louis' grand reforming moment of 1254 and then associating it with the later statutes.
[225] "De cauterio labiorum quod infligi fecit blasphemo." This title is found only in *B*, where it follows directly on the title of 32*bis*. We have separated it here and presented it as a new

oath. The just[226] king, with no pity, ordered that he be branded on the lips with a white hot iron, as a perpetual reminder of his sin and as an example to others. Many worldly-wise[227] persons spoke evil of this against the king. But hearing this, the king was magnanimous, knowing that it is written, *Blessed will you be when men will revile you,*[228] and equally *They will curse, and you will bless.*[229] And he made a most catholic comment; that is, that he would wish that[230] a similar branding be done to his own lips and that he bear this infamy for his whole life, if only thereby this pernicious vice would be completely removed from his kingdom. Moreover, at just this time the lord king had ordered that a special project be carried out in Paris,[231] which seemed to be of no small benefit to the public, and those who were benefiting from it[232] gave many blessings to the king. But he remarked that he was anticipating a greater reward from God for all the evil words he had received for the branding incident, than for all the blessings that came his way[233] for the project of public benefit. Therefore our king is rightly seen to be a strikingly close match for King Josias, in whose praise it is written, as has been earlier remarked, that *He took away the abominations of wickedness, and he directed his heart toward the Lord: and in the days of sinners he strengthened piety*[234] in divine worship.

[34] On the honor which he said was done him at Poissy.

It is also relevant in praising his devotion to the faith,[235] that once when he was at the castle of Poissy, in front of some of his own household,

---

chapter title, in an attempt to match what seems most likely to us to have been Geoffrey's original intention.

[226] *RHGF, A:* iustus] intus *B*
[227] *RHGF, A:* secundum seculum sapientes] sapientes secundum *B*
[228] Cf. Matt. 5:11.
[229] Ps. 108:28.
[230] *RHGF:* desiderabat potius] desiderabat *A B*
[231] It is not possible to specifically identify this "special project," but on Louis' pious building initiatives after 1254 see Jordan, *Louis IX and the Challenge,* 185–90.
[232] *RHGF, A:* Ab illius beneficia habentibus] ab illo beneficio utentibus *B*
[233] *RHGF, A:* quas habebat] *om. B*
[234] Ecclus. 49:3–4.
[235] *RHGF, A:* fidei] *om. B*

he proudly and joyfully remarked that in that very place the Lord had once[236] rendered him a greater good and a higher honor than any that he had ever received in this world. Everyone present wondered what honor he could be talking about, since they supposed that he would rather have said this about Reims where he had received the crown and holy unction of coronation. He replied with a smile that it was there, at Poissy, that he had received the grace of sacred baptism, which he considered to be a gift and honor without comparison, above all other honors and dignities of this world. And thus when he would send a secret letter to a close member of his household, and for some reason did not wish to use the title of king, he would sign himself "Louis of Poissy" or "lord of Poissy," choosing to be called by his place of baptism rather than by any one of his other renowned towns.

[35] That in touching the sick he added the sign of the Holy[237] Cross.

Likewise,[238] when it came to touching the sick, those suffering from what is commonly known as scrofula—which the Lord has granted to the kings of France the unique grace of curing—the pious king wished to observe this practice above and beyond previous kings: for since all the kings who had gone before him had only touched the afflicted place and pronounced the usual and fitting words, which indeed are holy and catholic, and it had not been their practice to make any sign of the Cross, he added to the practice established by others that while pronouncing the words over the afflicted area he would trace a small sign of the Holy Cross, so that the ensuing cure would thereby be attributed to the power of the Cross[239] rather than to the majesty of the king.[240]

---

[236] *RHGF, A:* fecerat sibi Dominus] fecerat sibi semel Dominus *B*
[237] *RHGF, A:* sancte] *om. B*
[238] *RHGF:* in tangendis] item in tangendis *A B*
[239] *RHGF, B:* sanctae crucis signaculum imprimebat, ut sequens curatio virtuti crucis attribueretur] *A* inserts "signaculum" again after the second "crucis." The *RHGF* editors must have rejected this as an obvious scribal error.
[240] Going back to King Robert "the Pious" (r. 996–1031) the Capetian kings were credited with the ability to heal scrofula (a skin disease also known as the "king's evil") with their touch.

[36] On[241] the many-faceted zeal of his faith.

Moreover, as a true worshiper of the Cross, he displayed such reverence for the sign of the Holy Cross that when he was passing through the cloister of a religious order and saw the crosses marked on the tombs of the deceased members, he did his best not to step on them.[242] Therefore, in those cloisters and cemeteries of religious orders in which he most practiced his faith he saw to it that the crosses of this sort were removed[243] from above the tombs there. Likewise, he saw among certain religious the use of a certain pious[244] practice; that is, when during the singing of Mass, "I believe in one God," is recited, "and He was made man," the choir would bow down deeply and humbly. He liked this practice immensely, so he had it implemented and maintained; not only in his own chapel for his own use, but also in many other churches, so that at that line the choir would not only bow but devoutly genuflect.

In like fashion he learned that in certain monasteries, when these lines are recited in the four "Passions" (commonly called penitential) that are said during Holy Week, "With bowed head He breathed out his spirit," or "He expired," the congregation would devoutly genuflect and lie flat down for the prayer.[245] Our pious king then made sure this practice was similarly observed in his own chapel and in many other churches. Therefore, at his request, this practice was also approved in the Order of Preaching Brothers and made a regulation.

Moreover, it seemed inappropriate and unworthy to his devotion that new images of the Crucifixion or the Blessed Virgin or of the other saints ought to be placed immediately in church to be adored just as they came from the house of the painter, without any benediction. Therefore he had

---

[241] *RHGF, A:* de] item de *B*
[242] *RHGF:* quantum poterat reformidabat] quantum poterat reformidans *A* reformidans quantum poterat declinabat *B*
[243] *RHGF, A:* Tumulos ejus removeri] tumulos huiusmodi removeri *B*
[244] *RHGF, A:* consuetudine] pia consuetudine *B*
[245] From "Tenebrae" services, performed during Holy Week in the days preceding Easter. The line is *Tenebræ factæ sunt, dum crucifixissent Jesum Judæi: Et circa horam nonam exclamavit Jesus voce magna: Deus meus, ut quid me dereliquisti? Et inclinato capite, emisit spiritum.* Compare the Office of the Lord's Passion composed by the Franciscan Bonaventure, reportedly at Louis' request, in Bonaventure, *Decem opuscula ad theologiam mysticam spectantia* (Quaracchi: Collegium S. Bonaventura, 1926), 388–408.

a careful inquiry made in the early records of the bishops, and there was discovered a devout prayer specifically intended for the blessing of new images prior to their exhibition to the public for adoration.[246] The holy king desired that this preliminary rite be employed in the images of his chapel and his devotions thereafter.

Many other things of this type dealing with his fervor and devout dedication to the faith could be written down, but in the name of humility[247] let these already mentioned suffice. Now let us proceed to his second and last pilgrimage overseas.

[37] On the pious proposal of a second pilgrimage to the Holy Land.[248]

So then the holy king, waiting[249] until he was deprived of any hope of entering religion, and yet hearing about so many disasters, so many forsaken places, and so many repeated perils threatening the Holy Land, yearned at the end of his days to attempt some lofty work for God, and it was not easy to stop him. He therefore devoutly conceived the holy proposal of crossing over the sea, so that, to the extent that divine grace would allow, he might supply saving aid and counsel against the dangers to the Holy Land that seemed so imminent. And then, to the astonishment of many,[250] he began as much as possible to cut back on the money

---

[246] The best-known blessing for images comes from William Durandus's Pontifical of 1293, which includes formulas "De benedictione ymaginis beate Marie" and "De benedictione ymaginum sanctorum" that were widely copied in the later Middle Ages. See Michel Andrieu, ed., *Le Pontifical romain au Moyen-Age*, vol. 3: *Le Pontifical de Guillaume Durand*, Studi e Testi 88 (Vatican City: Biblioteca apostolica vaticana, 1940), 525–27. We know of several earlier examples from English manuscripts, including Cambridge, Corpus Christi College ms. 146 (the so-called Samson Pontifical, ca. 1100), p. 4, including two prayers, "Benedictio super imagines," and ms. 44 (ca. 1100), fol. 138, "Benedictio ad imaginem sanctae Marie vel auro vel alia venustate fuerit compta"; Bangor Cathedral Library, Pontifical of Aniane, 13c, "Benedictio super imaginem vel imagines."

[247] *RHGF, A*: sed humilitatis causa] sed brevitatis causa *B*

[248] *RHGF*: De proposito peregrinationis in terram sanctam secundo] De proposito pio secunde peregrinationis in terram sanctam secundo acce (with the final two words crossed out in the original red ink) *A* De proposito pio secunde peregrinationis in terram sanctam *B*

[249] *RHGF*: audiens] attendens *A B*

[250] *RHGF*: cunctis] multis *A B*

spent on his household. Yet he was unwilling to undertake such an endeavor[251] rashly and merely at his own heart's desire. Therefore, by means of a secret, discreet messenger, he humbly and devoutly sought the advice of the lord Clement, the highest pontiff, of happy memory, concerning this project.[252] Clement, a sensible man, was at first reluctant and gave the matter long consideration, but finally he gave his kind permission and approved this holy endeavor. Concerning this matter, and at the king's request, he dispatched into France his legate; that is, lord Simon, at that time[253] cardinal priest of Saint Cecilia.

[38] How he took[254] the Cross for the second time.

Intending to take up the Cross, [Louis] called to Paris a large crowd of leading prelates, princes,[255] barons, knights, and others. When they were all assembled in the presence of the lord legate, the catholic king himself delivered a very effective and glorious exhortation in front of everyone, rousing them to avenge the injury to the Savior in the Holy Land endured now for so long, and as Christians to recover their rightful inheritance which for so long has been in the hands of infidels due to our own sins. Our pious king spoke most elegantly of these things and many others relevant to this subject. Then, after the lord legate had finished his sermon, the king himself, with deep devotion, was the first to take up the Cross, and then his three sons right after him, along with a host of counts and barons and knights, both those with whom the king had secretly discussed the project in advance[256] as well as others whose hearts God alone had touched.[257]

---

[251] *RHGF, A:* opus] *om.* B
[252] Clement IV (Guy Foulquois) was well-known to Louis as a former bishop of Puy and archbishop of Narbonne, and reigned as pope from 5 February 1265 to his death on 29 November 1268.
[253] *RHGF:* tunc titulo] tunc *A B*
[254] *RHGF, A:* accepit] assumpsit *B*
[255] *RHGF, A:* principum] *om.* B
[256] *RHGF:* rex pius] rex prius *A B*
[257] Louis took the Cross again on 25 March 1267.

[39] How careful he was in preparing for the pilgrimage.

After he had taken the Cross, those who were party to his careful efforts can testify to the heated interest with which he moved to attract great nobles to the Cross through promises and support; how eagerly he hastened the preparation of the fleet, the acceleration of departure, and the provision of necessities.[258] Seizing his opportunity, he proceeded with his forces at the appointed hour to the port of Aigues-Mortes. But there he had to put up with great grief and annoyance,[259] for the sailors had let him down, and the ships, which were not ready at the stated and promised time, failed him. And thus it was that he boarded ship much later than he had planned.[260]

[40] On the council held about going to Tunis.

When, therefore, all the ships which could be mustered had assembled at Sardinia—as had been ordered—and the commanders of the army were gathered before the king, common counsel was taken and the decision was reached that they should begin by conquering the kingdom of Tunis before traveling on to the Holy Land or to Egypt.[261] At this point it is most helpful, in our opinion, to lay out the particular reasons that led the lord king to this decision, because of the surprise and complaints of many to whom it seemed that he ought to have sailed directly to the aid of the Holy Land.

[41] The reasons for which the king agreed to go to Tunis.

Accordingly, even before the lord king took the Cross for the last time, he had received a number of envoys from the king of Tunis, and likewise our

---

[258] Necessarium provisionem *add.* B
[259] *RHGF:* moestitias] molestias *A B*
[260] Louis left Paris on 15 March 1270, and embarked at Aigues-Mortes on 1 July.
[261] The fleet was at Cagliari on 10–15 July 1270.

king had sent envoys back to him.[262] He was led to believe by trustworthy men[263] that this king of Tunis had great good will toward the Christian faith, and that[264] he might quite easily become a Christian, if he could find an honorable moment and if he were able to do it while maintaining his honor and without fear of his own Saracens. And thus our catholic king, with great longing, would say, "Oh, if only I could see this come about—that I should be godfather and sponsor to such a son!" And it was for this very hope that he once wanted to go to the region of Carcassonne and Narbonne, as though visiting his own lands, so that if the Lord should so inspire the said king to carry out his plan of receiving baptism, he would be able to be closer for this holy undertaking.

I do not think that it should be passed over in silence here that, in the very year that the king was due to go overseas for the last time, the king of Tunis sent to him important envoys. And when, during the feast of the blessed Denis,[265] the king was having a certain well-known Jew solemnly baptized in the church of that same blessed Denis—such that the king himself, together with the great nobles of the realm, was lifting this Jew from the sacred font—he wished these same Tunisian envoys[266] to take part in the solemn moment of baptism. Summoning them, with great emotion, the king said, "Tell your lord the king on my behalf, that I long so earnestly for the salvation of his soul that I would choose to spend all my life in a Saracen dungeon and never again see the clear light of the sun, if only your king and his people would become Christian in good faith!" O, *faithful saying and worthy of all acceptation!*[267] O, words so catholic, bursting with complete love and faith! And the most pious catholic

---

[262] This was Sultan al-Mustansir (d. 1277).
[263] Lower, "Conversion and St Louis' Last Crusade," 226–28, considers the question of who these men might have been, and notes the close ties between King Louis and Dominicans with experience in Tunis, such as Raymond of Peñafort, Francis Cendra, Andrew of Longjumeau, and Raymond Marti.
[264] *RHGF:* et valde] et quod valde *A B*
[265] 9 October, presumably of 1269, on which date Louis is indeed known to have been at Saint-Denis with a host of important churchmen (see Adam J. Davis, *The Holy Bureaucrat: Eudes Rigaud and Religious Reform in Thirteenth-Century Normandy* [Ithaca: Cornell University Press, 2006], 43).
[266] *RHGF:* nuncii regis Tunicii] nuncii Tunicii *A B*
[267] I Tim. 1:15, 4:9.

king desired[268] that the Christian faith, which had flourished so gracefully of old in Africa and especially in Carthage in the days of the blessed Augustine and other orthodox doctors,[269] should spring into blossom in our[270] day and should spread abroad to the honor and glory of Jesus Christ. He thought that if such a great and renowned army should suddenly arrive at Tunis, the said king of Tunis could hardly have a more reasonable moment in the eyes of his Saracens to receive baptism; that is, he would be able to avoid not only his own death but also that of those who desired to become Christian with him, and thus his realm would remain peacefully his.

Moreover, the king was given to believe that should the said king flatly refuse to become Christian, the city of Tunis could be very easily captured and then the whole land as well. As a further incentive, the king was informed that this city was as full as possible of silver and gold and limitless wealth, for it had not been plundered for a long time. Therefore it was hoped that, God willing, if the said city were taken by a Christian army, he would be able, with the treasure found therein, to help effectively in the capturing and restoring of the Holy Land. In addition, our men[271] believed that if that pestilent root of Tunis could be ripped out, it would greatly benefit the Holy Land and Christendom, because a great deal of military support usually came to the sultan of Babylon[272] from Tunis, as much in cavalry as in warriors and arms, all to the great harm and detriment of the Holy Land. Therefore, since it has been written that "where one thing exists because of another, in that case there is really only one thing,"[273] and since the way through Tunis would have advanced the increase of the honor of the Christian name and been of great use to the Holy Land and more easily aided it, the route by way of Tunis did not

---

[268] *RHGF:* desiderabat quoque] desiderabat que *A* desiderabat quidem *B*
[269] *RHGF, A:* doctorum] *om. B*
[270] *RHGF, A:* nostris] *om. B*
[271] *RHGF:* barones nostri] nostri *A B*
[272] That is, Egypt.
[273] "ubi unum propter alterum ibi tantum unum." This is a quotation from Aristotle (II *Topics* cap. II) cited in commentaries on Peter Lombard's *Sentences* by Aquinas, Bonaventure, and others. (*RHGF* reads "tantum alterum unum" but "alterum" is canceled in *A* [probably by the original scribal hand] and not present in *B*.) Geoffrey is thus employing a bit of Aristotelian logic to demonstrate the reasonableness of Louis' decision.

seem counter to the oath of the Cross but, rather, was one and the same, as a viable support and preparation for a swift and easier recovery of the Holy Land.[274] Because of these and certain other reasons, they advanced along the route to Tunis. And if matters turned out otherwise on this route than the faithful had hoped, then we must blame our own sins and ourselves in accordance with the hidden, just[275] judgment of God.

[42] On the arrival of the king before Tunis.

Therefore, quite easily and without opposition, our fleet and army arrived in Africa, by way of Tunis, and our troops made camp near Carthage.[276] After a short while our forces swiftly and victoriously took the renowned castle of Carthage and the region belonging to it. And there they killed many Saracens and gained huge food supplies and other military necessities. I leave it to others who know about these things better than I to write[277] of the daily encounters with the Saracens and the massacres that took place and other things of this sort.

[43] On the deadly disease that struck there.

The Christian army remained encamped at that place for about four months, and a great and deadly disease followed, as much because of the inclement nature of the air and land as because of the lack of healthy food[278] and the scarcity of fresh water. And thus did many knights and

---

[274] Note that by the time Geoffrey was writing, Gregory X had made it clear that he did not consider the crusaders' vows of 1270 to have been fulfilled by the expedition to Tunis. See Hélary, "Les rois de France et la terre sainte."
[275] *RHGF*, A: occulto Dei iudicio] occulto iusto Dei iudicio B
[276] The fleet landed in North Africa on 17 July 1270. Geoffrey is probably distinguishing between the port of Tunis, the old city of Tunis, and Carthage (geographically separate to the northeast).
[277] *RHGF*: qui melius ista noverunt scribere derlinquo] qui melius ista noverunt scribenda relinquo A B
[278] *RHGF*: arborum] ciborum A B [This misreading in *RHGF* has caused several modern commentators to see in Geoffrey's text evidence of a medieval belief that a lack of trees led

noble counts[279] die. Among those who died was the famed count of Nevers, lord Jean, the son of our pious king,[280] over whose death the heart of his pious father grieved not a little. But the steady, sensible king received quickly enough such consolation as he could in his own death.

[44] On the pious and sorrowful death of the pious king and how he behaved in death.

After a short time in these quarters this same king—of famed and pious memory, beloved of God and honored by men, after many praiseworthy acts of faith and charity,[281] after many burdensome struggles that he undertook with tireless spirit, faithfully and earnestly, for the faith and for the propagation of the Church—now weakened by continuous fever, took to his bed.[282] This was ordained by God, who wished to bring his endeavors to a joyful[283] end, and to bring his good efforts to glorious fruition. And as the king's illness worsened, he received all the church sacraments in a most devout and Christian manner, with sound mind and clear understanding. Thus, as we were offering the sacrament of Extreme Unction and as the Seven Psalms and the Litany were being recited, he said the verses of the psalms himself, naming the saints in the Litany and invoking their efforts with great devotion.

When clear signs showed that he was approaching the end, he worried about nothing except those things that properly concerned God alone and the exaltation of the Christian faith. Thus, when he could speak only softly and with difficulty, this truly catholic man filled with God said to those of us who were present and inclining our ears to his words, "For

---

to plague; in fact, Geoffrey makes only the commonsense equation between the onset of disease and a scarcity of healthy food and water].

[279] *RHGF*, A: Multi milites et nobiles comites] multi comites et nobiles milites B

[280] See note 16 on Jean Tristan; he died on 3 August 1270.

[281] *RHGF*: charitatis] claritatis A caritatis B

[282] Geoffrey here closely follows the account set out in Philip III's letter of 1270 announcing Louis' death. He even adopts the precise phrasing of the letter at some places, and will do so again later in this chapter.

[283] *RHGF*, A: feliciter] *om.* B

God's sake, let us strive to see how the true faith may be[284] preached and implanted in Tunis! O, who would be suitable to be sent there to preach?" And he named a certain brother of the Order of Preachers who had gone there at another time and was known to the king of Tunis.[285] Behold how a true promoter of God and a tireless zealot of the Christian faith culminated his life in a confession of true faith! As the strength of his body and speech ebbed away little by little, striving as best he could to speak, he did not stop asking for the prayerful support of the saints dear to him, and especially of the blessed Denis, his special patron.[286] Then at that point we heard him repeat many times in a whisper the end of that prayer which is sung of the blessed Denis, that is: "Grant us, we ask,[287] for the sake of your love, that we may despise worldly success and fear none of its misfortunes."[288] Again and again he repeated these words. Likewise he recited the beginning of the prayer to Saint James,[289] that is: "Lord, be the guardian and sanctifier of your people,"[290] and similarly[291] repeating this many times, he also remembered other saints in devotion. Therefore, the servant of Christ,[292] approaching his last hour, and lying down on a bed of ashes spread out in the shape of a cross,[293] rendered his joyful spirit to its creator, at the very hour at which the Son of God expired, dying on the Cross *for the life of the world.*[294]

---

[284] *RHGF:* possit] posset *A B*
[285] The later *Grandes chroniques de France* identified this Dominican as Andrew of Longjumeau, who had acted for Louis as envoy to Constantinople in 1238 and to the Mongol Khan Güyük in 1249, and then lived in the Dominican community of Tunis. See the discussion in Lower, "Conversion and St Louis' Last Crusade," 227.
[286] *RHGF:* specialis patroni regni sui] specialis patroni sui *A B*
[287] *RHGF:* quaesumus Domine] Domine *A B*
[288] This is from the *Oratio* in the *Suffragia* to Saint Denis from the *Horae Beatae Mariae ad usum Romanum.* See Robert Lippe, ed., *Missale Romanum Mediolani, 1474* (London: Harrison and Sons, 1899), 390 (or the "Hypertext Book of Hours" at http://medievalist.net/hourstxt/suffrage.htm).
[289] *RHGF:* Jacobo apostolo] Jacobo *A B*
[290] See the *Oratio* from the *Suffragia* to James the Apostle, in Lippe, *Missale Romanum,* 356 (or the "Hypertext Book of Hours," as at note 288 above).
[291] *RHGF:* pluries replicabat et] et hec similiter pluries replicabat *A B*
[292] *RHGF, A:* Christi servus] *om. B*
[293] *RHGF:* super stratum cinere respersum in modum crucis recubans] et superstratum in cruce cinerem recubans *A B*
[294] John 6:52. Here Geoffrey again echoes closely the content and language of Philip III's letter of 1270.

Certainly it is pious to weep over a death so Christian and joyous; and it is also pious to rejoice. It is pious and fitting to weep over the loss and desolation of the universal mother Church, whose most devout supporter and defender he was. One must particularly weep and grieve for the whole kingdom of the Franks, which was uniquely glorified by the merit of such a worthy and superior prince. But if the force of grief can give way to reason, we must rejoice[295] rather than grieve, both because of the most Christian manner of his death, and because of the solid hope held for him by everyone aware of his glorious life and most holy deeds, that he is now carried off from the cares of the temporal kingdom into the joyous court of the heavenly kingdom, which is entirely foreign to earthly trials, where, reigning forever with the elect of God, he enjoys blessed rest without end.[296] He passed to the Lord the day after the Feast of the Blessed Bartholomew the Apostle, around Nones, in the year of the Lord 1270.[297]

[45] On the arrival of the king of Sicily at Tunis.

It should not be passed over, that when the spirit of the blessed king was departing from his body, at that hour—almost at the very instant—the renowned king of Sicily, the brother of the glorious king of France,[298] sailed into port by divine direction and entered our camp.[299] At his happy arrival our hearts, which had been gravely wounded by the death of the pious king, were to no small extent consoled, and great joy came into them from such powerful assistance. In like fashion, the hearts of the

---

[295] *RHGF:* gaudendum] gaudendum est *A B*
[296] Once again Geoffrey is closely following the content and language of the 1270 letter.
[297] 25 August 1270. The Feast of Saint Bartholomew is 24 August.
[298] *RHGF, A:* Francie] *om. B*
[299] Youngest sibling of Louis IX, Charles of Anjou was count of Provence from 1246 (when he married Beatrice of Provence), accompanied Louis on his first crusade, and defeated the heirs of Emperor Frederick II to become king of Sicily by 1266. He had wider ambitions in the Mediterranean, and it has often been thought (without much evidence) that he helped steer Louis' second crusade toward Tunis. In 1282 he was expelled from the island of Sicily during the rebellion known as the Sicilian Vespers and his attempts to regain his kingdom led to Philip III's "crusade" against Peter of Aragaon after Peter (married to a member of Frederick II's family) accepted the crown of Sicily offered to him by the anti-French rebels. Charles died the same year as Philip, 1285.

Saracens, which had been revived and made joyful by the death of the holy king, were now dismayed to no small degree by the presence of such a victorious and renowned prince

[46] That his sacred[300] bones were kept with the army.

Immediately after his death, in accordance with the wishes of our lord the new King Philip [III], we and certain others chosen for this purpose were asked to carry the sacred bones of his body back to France; that is, to the church of the Blessed Denis where he had chosen to be buried in the event that, by the will of God,[301] he should happen to die in a land not yet acquired for Christianity. But later, after, we believe, taking more sensible advice from the king of Sicily, the lord King Philip kept these sacred relics with him, believing strongly that the Lord would direct the army to the good and protect it from misfortune because of the merits of his saintly father.

[47] On his heart and intestines being translated to Sicily.

When the flesh of his body had been boiled away and separated from his bones, the devout king of Sicily sought and obtained from his nephew King Philip in particular the heart and intestines. Taking these sacred relics,[302] he sent them on to Sicily and ordered that they be installed near Palermo in a certain noble cathedral abbey,[303] with a very solemn and devout procession of all the clergy and people of the land. On our return from Tunis, as we were crossing through Palermo, we stopped at that truly noble and most beautiful abbey, and we learned from many trustworthy individuals that after the relics had been installed many miracles had occurred at that very spot, with the help of God.

---

[300] *RHGF:* sancta] sacra *A B*
[301] *RHGF:* Domino] Deo *A B*
[302] *RHGF:* qui suscipiens sanctas reliquias] qui susceptas sanctas reliquias *A B*
[303] The church of Monreale near Palermo.

[47*bis*] On the passage of his sacred bones through Sicily.[304]

Those who were present with the lord king as these things happened can now bear witness to the honor, devotion, and reverence with which his bones were taken up when his most devout son, the illustrious King Philip, carried them with him with great devotion during his entire return journey from Tunis. With what longing and devotion, the clergy, nobles, and a countless host of people came from all directions in solemn and devout processions to see or touch the little box in which his precious relics were carried, as the lord king made his progress through Sicily and Calabria, as well as through the holy city of Rome and at Viterbo—where the lord cardinals were taking their time electing a pope—and then through Bologna and the other cities of Lombardy![305]

[48] On the arrival of the sacred bones in France.

Now if the relics of these sacred bones were accompanied by such great honors and so many faithful people and holy processions as they passed through foreign lands, who indeed could have managed[306] to describe what transpired when the famous king entered France itself with the sacred bones of his pious father and passed through[307] the cities and castles of his realm, [and] with what tearful and devout processions the clergy and religious reverently ran to meet him and piously receive him, with all due dignity, and to follow behind most devotedly with countless crowds of devoted people?

---

[304] "De transitu sacrorum ossium per Siciliam"; this chapter division is found only in *B*.
[305] After Clement IV died in 1268, the conclave assembled at Viterbo took three years to elect a new pope. Eventually Teobaldo Visconti was elected on 1 September 1271, and took the name Gregory X. It was he who would commission Geoffrey's life of Louis.
[306] *RHGF*: sufficiat] sufficeret *A B*
[307] *RHGF*: transivit] transiret *A B*

[49] On his burial at Saint-Denis.

Finally, reaching Saint-Denis in France, where, as we said, the holy king had chosen to be buried, with a vast gathering of prelates and barons and religious, his very holy bones were consigned to his tomb next to his father, the most pious King Louis [VIII], in the presence of his son, the lord King Philip who, like the best son of the best father, most faithfully and devotedly always stood by him as much in life as in death. He was buried in the year of Our Lord 1271, the Friday before Pentecost.[308]

[50] On the miracles after his burial.

After his most sacred bones were buried, there was no dearth of great wonders, but soon *the Lord made his holy one wonderful*.[309] Through the power of Christ and prompted by the merits of our holy king, many miracles shown forth over his tomb, which have been faithfully written down on the order of the lord abbot of Saint-Denis,[310] and, as it is said, carefully tested, as described, in order to declare the merits of this most holy man and to the honor and glory of God almighty, who is ever miraculous and praiseworthy[311] in his saints. *To him be glory and empire for ever and ever. Amen.*[312]

---

[308] 22 May 1271.
[309] Ps. 4:4.
[310] Matthew of Vendôme was abbot of Saint-Denis from 1258 to his death in 1286, and one of the council charged with guarding the realm during Louis' absence in 1270. A specific record of miracles written at Saint-Denis at this moment does not survive, but there are other indications from the canonization hearings that such a record existed. William of Chartres records his own version of early miracles, some of which are likely to have been noted at Saint-Denis as well.
[311] *RHGF atque laudabilis*] *add. in marg A* (but probably by original scribal hand) *om.* B
[312] Apoc. 1:6.

[51] How the memory of Josias is fitting to his memory.

Finally (so that the end of this work may be joined to the beginning), truly and worthily the *memory of* our King *Josias*—that is, of King Louis, because of the previously mentioned merits of his holy comportment and the great event of his happy death—*is like the composition of a sweet smell made by the art of a perfumer, and his remembrance shall be sweet as honey in every mouth, and as music at a banquet of wine.*[313] Indeed the memory of his praiseworthy life and comportment can rightfully be compared to[314] *the composition of a sweet smell made by the art of a perfumer* because of the fragrance[315] of his most sweet fame.

For those who were not there and who did not see him in the flesh, this was spread and carried far and wide throughout the whole world, so that it can truly be said, *We are the good odor of Christ, in every place,*[316] and that the entire universal house of the Church, and even of the whole world, has been suffused with his fragrant oil. For I do not believe that in many ages past a living person has stood out whose extraordinary deeds and fame have been more widely diffused throughout the whole world, so that of him it may be said *Your name is as oil poured out.*[317] And just as it is said in praise of Mardochai *the fame of his name increased daily, and was spread abroad through all men's mouths,*[318] and indeed, as is said of King Solomon *he exceeded his fame with his virtues,*[319] in this way hardly the half of his wisdom and virtues is really related in these accounts.

The passage continues: *and in every mouth as sweet as honey.* This is for those who were with him and conversed with him personally, who were worthy to frequently observe his holy works close at hand, and *as sweet as honey in the mouth* to test and taste his praiseworthy life. His comportment, indeed, was most sweetened with honey. And just as with

---

[313] Ecclus. 49:1–2.
[314] *RHGF* (with note that a word must be missing), *A:* merito] merito comparatur *B*
[315] *RHGF, A:* Factam gratiam] fragranciam *B*
[316] 2 Cor. 2:15,14.
[317] Cf. Cant. 1:2.
[318] Esther 9:4 ("et per ora omnium volitabat" found only in *B*).
[319] Cf. 2 Par. 9:6.

honey itself, the more you savor it, the sweeter is its taste, and the more it thus moves you to love.

And so the passage ends by adding *and as music at a banquet of wine.* This pertains particularly to the intimates of his household and his counselors and especially those who knew the innermost secrets of his heart, who heard him many times speaking with much grace, both in secret councils and in the friendly sermons of his sweet conversations, and most especially to those to whom he laid bare intimately his secrets, his pious longings and holy desires; because it was all like simple, pleasant *music* to be heard, and a *banquet of wine* to be pleasantly tasted.[320]

So of him it can be said, as was said in praise of Elias, *Blessed are they who heard you* (like harmonious *music*), *and were honored with your friendship* (like *a banquet of wine*),[321] and as the queen of Sheba said admiringly of Solomon, *Happy are your men and happy are your servants who stand always before your face and hear your wisdom.*[322] Thus indeed was our Josias like the *sweet smell of the perfumer,* fragrant through his most sweet reputation to those far away; *as sweet as honey in the mouth,* to those present who tasted in approval his holy comportment; *and like music at a banquet of wine* to his very special friends who, hearing the secrets of his wisdom and his virtues, were like those experiencing melodious *music* and a delicious *banquet of wine.*

[52] That he is worthy to be enrolled among the saints.

Therefore, after all these great efforts of praise, what else would seem to remain, if not that the memory of our own Josias—so sweet-smelling, honey-sweetened, and melodious—should be perpetually preserved in the Church of God, as it so well deserves? That is, that our just man will be established in everlasting memory. And then the memory of

---

[320] In good Dominican fashion, Geoffrey here performs a quick tripartite explication of the biblical passage, in the manner Preachers were trained to do in their sermons.
[321] Cf. Ecclus. 48:11. The comments "quasi musicam armoniam" and "quasi convivio vini" are found only in *B*.
[322] 2 Par. 9:7 (Cf also 3 Kings 10:8).

this just man will be accompanied by solemn and devout praises, and truly *beloved of God and men, whose memory is in benediction*[323] of all the ages. *And He may make him like the saints, in glory*[324] and honor of his saints, He who is always glorious and exalted in his saints, for ever and ever. Amen.

---

[323] Ecclus. 45:1.
[324] Ecclus. 45:2.

Chapter Three

On the Life and Deeds of Louis, King of the Franks of Famous Memory, and on the Miracles That Declare His Sanctity

Compilation of Brother William of Chartres, once a personal cleric of the blessed King Louis, eventually a member of the Order of Preachers[1]

[1] *The wonderful Lord on high*[2] does not cease to bring forth wonders around us in our own times, creating signs and changing wonders in these days. For a new sun—having risen in the western region and pouring forth its rays of light and heat over the world, setting now[3] *in the south*—has not cooled in its setting; but, *keeping a furnace* of heat and light *in the works of heat*,[4] has left behind *a light that is sweet and delightful for* sound *eyes*.[5] On a spiritual level, we understand truly in this sun a man shining uniquely[6] among the princes of our age and the rulers of

---

[1] This identification is added by a later hand in *A*, bottom of fol. 41v (see figure 4). Although generally we have not included later marginalia, this early modern addition seems worth including in the body of the text, as long as it is clearly remembered that it was not part of the work of the original scribe. In the left-hand margin a third hand has added "Guillelmus Carnotensis."
[2] Ps. 92:4.
[3] *RHGF* has "nec" (rendering the passage nonsensical) where the abbreviation in *A* should properly be expanded as "nunc."
[4] Cf. Ecclus. 43:2–3. The phrase *in meridiano* that we have translated here as "in the south" is translated as "at noon" in the Douay-Rheims New Testament. Either is possible, but it seems to us that William is playing on the opposition between Louis' birth in the west and his death in the south (Africa).
[5] Cf. Eccles. 11:7.
[6] *RHGF* has "solem" where *A* has "solum."

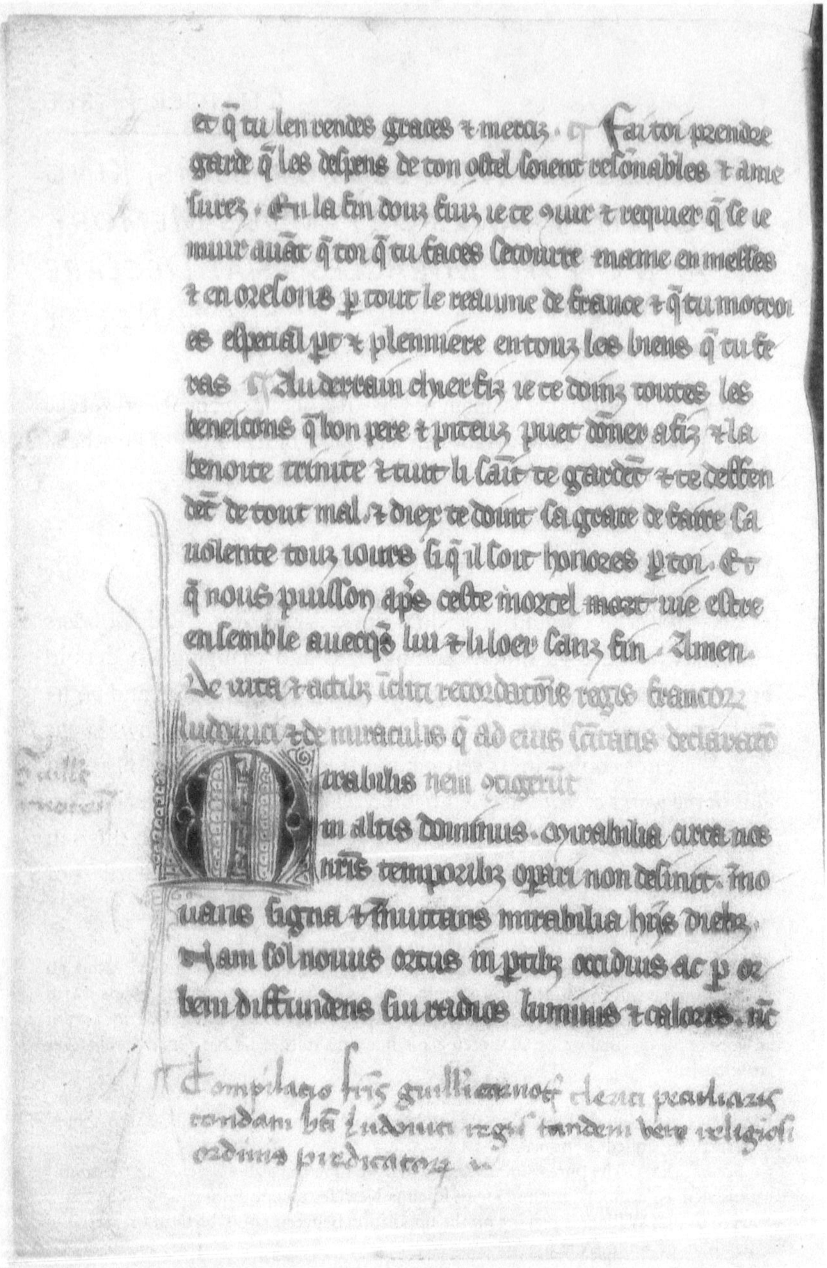

et q̃ tu l'en rendes graces ⁊ merciz. Fai toi prendre
garde q̃ les despens de ton ostel soient resonables ⁊ a mesures. En la fin douz fiuz, ie te pri ⁊ requier q̃ se il
muir auant q̃ toi q̃ tu faces secourre m'ame en messes
⁊ en oreisons p tout le reaume de france ⁊ q̃ tu m'en soies especial pa ⁊ pleniere en touz les biens q̃ tu feras. Au derrain chier fiz, ie te doinz toutes les
beneicons q̃ bon pere ⁊ piteus puet doner a fiz ⁊ la
benoite trinite ⁊ tuit li saint te gardent ⁊ te deffendent de tout mal. ⁊ diex te doint sa grace de faire sa
uolente touz iours si q̃ il soit honores p toi. Et
q̃ nous puisson apes ceste mortel mort uie estre
ensemble auecq̃s lui ⁊ lu loer sainz fin. Amen.

De uita ⁊ actib; i[n]cli[t]a recordac[i]o[n]is regis franco[rum]
Ludouici ⁊ de miraculis q̃ ad eius sa[n]cta[n]s declaracio[n]em
[mi]rabilis rem pagru[n]t

[I]n altis d[omi]n[u]s · mirabilia circa nos
[n]ris temporib; operari non desinit. imo
nouans signa ⁊ inmutans mirabilia h[ii]s diebz.
⁊ iam sol nouus ortus in p[ur]b; occiduis ac p orbem diffundens suu radios luminis ⁊ caloris. &c.

Compilacio fr[atr]is guillielm[i] de ca[r]n[oto] de s[an]ca p[re]dicac[i]o[n]is
quondam b[eati] ludouici reg[is] tandem u[er]o religios[i]
ordinis p[re]dicator[um].

Figure 4. Opening of William of Chartres' *vita*, from BnF ms. lat. 13778, fol. 41v. In the left and bottom margins, later hands have added the attribution to William of Chartres. Above can be seen the end of the copy of Louis IX's *Enseignements* that appears in this manuscript after Geoffrey of Beaulieu's *vita* and before William's. Reproduced by permission of the Bibliothèque nationale de France.

this world, just as the sun shines forth *among the stars;*[7] that is, the king of France, of fame and cherished memory, Louis. Born in the west, he lit up the world with the rays of his shining life. Finally setting in Africa, he waxed strong with heat as the sun at midday and *with his beams blinds the eyes.*[8] And thus he flared forth in dying, afire with the heat of faith and divine love, and shone bright to all with the holiness of his works and good deeds. And even after his final setting, he did not cease to shine with the light of his visible miracles.

[2] It might seem that for the honor and glory of the Creator and the praise of this same glorious king, and as evidence of his holiness, the odor of his most sacred fame now wafted throughout the world would suffice. There is, as well, all that has been written by our father of sacred memory, that mirror of all religious life, Brother Geoffrey of Beaulieu of the Order of Preachers, who was Louis' confessor and shared his secrets, and who, at the close of his own life, as he was able and with his own hand, bidden by our lord pope Gregory, wrote down his text and left it to be given to our lord pontiff himself. Nevertheless, among certain other things worthy of remembrance that Louis did in his lifetime, both during the good days of his rule as well as in the trials of his imprisonment and the distress of his death, there are certain matters that have been passed over or left out entirely; likewise concerning miracles known to have happened around his tomb and elsewhere. For the increase of divine praise and as a declaration of the merits of this king, I have tried to gather a few facts about these matters and to supplement in a plain style what has already been written.

[3] Now, the father just mentioned [Geoffrey] began his work by taking a line of Scripture from Ecclesiasticus for his theme: *The memory of Josias is like the composition of a sweet smell made by the art of a perfumer. It shall be sweet as honey in every mouth, and as music at a banquet of wine*[9]—thus appropriately referring to our own king by the name of Josias, for he was very like him in thought and deed. And as the simile is rightly applied to Josias, so should the sweet memory of our king be compared in these three things: to the smell of the art of a perfumer, to

---

[7] Abdias 1:4.
[8] Cf. Ecclus. 43:4. The Vulgate reads "obcaecat" where *A* has "obfuscat."
[9] Ecclus. 49:1.

the sweetness of honey, and to the harmony of instrumental music; like something quite pleasant to the heart, the taste, and even the ear. And this is because of those three things which, we read, were in this same king; that is, his well-known reputation for virtue, more fragrant than any scent; the sweetness of his holy, modest way of life, which rose above all corporeal delight; and his dedication to divine honor and praise, more appealing than any song or melody of this world.[10] Granted that enough has been said on all other points, our king's acts, his words and deeds, were not only sweet and delightful to those who heard and saw them clearly—that is, they carried the scent of true holiness—but they also aroused many hearts to dedicated worship. For divine virtue had bestowed upon him this unique grace such that, as was seen over and over again, his very countenance and speech would straightaway render peaceful and calm the minds of the many people, even the great, who came to him in alarm and confusion. Many people, in fact, who seemed more religious than others, after they had seen and heard him, went away greatly edified. The more these people came to know firsthand his holy and humble ways, the more they realized that they themselves were, by and large, not really all that religious or perfect or humble. His principles, his acts, and his deeds were not only regal but well-regulated,[11] wholly devoid of any flavor of this vain world. And then one cannot easily say how *sweet to the palate* his divine *words* always were.[12] For his public proclamation of divine praise, not only *more than honey to his tongue*,[13] but more than all the other delights about him flowed into the ears and hearts of people. Loathing and despising the vain songs of this world and the idle plays of actors, rejecting the attractions of musical instruments in which most nobility find enjoyment, he shielded his sons and his household from such folly. He was wholly inspired by and given to hymns of divine praise, greatly delighted by the voices of the sweetly sounding Church, to such an extent as to be able gloriously to proclaim about himself, as did that outstanding

---

[10] *RHGF* has "secularem melodiam" where *A* reads "secularium melodiam."
[11] The Latin pun here is difficult to translate; his deeds were not only "regales" (royal or regal) but "regulares," implying they were "regulated" in the sense of resembling a monastic rule.
[12] Cf. Ps. 118:103. *RHGF* has "semper fuerint" where *A* reads "semper fuerunt."
[13] Cf. Ps. 118:103.

teacher of the Church, "Oh Lord, your praises have held up the young vine of my heart toward you, lest it be carried off through empty things, defiled, a prey to flighty whims."[14]

[4] With what honor-inspiring reverence for our Savior, with what throngs of devoted people did he annually carry out the solemn religious processions that he established in his royal chapel! He established one for the most sacred Crown of Our Lord, on the day after the Feast of Saint Lawrence,[15] which is observed in the entire province of Sens; and another for all of the other holy relics, on the day after the Feast of Saint Michael the Archangel.[16] Or how reverently and solemnly he arranged to have the most precious wood of the Cross of Our Lord, His most holy Crown of Thorns, and the venerable iron spear that pierced His side, carried in public procession, all richly decorated with gold and very precious stones. In each of these just-mentioned sacred processions were Church prelates, members of the orders, the clergy, wearing silken capes, singing holy praise in the highest—while our pious king would come behind, humbly following with his chief nobility and the whole of the people in devout adoration of these sacred relics. Even though I would like to, it is quite beyond my strength and ability to describe this. Moreover, our pious king desired that these solemnities be observed as much in his absence as in his presence, even while he was gone overseas, thinking and acting with religious justification that just as Our Lord of Majesty was dishonored by the infidel Jews through these things—the Cross, the Crown of Thorns, and the spear—so would He now be honored through them by the faithful devout. And after the cursing and shameful mockery, which He endured for us, the glory of His praise would be manifold.

[5] In addition I should not be silent about how our pious king observed the holy Sabbath year in and year out. After having Matins sung in his presence before daybreak, as it should be, and after a short prayer,

---

[14] Augustine, *Confessions*, book I, ch. 17, where the text actually reads "laudes tuae, domine, laudes tuae per scripturas tuas suspenderent palmitem cordis mei, et non raperetur per inania nugarum turpis praeda volatilibus." *A* reads "Laudes tue domine suspenderunt planitiem cordis mei ad te ne raperetur per inania turpis preda volatilibus." Our translation follows *A*, except that it assumes that William intended "palmitem" instead of "planitiem."
[15] Saint Lawrence's Day was 10 August; the new feast was therefore 11 August.
[16] Saint Michael's Day was 29 September; the new feast was therefore 30 September.

coming in silence to his own room and remaining there alone, he would go through all the psalms in order with only his chaplain, reading through them all with complete and attentive devotion. After a short while, without returning to bed or sleeping, at about sunrise, with naked feet and in simple garb, with but a few companions, walking through the muddy cobblestone streets of whatever town or village he was in, he would enter churches and pray. With his almoner coming along behind him and pouring forth alms to all the poor, the king himself would hand out money with his own hands. Then he would return home, entirely worn out but still filled with all devotion, and listen, after a while, to a public sermon in which the full story of Our Lord's Passion was proclaimed to the assembled people, after which he had the Divine Office[17] celebrated in devotion and solemnity. In all truth it is not easy to describe how humble and reverent he was in his adoration of the Cross. Leaving his seat or his place, barefoot, with uncovered head and bare neck, in a thin belt[18] and humble dress, as though he were the poorest of the poor coming from afar, on bended knee, followed by his children dressed just like him, he thus humbly worshiped at Our Lord's Cross, which brought most of the spectators standing around to tears of moving devotion. Having thus fulfilled his obligation, the most Christian king went on to his very meager meal of plain bread and water. Behold how our pious king, beginning at midnight, spent his entire day in many vigils, in toil and weariness, in fasting and hunger, in almsgiving and in divine praise and prayer. Thus did he endeavor to devote the rest of his life to divine service and pious works that he might leave to people, great and small, the very mirror and image of pure and sacred virtue. For it is rightly said, "The whole world follows the example of the king."[19] And thus the Lord said to Moses, *Look, and act according to the pattern that was shown to you on the mountain.*[20] And thus, indeed, what we must do is shown and revealed to each and

---

[17] *RHGF* has "dominicum officium" where *A* reads "divinum officium."
[18] This word is given as "semiciis" in *RHGF* with a note suggesting the possibility of "semicinctiis." There is an abbreviation mark over "semiccis" in *A* that should indicate a missing "a." Unfortunately this is nonsensical, and the reading "semicinctiis" may be the best.
[19] The earliest source of this maxim appears to be Claudius Claudianus, *Panegyricus dictus Honorio Augusto quartum consuli (Carmina maiora, VIII)*, dating from the end of the fourth century.
[20] Exod. 25:40.

every one of us on the heights of this mountain; that is, on the summit of the noble worth of this our famous king, on his shining goodness and the superiority of his life.

[6] In truth, as a result of such pious devotion and his many, many deeds of charity and mercy, he found favor with God. Just as is read of Tobias, it was necessary *that temptation should prove him*[21] and that this proving be manifestly shown, just as the finest gold and silver are tried in the furnace. Therefore it should not be hidden in silence that, when he was made prisoner by the infidels in Egypt, during the entire time he was in prison, he never once deviated from his accustomed prayer and devotion. For as long as he was kept imprisoned in that foul dungeon,[22] he recited the Divine Office in the very same way as at church in Paris; that is, Matins and the canonical hours, both of the day and of the Blessed Virgin, and all of the Mass, save only the consecration of the sacrament, diligently reciting all at the appropriate time, together with a priest, a Preaching Brother who knew Arabic, with me there as his cleric at that time. And with the Saracen guards listening to him, he continually performed the appropriate hours with devout heart and mouth, having a breviary from his own chapel, which the Saracens had given to him as a gift after his capture, and a missal.[23]

[7] Despite the fact that I was almost always with him at all times and places, it is beyond my power to lay out just how wisely, how faithfully, and how constantly he bore himself in all things with respect to the Saracens, who came at him with frightening, overbearing threats and demands. This, however, I can assert in all truth and desire for brevity: that in everything he did he was utterly honest, shrewd in his answers, careful and true in his dealings, and fearless in his refusals. Under all pressure he always remained the soul of constancy, so that even the leading emirs marveled at him and said to the king, when he remained so unmoved

---

[21] Tob. 12:13.
[22] The word "ergastulo" ("work prison," or literally "slave quarters") used here in the context of Egypt, evokes Exodus 6:6, where the Lord promises to bring the children of Israel out of the "ergastulo" of the Egyptians.
[23] This episode furnished the kernel of what would become one of the most often-told miracle stories associated with Louis. Note, however, that in William's telling there is nothing miraculous about the episode.

in the face of their unrelenting demands, "It is a great wonder to us that you—whom we have considered to be our prisoner and slave and find you such in all things—consider that it is we who are these things, as though it were *you* who held *us* in prison." He would never have agreed to turn over Damietta to them if the Christians had been able to hold it at that time. Earlier he had asked and been told that, if the Saracens besieged the place, it could not be defended against the strength of such an army. But he could not be swayed in the least by their fierce pressure and threats, or be made to promise anything, or concede or swear to anything that would result in harm to Christianity or burden his conscience. All who were there, even the higher Christian nobility, were amazed at how confident and unperturbed he was, while they themselves were quite afraid. He himself, as a just man, was used to placing his trust in the Lord, and thus was unafraid, in accordance with the words of a wise man: *The just, bold as a lion, shall be without dread.*[24]

[8] The king showed one of his virtues—this one by far the greatest sign of virtue and grace—on the following occasion: after a truce was proposed and confirmed between the sultan and our king, we had met, discussed, and confirmed it late on a Sunday, with the archbishop of Jerusalem, Robert[25] of good memory, whom the king had summoned from Damietta for consultation, present with many others of the Christian nobility. Very early the next morning, the leading emirs of Babylon, plotting revolt, had the sultan cut down by some of his own staff as he sat to eat, and they had his body thrown out on the dirt like a dead, stinking mongrel. The guards who were protecting the king and his party[26] were at once forced out. And as everyone stood by, now without any protection to look to, and awaiting nothing more than a sword stroke or death, suddenly some of the slayers rushed in upon them with some of the leading emirs and the foremost killers, *like lions*[27] or raging bears in high fury, with bloody hands still steaming with hot gore and arms dripping with fresh-spilled blood. At the sight of our glorious king, they

---

[24] Prov. 28:1. The "wise man" is Solomon, presumed by medieval scholars to be the author of the Book of Proverbs.
[25] Robert of Nantes was patriarch of Jerusalem from 1240 to his death in 1254.
[26] *RHGF* has "qui Regem et suos servabant" but the word "qui" is not in fact found in *A*.
[27] Soph. 3:3.

straightway lost all earlier ferocity; and, *like lambs*,[28] with meek expression, heads downcast, greeting him with hands in prayer, said, "Fear not, lord, be free of care. You need not be concerned about what has occurred. This had to be done. Please carry on according to the requirements of the agreements that have been reached and soon you will be set free." And so it came to pass. After three days came the truly swift and solemn release of the king and of the nobility, with the Lord of Hosts miraculously arranging that those people who just recently in such vile fashion had slaughtered their infidel lord sultan, so pompous and proudly exultant over our defeat, and had tossed him out as though a filthy, rotten mongrel, now honorably set free the captive king—a humble man, their enemy, a faithful Christian. Thus, as has been said by a wise man, *The just man is delivered out of distress, and the wicked shall be given up for him*.[29] After this, as many captives as could be found in all of Egypt, even those held from olden times, were set free. Among them the master of the Hospital of Jerusalem,[30] who had been some long time held in prison, and many others were freed and restored to their old liberty. This came about not without a miracle of divine power, and the fact that so many and such men were set free, safe and sound, from out of the hands of wicked infidels so easily and for so little, must be ascribed to the king's own merits. Later on, the Saracens themselves, complaining bitterly to one another in regret, said to some of our men that, at that time, they simply did not know what they were doing. And, truly, that was the case. For thus is read in Isaias: *The Lord mingled in the midst of them the spirit of giddiness: and they have caused Egypt to err in all its works, as a drunken man staggers and vomits*.[31]

[9] Also I must not pass over in silence this thing, which perfectly pronounces the fervor and humility of the faith of this king: while on his way to Sidon he heard about the Christians sent there by the one who had begun to rebuild the city, but who had been slain there by the army of

---

[28] Cf. 1 Peter 1:19. The biblical echo of "quasi agni" may be unintentional, since it would seem to cast the "infideles" in a Christ-like light.
[29] Prov. 11:8.
[30] William of Châteauneuf, who had been taken prisoner in October 1244.
[31] Isa. 19:14. *RHGF* renders the last word of the quotation as "amens," but *A* actually follows the Vulgate reading of "vomens."

Damascus; that many of their bodies and limbs lay completely unburied on the shore. Our pious king, without pausing to eat, went there straightaway together with the well-remembered venerable father, lord Eudes, bishop of Tusculum and legate of the apostolic see.[32] Now, although all the others who were present reacted as though they had some sort of loathing and dread of picking up the bodies and gathering the now half-rotten, hacked-off limbs or touching the bones, our devout, greathearted king himself, as though having and sensing no repulsion, was there *from morning even until noon,*[33] as though lingering in a perfumed chamber, with his very own hands so benevolently gathering up the limbs and entrails of these Christians, whom he considered to be martyrs, so sweetly handling and gathering them up and placing them in containers to be carried to their place of burial, which he had made near the camp. Everyone there, and many who had fled the ghastly endeavor, marveled at his magnanimous humility. So it was that nothing at all (or just the merest fragments of bone) was left there, and what was found was most honorably delivered for solemn last rites and church burial, so that in these things could plainly be understood that psalm verse which says: *The Lord keeps all their bones, not one among them will be broken,*[34] and that other saying of a wise man: *The bodies of the saints are buried in peace and their names will live in eternity.*[35]

[10] The king himself was so full of a spirit of piety for such deeds that out of charity he would freely go to see those who were sick, even those in their hour of death. And he would offer them words of pious salvation and consolation, advice they sorely needed, even though many people argued that he should not because of the danger involved. Once it came to pass at Mansura, in Egypt, that I, who served then as his cleric, had gone to see a certain man among the troops, his attendant and bedchamber servant, a good man especially well known to him named Jacques,[36] who was then so near to death as to believe that he would at any moment breathe his last. And, as I was about to go, he said to me, "I am waiting for

[32] See chapter 2, note 157 on Eudes of Châteauroux.
[33] 3 Kings 18:26.
[34] Ps. 33:21.
[35] Cf. Ecclus. 44:14.
[36] The Latin name here is "Gauquelmus."

my lord the holy king to visit me, and I will not depart this world until I have seen him and spoken with him, and I will then quickly depart." And this is indeed what happened. Presently the king came to see this man, for whom few of his men held out hope, and he gave him the consolation of pious personal conversation. Upon his return, before he had reached his royal pavilion, he was told most truly that Jacques was dead.

[11] Moreover, he knew quite often the character of men and what they would do—a thing I once proved true. And sometimes he predicted it, not by any human means but by divine revelation. Because of all that I have had to do, these things have slipped away from my feeble memory. This episode however, because it happened to me, I am able to faithfully relate. Once the king was talking quite casually with two of us—that is with Brother Geoffrey [of Beaulieu] of good memory and with me. I was then living a secular life, since the king had recently given me a rich position as treasurer. He turned to Brother [Geoffrey] in the course of conversation and remarked, speaking in reference to me, "Master William will toy with his position as treasurer for only five, maybe six years; but then he will enter into religion." I was entertaining no such idea at the time and did not agree with him about this, but the final turn of events proved that he had predicted most accurately. In fact, five and a half years later, by God's grace, though unworthy, I entered the Order of the Preaching Brothers where I now am, just as our devout king foresaw it in spirit and foretold it.[37] At that time I did not recall his words, but only a while later did I remember what I had heard.

[12] He was not only worried by and concerned with the safeguard of bodily or temporal matters[38] in governing the kingdom, so far as this pertained to the royal office, watching out day and night in order to preserve everyone *as the apple of his eye*;[39] but he was also moved, more than

---

[37] William was probably made treasurer of Saint-Frambaut in Senlis in 1258 or early 1259; he would therefore have entered the Dominican order around 1264 or 1265. See Louis Carolus-Barré, "Guillaume de Chartres clerc du roi, frère prêcheur, ami et historien de saint Louis," *Collection de l'Ecole française de Rome* 204 (1995): 52, and our introduction to the present volume.

[38] *RHGF* has "de corporum aut rerum corporalium custodia," but *A* has "temporalium" rather than "corporalium."

[39] Deut. 32:10.

I would have believed possible, by a sort of pious usurpation,[40] to concern himself with the salvation of souls, about which he was so actively concerned that he seemed to exercise equally a priestly rule or a royal priesthood. Exerting his royal authority, he reined in many quite arrogant nobles who were eager to plunder his poor subjects; and by private entreaties he brought a host of others, lusting and wicked, to the fruits of an amended life. And there were even some quite powerful nobles who had long kept concubines but repudiated them after the advice and direction of a royal warning. And one or several of these nobles actually later wed these ladies of lesser standing whom they had previously kept as concubines.

[13] Out of respectful reverence for his majesty or honesty, everyone, both great and small, was afraid to come into his presence or to approach him dressed ornately in grandiose fashion, lest they receive shame rather than honor if they appeared at all haughty before so humble and honored a king.

[14] Indeed, it once happened at a council of the king that a certain lady, adorned with no little care, after her business had been addressed at court, entered the king's chamber with only a few others. The king took notice, seeing that (according to the false and deceiving judgment of the worldly and the vanity of physical beauty) she had been notoriously attractive. Our king, wholly given to God, deciding that he[41] would speak personally with her concerning her salvation, called aside Brother Geoffrey, who was there at hand, and said to him, "I want you to stay here and listen to what I intend to tell such a lady as this who is here and wishes to speak with me." After he explained what he intended to say, and she was alone with the king and the aforesaid brother, the king spoke as follows: "My lady, I want you to call to mind something concerning your salvation. It is said that you were once a beautiful lady. But what once was, now is passed, as you are well aware. You can, therefore, consider that such swiftly fading beauty is vain and useless and does not

---

[40] William's point seems to be that Louis not only fulfilled a king's duty to guard his subjects' bodily safety, but veered over into the responsibilities of the Church by tending to souls as well. His phrase "pia usurpatione" is quite striking, as is his juxtaposition of "regale sacerdotium" with "sacerdotale regimen."

[41] *RHGF* omits the word "rex" where *A* reads "quod de salute sua rex ei familiariter loqueretur."

last, like a quickly wilting flower. And with all your care and effort, you cannot bring it back. Rather you must concern yourself with achieving another beauty, not of the body, but of the soul, whereby you may be able to please our Creator and atone for those things done thoughtlessly in bygone elegance." The lady of whom we are speaking listened patiently and took it all in. Afterward, having changed for the better, she was careful to act more humbly and honestly.

[15] He himself was the very mirror of all honesty and modesty. He especially loved honest and modest men and welcomed them to his inner circle, edifying his children, his friends and relations, and the nobility who were close to him, by his words of salvation and his example.

[16] Moreover, the king was a man of peace. Like an ardent suitor of peace and religion, he was vigilant in all his efforts for the reformation and peace and conservation of all the churches and monasteries of his realm, by settling disagreements, shielding them from the harm and vexation that so many cathedrals and convents of the Church so often endure. Like a pious father and tireless patron, he was ever present in his support, and he saved from many troubles many worthy monasteries—especially Cluny with its daughter houses; and Marmoutier in Tours, Saint-Denis, Saint-Benoît of Fleury; and also Cistercian houses, Clairvaux and many others—when they were in an hour of need or dissension or oppression.[42]

[17] With a certain unique and tender affection, he took on the burdens, needs, and troubles of the religious poor, like a father of the poor,[43] nourishing and supporting them with timely benefits and aids.

[18] Those who stayed near him in his inner circle certainly know how reverently and humbly he always behaved toward the most holy Roman Church, how devoutly and obediently he would receive apostolic orders and decrees, and how obediently and effectively he fulfilled them as a true son of obedience. Considering the business of mother Church more important than his own, he devoted every effort to accomplishing it.

---

[42] Cluny was founded in 910 and controlled a vast family of reformed "daughter houses" by the thirteenth century; Marmoutier in Tours, Saint-Denis north of Paris, and Saint-Benoît of Fleury-sur-Loire were venerable Benedictine houses; Clairvaux (founded 1115 by Saint Bernard) was the most famous house of the Cistercian order.

[43] Note that this title is also given to Louis in Philip III's letter.

[19] He also welcomed with kind indulgence the inquisitors of heretics, who were working on behalf of the faith and the Church. Whenever they came to him for help, he put aside all other business, no matter how grave, giving them his attentive ear, assisting them with all thankful support, and insisting that the work of the faith ought to be put ahead of everything else.[44]

[20] He continually ordered that unfair and wrongheaded customs, no matter how long-standing, be abolished, and that unwarranted exactions be ended, where[45] this could reasonably be done. Even if it meant some loss of money or income, he wanted offices[46] to be entrusted only to people who were upright and trustworthy, rather than to have them sold for his own gain or profit. He considered that what came to him through injustice and public harm was no gain or profit at all.

[21] He so loathed the Jews, people hateful to God and man, that he could not look at them, and refused to benefit in any way from their wealth, insisting that he did not want to keep their poison and have them practice usury, but to have them earn their bread in lawful trade and service as was customarily done in other places. Many of his councillors argued against him, pointing out that people cannot live without loans, or farm the land, or develop commerce and service, and that it was better and more acceptable that the Jews, who were already damned, should see to this damnable duty than certain Christians—who, given the opportunity, were oppressing the people with even higher interest rates. The king himself, as a catholic man, gave this answer: "The issue of Christians charging interest and practicing usury seems to be a matter for prelates of the Church. The Jews, however, who bear the yoke of servitude to me,[47] are my concern, to see that they oppress no Christians by usury and that they not be allowed to commit such depravity[48] under my protection and

---

[44] The first "inquisitors of heretical depravity" (see chapter 2, note 31) were appointed by Pope Gregory IX in the 1230s, following the Albigensian Crusade. Many, though not all, were Dominicans. This new office was thus of particular interest to Louis' Dominican biographers, having come into being during Louis' reign as a result of developments within his realm.
[45] *RHGF* has "ut" where the abbreviation found in *A* should be expanded as "ubi."
[46] "Preposituras" here probably indicates the offices of *prevôt* and *bailli*.
[47] Jews within the royal domain were legally considered serfs of the crown.
[48] *A* reads "et sub umbra protectione mea talem pravitatem exerceant." This reading is given in a note to *RHGF*, but amended to "et sub umbra protectionis meae talia permittatur ut exerceant."

infect my land with their poison. Let the prelates act as they see fit for the Christians answerable to them, and I wish to attend to my business with the Jews. Let them abandon usury or leave my land, lest it be further befouled by their filth."

[22] He sometimes had their property seized with them; not to keep it for himself, but to return it, upon receipt of lawful proof of their claim, to those from whom they had wrung it through usurious depravity. And he assigned diligent and thoughtful *enquêteurs*[49] to do this, putting the property in their hands so they might freely restore it on their own. If any property remained whose owners were not known or could not be found, he allocated it with Church approval for pious uses and alms.[50]

[23] Although he was concerned for and dedicated to rendering due justice to all, by justly pursuing what was just with all good will, yet tempering the letter of the law with the mildness of mercy, he was often not a little inclined by his innate clemency toward those things that exalt a judgment,[51] though he always held to the truth, knowing that it is written, *Mercy and truth preserve the king, and his throne is secured by clemency.*[52]

[24] He called for the counsel of discerning men learned in the law, from all parts of his realm, to discuss the matter of trial by combat, which is called a battle or a duel. And understanding from them that it could not be carried out without mortal sin, for it seems not to be justice but rather tempting God, he decreed that it be entirely abolished within his domain. In its place an alternative method of proceeding and proving was established, consonant with law; that is, by witnesses and written instruments or even reasoning, as the legal process requires.

[25] When it came to higher transgressions, where leniency can have no place without divine offense, he showed himself not lenient but effectively firm and undeviating, no matter what the rank of the offender.

---

[49] The Latin word here translated as *enquêteurs* is *inquisitores*, the same as for papal "inquisitors of heretical depravity" though the offices were entirely different (see chapter 2, note 31). Note, however, the way the juxtaposition of *inquisitor* and *pravitas* ("depravity") colors the Jews in shades of heresy.

[50] *RHGF* reads "ecclesias erogabat" where the abbreviation in *A* is properly expanded as "elemosinas erogabat."

[51] *RHGF* has "super exaltabant" where *A* reads "super exaltat." The emendation to the plural verb "superexaltabant," however, seems necessary.

[52] Prov. 20:28. The Vulgate reads "roboratur" where *A* has "firmatur."

If the offender were of his own household[53] he was at pains to right the wrong or the transgression more severely than if the offender were an outsider. Examples of these things could be given from many certain cases. We leave them out for the sake of brevity, and lest individuals living or dead be exposed through such a recital.

[26] With extreme diligence he sought out trustworthy, sensible men of good behavior and reputation, especially those whose hands were clean of graft, appointing such men as his *baillis* and *sénéchaux*. And from among these men, after they had governed their districts for some time, he would choose his household and advisers. He would remove from their positions or their districts those who received graft or plundered the poor, avoiding them like the plague.[54]

[27] Many a person marveled—and the wicked grumbled—that one man, so humble, so mild, not strong of body or harsh in approach, was able to rule peaceably over such a realm, over such and so many princes and mighty lords, especially since he was hardly affable or generous with rewards for some people. This must be ascribed not to temporal power but to divine virtue; not to cruel tyranny but to royal clemency; to love, and to the faith of a devout people who are known to have before all else a certain special and innate affection for their natural lord, and are ruled not by a repressive fear but rather by a mastering love.

[28] With respect to his abstinence and frugality, I believe we may generally conclude that in every way through which he possibly could receive bodily or worldly pleasure he displayed particular self-denial, by laying forceful restrictions upon his spirit in all these things.

[29] Concerning his food, which was served to him first and of which he freely ate, it was his regular practice to take some of it away, or sometimes all of it, and bestow it upon one of the poor people who in his daily routine ate in his presence. Once it happened that he had sent to a wretched and sickly one of these poor people a plate[55] full of rich pudding,[56] which he freely ate himself and which he had portioned out

---

[53] *RHGF* has "Quod si etiam esset persona de propria familia," where *A* reads "Quod si etiam de propria esset familia."
[54] Louis formalized these decisions in the Grand Ordinance of 1254.
[55] *RHGF* has "quod cum scutellam" but the word "cum" is not found in *A*.
[56] "Offis pinguibus" suggests a rich and greasy dish, perhaps like an old-fashioned English pudding.

and heaped on the dish with his own hands. And that person had eaten part of it with his own filthy, ulcerous hands and did not want any more, asking that it be taken away. And then our renowned king, seeing this, out of his innate virtue of humility, asked to have back what the poor man had left and in which he had stained his dirty hands, saying, "Give me back my pudding!" And, to the amazement of many,[57] as much as the mind was horrified, he began to eat from this with such relish and enthusiasm as if no one had touched it at all.

[30] Moreover, quite trustworthy individuals, who personally observed it, say that at his monastery of Royaumont, the humble king knowingly washed the feet of a certain leper, and diligently drying them in his accustomed fashion, kissed them humbly and devoutly.

[31] And this should not be passed over in silence: once, when he had devoted himself to washing feet in this fashion, he came to a certain poor man who had been called for this purpose and, getting down on his knees in the usual way, he began to wash his feet. The pauper did not know that it was the king, so he asked him, in his simplicity, to wash and clean between[58] the toes where the grime was hiding. The bystanders were, of course, amazed and reproached the pauper for daring to ask such a thing of the king. But then our pious king kindly acquiesced to his request and benignly fulfilled this duty of humility, washing and drying with his own fingers inserted between his toes, and finally bent down with a kiss of charity.

[32] He observed the prescribed fasts so completely that even when he was sick he did not want to break them in any way. So it was that in his final illness, from which he died, he refused to taste chicken broth on the Sabbath, which was offered him on the advice of his doctors, on the grounds that he had not received special permission to do so from his confessor, who was absent at the time. In addition to the other personal fasts, about which the above-mentioned Brother Geoffrey has explained at length, he was accustomed to make other special demands on himself. He fasted throughout Advent on Lenten foods, as well as on those holy days from Our Lord's Ascension until Pentecost. He also fasted on all the

---

[57] *RHGF* has "cunctis" where *A* reads "multis."
[58] *RHGF* has "iterum digitos pedum," where *A* reads "inter digitos pedum."

vigils of the apostles, although for some of them this was not the practice at Paris or in whatever diocese he was in; but he offered this justification to those who spoke to him about it, that he came from[59] the diocese of Chartres, where fasting was observed for this vigil.[60]

[33] Among his other deeds of mercy and piety, with which he wholly overflowed like a stream of charity, I ought not be silent about *his alms which the whole church of the saints declares*,[61] by generally asserting[62] that no kind of pauper ever came to his attention who did not feel the benefit of his largess or help in some way.

[34] I particularly wish to add this point, that when famine loomed he poured himself more freely into almsgiving, sending funds for disbursement to various places all around, especially ordering that distributions be most abundantly made to those areas where he secured the most returns and revenues. When a famine once befell parts of Normandy, he designated such a large supply of money for the poor of that area that, just as from there was usually brought[63] to Paris a treasure of revenues in coffers and wagons, now by contrast just as much money was carried back from Paris in boxes and vehicles for distribution to the poor. He considered it right and just that, where he reaped in plenty, there in time of need should he sow. Because,[64] as it is written, *The lips of many shall bless him that is liberal of his bread*.[65] He further was hoping that from the seed of this blessing he would in the last harvest reap a glorious blessing of eternal recompense.

[35] I must not be silent about this thing that once occurred in my presence. As he augmented at great cost many necessary buildings for the Hôtel-Dieu in Paris,[66] where a truly large swarm of poor sick people came for refuge every day, and where space was lacking, the master of the

---

[59] *RHGF* has "existebat," where *A* reads "extiterat."
[60] Louis was born at Poissy, in the diocese of Chartres. See Geoffrey of Beaulieu, ch. 34.
[61] Cf. Ecclus. 31:11.
[62] *RHGF* has "adserens" where *A* reads "asserendo."
[63] *A* reads "afferre" which *RHGF* silently emends to "afferri."
[64] *RHGF* reads "quod" where *A* has "quia."
[65] Ecclus. 31:28.
[66] The thirteenth-century Hôtel-Dieu was situated on the southern side of the Ile de la Cité, just west of Notre Dame and the bishop's palace.

house came to him and asked him for a certain aid of alms,[67] especially since they had endured a huge wine shortfall for the house that year. The king, this man so full of piety, upon hearing this, giving bountifully from the bounty of his pious heart, called his chamberlain and bid him at once to deliver to this house one thousand Parisian livres for wine and other immediate needs. The master stood amazed, and could scarcely believe it, until the king repeated it, saying "Deliver a thousand livres to the poor of the Hôtel-Dieu of Paris!" The master would have thought it enough of a benefit if only a hundred livres had been given there for alms!

[36] About that same time, in brief, he saw to the construction of three notable hospitals for the poor in three of his towns at great expense, with ample accommodations. He built the house of the Preaching Brothers at Compiègne at great cost, and the entire church of the Brothers Minor at Paris, and many other structures there, with great expense. He also built the dormitory of the Preaching Brothers with its dining hall in Paris. In brief, he was thus hoping and trusting in the mercy of the greatest giver of largess that, by the building of houses of the Lord and other acts of piety, he would receive *a house not made with hands, eternal in heaven*, after his *earthly house was dissolved*.[68]

[37] As his earthly struggle came to an end, it was time for the glorious king[69] to pass beyond the end of this life[70] and the care of his realm to the heavenly kingdom to receive the incorruptible crown[71] in reward for his toil. Brother Geoffrey, who was there and whom we have so often mentioned, has proclaimed how utterly firm the king was[72] in his faith, how warm in his love, how lofty in the sublime hope of receiving his reward, and how clearly resplendent to the very end of life in his final illness, from which he suffered greatly. And I too was there, standing by him in sickness and in death. As to the extent and nature of his faith, which he strove with loving ardor to increase with every fiber of his being, it was like a

---

[67] *RHGF* has "aliquam eleemosynam," where *A* has "aliquam elemosine."
[68] 2 Cor 5:1.
[69] *A* reads "gloriosus rex," which *RHGF* amends to "gloriosam" to modify "curam."
[70] *RHGF* has "quo post finem certaminis" where the first word in *A* is "quod."
[71] *A* reads "incorruptibilem coronam" which *RHGF* amends to "incomparabilem coronam."
[72] *RHGF* has "quantum fuit" where *A* reads "quantum fuerit."

mustard seed,[73] in that the more it is ground, the more its pungent smell increases. Thus for this man, so wholly established in his faith, wholly distilled in spirit, the more he was wracked in turn by the hammer blows of adversity and ill health, the more, by the stoking of his passion, he made manifest the perfection of faith within him. Not wanting to hear a word about anything of this world or of the flesh, he concentrated instead only on spiritual things, encouraging and inspiring his men as far as was possible to strive[74] to envision the propagation and multiplication of the faith in those parts of Africa. He displayed the intense[75] and burning passion of charity within him, which the many waters of suffering and bodily sickness could not[76] quench but seemed rather to intensify. For, just as we read of Our Lord the Savior, that *in his agony he prayed the longer,*[77] thus did this holy man, agonizing at the end, begin to pray at length. And among other prayerful supplications, as he was calling upon his well-known saints, he began to recite that short prayer, which is sung of the blessed apostle James the Elder, "Lord, be the guardian and sanctifier of your people,"[78] saying it over and over in a gentle whisper. And so he was sweetly drawing forth that warmth of love which he bore in his heart for the spiritual as well as the temporal salvation of his people, as if he were saying "Lord, *it is enough*[79] that I have struggled on until now, that I have toiled on in your service with all my powers, that I have preserved your people and realm entrusted to me with such dedication as I could command. Now, called to you by your dispensing mercy, I am no longer able to protect them with my body. I pray you, I beseech you, o Lord, be with them now a sanctifier of their souls, a guardian of their bodies! I commend them to your piety,"

---

[73] Cf. Matt. 18:19, Luke 17:6.
[74] *RHGF* has "prout enim possent" (with a note indicating ms. reading of "poterat") where *A* has "prout eniti poterat."
[75] *A* has "intense" which *RHGF* amends to "incensae."
[76] *RHGF* has "potuerant" where *A* reads "poterunt." This silent emendation, however, seems warranted.
[77] Luke 22:43.
[78] See the *Oratio* from the *Suffragia* to James the Apostle, in Robert Lippe, ed., *Missale Romanum Mediolani, 1474* (London: Harrison and Sons, 1899), 356 (or in the Hypertext Book of Hours, at http://medievalist.net/hourstxt/suffrage.htm).
[79] Luke 22:38.

[38] Moreover, though he was pressed down by the pains of great bodily suffering, his spirit soared in hope of the desired reward. The previous night he had been heard saying in French "We will go to Jerusalem!"[80] Completely desiring heavenly things, his whole spirit immersed in realms above, he ceaselessly sighed in aspiration for that heavenly Jerusalem which is the vision of true peace. Then around Terce, when he had almost entirely lost the power of speech, he was gazing at his household, which was standing around him, as though he were quite sweetly smiling at them and sighing. Then, between Terce and Sext, he seemed to rest, sleeping for half an hour.[81] Then, opening his eyes and raising them to heaven with a serene countenance, he spoke this Psalm verse, *I will go into your house, I will worship toward your holy temple, and I will give glory to your name.*[82] For this, as we sincerely believe, he was able to say truly, because he had longed, because he had waited, because he was hoping to go into the dominion of the Lord—that is, into the house of God—and come into the sight of God, not empty-handed but *bringing burnt offerings full of marrow.*[83] He had offered himself and his own from devotion born of burning love, and thus could he say with the psalmist, *I will go into your house with burnt offerings.*[84]

[39] So, finally, having earlier in royal fashion arranged all that concerned him, having received with solemn devotion[85] all the final sacraments of the church, the day after the Feast of the Blessed Bartholomew, around Nones, he ended his last day, returning his happy soul to the Creator at the very time of day, it would seem, that our Savior, dying *for the life of the world,*[86] breathed his last.[87]

[40] From that very moment until that time when his body had to be prepared in order to separate the bones from the flesh, he appeared, to all those who gazed upon him, graciously handsome of countenance, as if he were alive and well, and it even seemed as if he were smiling a little.

---

[80] The quotation is given in French in *A: Nous iron en Jerusalem.*
[81] *A* reads "dimidie leuce" which *RHGF* justifiably emends to "dimidiae horae."
[82] Ps. 5:8, 137:2.
[83] Cf. Ps. 65:15.
[84] Ps. 65:13.
[85] *A* reads "cum devocione sollempni" which *RHGF* emends to simply "devotissime."
[86] John 6:52.
[87] 25 August 1270. Note exact parallels with Philip III's letter describing Louis' death.

[41] I will pass over the sorrow and grief of the faithful and the wails and cries of the poor because we should rejoice over him, rather than grieve.

[42] Thus the sun and glory of kings and princes of the earth set in the southern regions, and in the midday of fervid love,[88] so that he passed over to him *who feeds and lies in the midday.*[89] The renowned king thus crossed over from the servitude of the temporal kingdom, as we certainly believe and hope, to the kingdom of eternal happiness. In this way the faithful and prudent servant, established above the family of the Lord, by multiplying his talents, deserved to enter from labor into rest, from the state of grief *into the joy of his Lord.*[90]

[43] For the honor and glory of the King of Kings and as a demonstration of the worth and holiness of our aforesaid king, there has been no lack of divine miracles both at his tomb and elsewhere. Many of these, perhaps from want of attention, were not written down or examined closely or established by proof. But others of them, which were truly tested and proven as clear as day, we have committed to writing and caused to be noted below.

[44: Mir. 1][91] Not long after the happy death of our most illustrious king, before news of it had spread, a certain respectable woman at Paris, praiseworthy for her faith and honesty, who was herself quite devoted to the king and whose husband had been part of his retinue, beheld the following vision in her sleep. It appeared to her that the king himself, clothed in a purple cloak such as he had not been accustomed to wear these many years,[92] was entering his royal chapel in Paris[93] from the right-hand side, luminous and glorious with a great throng of bystanders. And, approaching the altar, out ahead of the others, he bowed over it with joined hands as if he were offering a sacrifice on it. Then, after a short while, he turned

---

[88] *A* reads "in meridie fervide caritatis," where *RHGF* emends "fervide" to "foecundae."
[89] Cf. Cant. 1:6.
[90] Cf. Matt. 25: 21, and more broadly 14–28 (the Parable of the Talents).
[91] Later version in *BL* 13.1.
[92] *A* here reads "capa superindutus purpurea qua veste non consueverat …" Cf. John 19:2: "… inposuerunt capiti eius et veste purpurea …" The echoes suggest a parallel with Christ and the Crown of Thorns.
[93] The Sainte-Chapelle. *RHGF* has "capellam suam regiam parisiensem" but the last word is "parisius" in *A*.

toward the choir with a truly luminous and serene look on his face. A little way back on the right-hand side of the choir toward the altar another figure was standing, clothed in the same manner but not as luminous, with his face turned toward the altar and his hands clasped as in prayer. These two appeared, however, more luminous than all the others, and many bystanders marveled at this. And then the vision vanished. That very same day her aforementioned husband, coming home from the royal palace, threw himself down upon his bed in sadness and grief, weeping and moaning away. His wife asked why he was so afflicted and he told her the sad news, that he had just heard of the death of our lord his king and also of the king's son, Jean, the count of Nevers.[94] And thus this respectable woman, recalling and later thinking over this vision, related it to me as though consoled in spirit. From which it can be plainly understood that the acceptable sacrifice that the pious king had made had been shown to her; going beyond the memorable sacrifice of Abraham, he had offered not only his own son so dear to him, but, *in a savor of sweetness*,[95] had offered the sacrifice of himself, following in the footsteps of the highest King who once offered unto God the Father his immaculate self on behalf of sinners.

[45: Mir. 2][96] On the day in which the precious body was laid to rest at Saint-Denis,[97] a certain respectable woman of the diocese of Sées is said, then and there, to have regained the sight in her eyes which she had long since almost totally lost. Trustworthy individuals say they saw this, and especially Master William of Mâcon, canon of Paris, says that he saw her.[98] Many other miracles happened both on that day and at other times in that place to people suffering various illnesses, which have not come to public notice.

[46: Mir. 3][99] It then happened shortly thereafter that there was a certain young man, about twenty-five years of age, from the far side of

---

[94] See chapter 2, note 16.
[95] Exod. 29:41.
[96] Later version in *BL* 13.2.
[97] 22 May 1271.
[98] *RHGF* has "qui se adserit vidisse," where *A* has "eam" instead of "qui."
[99] Later versions in *BL* 13.3; WSP, *Miracles*, no. 15; Jean de Vignay, *RHGF* 23, 69e–f. For an English translation of the WSP version, with commentary, see Sharon Farmer, "A Deaf-Mute's Story," in *Medieval Christianity in Practice*, ed. Miri Rubin (Princeton, N.J.: Princeton University Press, 2009), 203–8.

Burgundy, *deaf and mute*[100] from birth, who for sixteen years or so had lived and been raised in a castle of the nobleman, lord Jean of Chalon-sur-Saône, which is called Orgelet.[101] And for a year or so he had worked as best he could in this nobleman's kitchen, neither hearing nor speaking, but using only gestures that almost the whole household knew; and thus he could show others his wants and desires, and they could do the same.[102] Learning in this way that through divine intervention miracles were happening at the tomb of the glorious King Louis of France, he joined a group of people going on foot to Paris and then he went on to Saint-Denis. And at the king's tomb, weeping and moaning, he poured forth at length his prayer, not from his lips but from his heart, in groans and sighs as best he could. At last, by divine intervention and the merits of our glorious king, out of devotion to whom he had come, *his ears were opened and the string of his tongue was loosed and he spoke right.*[103] He immediately began to speak at that very spot, not in his mother tongue, but in correct French as though he had been born and raised at Saint-Denis! This was the cause of wonder and astonishment to many. When some people, whom he knew by sight but not by name, asked him in French, "What is my name?" he answered in French, "You have the name 'my friends.' Because I don't know anything about another name."[104] He even said that he had never known such terror in his life as when he heard the church bells ring. He was afraid that the whole church would come down on top of him! For now he had begun to hear for the first time, so that trembling and wonder filled him in equal measure.[105] The aforementioned noble,[106] and many others who had known him for a long time, related these things. Many other beneficial deeds of divine piety are believed to have been conferred in that place upon variously afflicted

---

[100] Mark 7:32.
[101] Modern Orgelet, just east of Chalon-sur-Saône.
[102] *RHGF* has "per signa suam voluntatem" where *A* reads "per signa sua in voluntatem."
[103] Mark 7:35. This echo of Christ's healing a deaf mute again places Louis in a Christ-like position.
[104] The quotation is given in French in *A: Vous avez non mes amiz. Quar dautre non ne sai ie riens.*
[105] *RHGF* has "stupor et tremor potens eum invasit," where *A* reads "pariter" instead of "potens."
[106] *RHGF* has "praecedens nobilis" where *A* reads "predictus nobilis."

people, all done out of the king's merits, but which have not yet come to common notice.

[47: Mir. 4][107] Moreover it happened about that time that a certain cleric from Brittany,[108] one well known to the bishop of Saint-Malo[109] and others worthy of faith, was struck by a grave illness and confined to bed when he was passing through the city of Chartres. Growing worse and worse in continuous sickness, so that he thought he would surely die and was on the point of death, encouraged by the pious suggestion of certain people, he began to beseech divine help and to call for help to the pious King Louis, vowing and swearing that should God grant him recovery he would at once devoutly[110] go to the tomb of that very king. And as he did this, he at once felt a divine power at work and began a complete recovery. The next day, rising from his bed and rejoicing, he undertook his promised trip and completed it, restored to his former health. And many were amazed at such a sudden recovery of his despaired-of health.

[48: Mir. 5][111] Master Dudo, the royal physician and cleric who had been with king Louis of holy memory in the region of Carthage, attending him in his illness and death, had returned home with King Philip. Shortly after the interment of the glorious king,[112] while at Saint-Germain-en-Laye for Pentecost,[113] where the lord King Philip was celebrating the feast day in royal fashion, [Dudo] felt himself become gravely ill. Indeed, he was struck by a very high fever.[114] The next day, he made his way to Paris as best he could and lay ill at the king's palace, as his illness grew worse and worse so that all the doctors, himself included, had no hope of his

---

[107] Later version in *BL* 13.4.
[108] The Latin here, "Britannia," might normally indicate in the first instance "Britannia major" or Great Britain. But given the reference to Saint-Malo, it seems that here it should be taken to indicate "Britannia minor," or Brittany.
[109] Simon of Clisson, bishop of Saint-Malo from 1264 to his death in 1286, was a Dominican, former prior of Saint-Jacques in Paris, and well known to Louis IX. See Chapotin, *Histoire*, 548–51. Perhaps this incident took place when Simon was in Chartres in June 1273 consecrating an alter to the Dominican Saint Peter Martyr, if this cleric might have been traveling with him. Ibid., 550.
[110] *RHGF* omits the word "devote," found in *A*.
[111] Later version in *BL* 13.5; WSP, *miracles*, no. 38, p. 114; Jean de Vignay, *RHGF* vol. 23, 69 h-k.
[112] Louis' bones were buried at Saint-Denis on 22 May 1271, the day after Philip's return to Paris from North Africa via Italy.
[113] Pentecost in 1271 fell on May 24.
[114] *A* reads "febris fortis" which *RHGF* emends to "febris satis."

recovery. On the fourth day[115] he made his confession and disposed of all his goods. Seized by an unbearable pain in his head, he began to call upon the blessed Louis with great emotion, saying, "Oh lord King, I have been your cleric and I believe you to be a saint. Help me, I pray, in my hour of need, and I will keep vigil through the night beside your tomb!" As he finished speaking he fell into a deep slumber and in a dream found himself before the tomb of the king, above which there seemed to him to be, up high, a sort of bier that he had never seen. And there appeared to him King Louis, standing with both feet on the top of the bier, carrying his scepter in his hand, the lower part of which below his hand was of such length that he leaned upon it against the sloping part of the bier. And he wore a long white dalmatic robe[116] reaching to his feet with a fringe of golden tassels,[117] and *having on his head a crown of gold*[118] with *precious jewels*.[119] His face was more beautiful and he was more joyful than he had ever seen[120] him in life. He spoke to him in Latin, saying, "Behold, I am here. What do you want? You have called much upon me." And in tears the sick man said:[121] "Lord, in God's name, help me!" And he replied, "Fear not. You will be healed[122] from this sickness. But you have in your brain a corrupt tumor,[123] poisonous and dark, which precludes your knowing your Creator. This is the cause of your illness and I will remove it." Then he seized him by the head with one hand and with the thumb of the other hand, as it seemed to him, and split him open on the left side

---

[115] This would be Thursday, 28 May.
[116] "Dalmatica alba longa." A dalmatic robe was worn by bishops and deacons, but the label could also refer to a royal garment. Dudo (or William) thus seems to be emphasizing Louis' combination of royal and quasi-priestly posthumous attributes.
[117] "fimbriae ... deauratae," cf. Ps. 44:14.
[118] Apoc. 14:14: "And I saw: and behold a white cloud and upon the cloud one sitting like to the Son of Man, having on his head a crown of gold and in his hand a sharp sickle." This passage (between descriptions of the third and fourth angels of the Apocalypse) gives the comparison of Louis and Christ an overtly apocalyptic resonance.
[119] The phrase "lapidibus pretiosis" (with the adjective and noun in various cases) appears numerous times in the Bible. Most relevant here is Ps. 20:2–4: "Domine in virtute tua laetabitur rex et ... posuisti in capite eius coronam de lapide pretioso."
[120] A reads "videret" which *RHGF* emends silently to "vidisset."
[121] A reads "dixi" which *RHGF* emends silently to "dixit."
[122] A reads "curaberis" which *RHGF* emends to "convalebis."
[123] The original meaning of the Latin word used here, "humor," should imply a fluid, but clearly in this case it is a question of a solid mass, so we have chosen to use the most applicable English word for an unwelcome growth.

between his nose and brow! And inserting his thumb and another finger, he drew out the poisonous, corrupt, dark, and rotten tumor, as big as a large nut, and said "As long as you had this in your head you could not be well," and threw it down.[124] The said Master Dudo, waking up a little, realized that he was completely cured of the pain in his head and told those standing by him that this had happened, that he ought to be completely cured that night, and that he had been cured of the screaming pain in his head. Now *they were very much afraid*[125] lest he had lost his mind! But he himself told them of his vision. And on that very night, which was the fourth day of his illness, after a mighty stiffness and sweating, he was completely freed from illness. In the course of nature such a thing rarely or never simply happens without some symptoms of recovery preceding it, just as other doctors insist. The next morning, the said master related this vision to me, William of Chartres, who wrote these things down, and he insisted that he was freed from illness. And he gave me a much lengthier account of his vision, written with his own hand, and he is prepared to confirm all these things by his own oath.

[49: Mir. 6][126] At the Louvre castle in Paris, the knight lord Peter of Laon,[127] guardian of the sons of the lord King Philip, was beset by an unendurable pain in his right arm, so that for many days he could not lift it the least little bit or do anything with it. He took thought and recalled that he himself had some of the hairs of his lord the king, whose chamberlain he had once been, and, trusting in their divine power and the king's own merits, he touched the lame arm with them three times. And at the first touch he felt great relief, more on the second, and on the third he was completely freed of pain. He reverently laid these hairs away *in gold and silver*[128] and preserved them with devotion.

[50: Mir. 7][129] About this same time two Preaching Brothers were walking along the public street near Saint-Denis, intent on preaching, when

---

[124] *A* reads "illic" where *RHGF* emends to "illi."
[125] Matt. 17:6.
[126] Later version in *BL* 13.6.
[127] Peter of Laon (b. 1214) accompanied Louis on both his crusades, advancing from sergeant to chamberlain and knight. He testified at Louis' canonization hearings in 1282–83 and died before 1292. See Carolus-Barré, *Le procès*, 183–85.
[128] Exod. 35:32; Jth. 15:14.
[129] Later version in *BL* 13.7.

they saw, among the others coming back along the road from Saint-Denis, two women talking to one another and rejoicing over what had happened to them. One brother asked them what had occurred and one of them said, "Lord, it is in fact a great and manifest miracle, which God has truly done on account of this holy king! For this woman here, whom I brought here from Rouen as completely blind in her eyes as I am in the soles of my feet, now sees everything just as I do." That brother, indeed, asserts that he heard this and that he saw this woman then going along all on her own, without anyone's help, without a guide or a cane, freely and vigorously, though her eyes were still swollen from tears and vigils.

[51: Mir. 8][130] In that same year, that is 1271, on the Tuesday after the feast of Saint Urban the Pope,[131] a certain woman from Chambly named Emeline came to the tomb of King Louis of holy memory. For three years she had not been able to walk, except all bent over, using a small cane,[132] with which she went along very close to the ground, for her head was not more than a foot and a half off the ground. Having poured forth prayerful devotion, through the merits of the said king[133] she regained the ability to walk upright on the above mentioned day. This woman is known to many trustworthy people in the town of Saint-Denis, who had seen her when she was all bent over and again after she had been liberated and walked upright.

[52: Mir. 9][134] And in the same year, on the Friday following the feast of Saint Urban,[135] a certain girl named Petronilla, the daughter of Alice of Aube, who was not able to walk except by dragging herself along on the ground with her hands and feet, came to the said tomb and recovered her bodily health so that she was able to walk through the town with help from no one. And she has lived some twenty years in the town of Saint-Denis on the street of Saint-Remi, and is known to many people.

---

[130] This miracle was later recounted in the canonization hearings of 1282–83 by Thomas of Hauxton and several other witnesses; Delaborde, "Fragments," 19–20; *BL* 13.8; WSP, *Miracles*, no. 5; and William of Nangis, *RHGF* 20, 464b.
[131] The feast of Saint Urban was Monday, 25 May in 1271. Hence this date was Tuesday, 26 May 1271.
[132] *A* reads "baculi parvi" which *RHGF* emends to "baculi incurvi."
[133] *RHGF* has "domini regis" where *A* reads "dicti regis."
[134] Later versions in *BL* 13.9; WSP, *Miracles*, no. 54.
[135] 29 May 1271.

[53: Mir. 10][136] Again, in the same year, on the Thursday after the Feast of Saints Marcellinus and Peter,[137] a certain woman called Agnes la Maquine[138]—who had been staying at Paris near the house of the beguines,[139] and had been struck down with a paralysis the day after Easter[140] at a sermon delivered in the cemetery of the Holy Innocents[141] and lost control of the midsection of her body—coming to the place of the said tomb and praying devoutly, recovered the full health of the afflicted parts of her body through divine power and the merits of the king himself.

[54: Mir. 11][142] Again, in the same year and on the Wednesday after the feast of the above mentioned martyrs,[143] a certain woman of Villetaneuse[144] named Hodierne was so affected by a most serious bodily affliction for eleven years that for six of those years she could not get out of bed, and for the five years following she rose but once a year and this only on Easter when she went to church with great difficulty, supporting herself on a cane. This woman, coming to the said tomb and pouring forth her prayer, recovered her bodily health through the merits of the said king, to such an extent that from that very day and thereafter she was able to walk without any sort of assistance, having been restored to her former health.

[55: Mir. 12][145] Again, in the year mentioned, on the Saturday after the feast of the above mentioned martyrs,[146] Michael called Savage, abiding in Paris near the house of Barbeel in the parish of Saint-Paul,[147] had for

---

[136] Later versions in *BL* 13.10; WSP, *Miracles*, no. 44.
[137] This feast was 2 June (a Tuesday in 1271), so the following Thursday was 4 June.
[138] *A* reads "la maq¦ne." *RHGF* has 'la Maque" and suggests in a note "Lamarque."
[139] The Grand Béguinage on the Right Bank, in the parish of Saint-Paul, founded by Louis IX before 1264.
[140] This date would be Monday, 6 April 1271.
[141] On the Right Bank near Les Halles. See Philippe Lorentz and Dany Sandron, with Jacques Lebar and Bénédicte Loisel, *Atlas de Paris au Moyen Age: Espace urbain, habitat, société, religion, lieux de pouvoir* (Paris: Parigramme, 2006), 129–30.
[142] Later versions in *BL* 13.11; WSP, *Miracles*, no. 32.
[143] 3 June 1271.
[144] A village near Saint-Denis.
[145] Later versions in *BL* 13.12; WSP, *Miracles*, no. 48.
[146] 6 June 1271.
[147] The Porte-Barbeel was by the Seine on the Right Bank in the parish of Saint-Paul. For a map of parishes see *Atlas de Paris au Moyen Age*, 129.

six years been unable to walk without two crutches. But, coming to the oft-mentioned tomb, through the merits of the oft-mentioned Louis, he achieved such whole and complete health that he returned to Paris walking upright, joyfully and without help from anyone.

[56: Mir. 13][148] Again, in the mentioned year on the Vigil of the Blessed Apostle Bartholomew,[149] Jeanette of Porte-Baudéer,[150] abiding in the parish of Saint-Paul at Paris, was constrained by bodily affliction so that for four years she was unable to walk without two crutches. Coming to the tomb, through the merits of King Louis, she regained the ability to walk.

[57: Mir. 14][151] Again, in the said year, on the Sunday before the Feast of the Blessed Apostle Bartholomew,[152] Jean called Camus, abiding in Paris in the parish of Saint-Merri, on the street of Ralph of Saint-Laurent,[153] was unable to move for a period of four years except on his knees while supporting himself with his hands. Coming to the oft-mentioned tomb, through the oft-mentioned merits, he was easily walking nimbly without any support at all.

[58: Mir. 15][154] Again, in the said year, on the Saturday after the Feast of the Blessed Barnabas the Apostle,[155] Emeline Labrece,[156] wife of John the Englishman, of the parish of Saint-Merri, in similar fashion had lost [the

---

[148] Later version in *BL* 13.16.

[149] This feast was 24 August, so the vigil would be 23 August (note that August 25 was the anniversary of Louis' death and his future feast day).

[150] The old Porte-Baudéer, just north of Saint-Gervais, stood at the western end of the rue de la Porte-Baudéer which ran east through the parish of Saint-Paul toward the Porte-Saint-Antoine. *RHGF* emends to "Port-Baudet."

[151] Later version in *BL* 13.14.

[152] This would be 23 August 1271. The scribe of *A* wrote "die sabbati post festum predictorum die dominica ante festum beati bartholomei apostoli." The first five words are crossed out, perhaps by the original scribe but more likely by a later hand. The Saturday after the Feast of Saint Bartholomew would be 29 August (which is what *RHGF* assumes) but the plural "predictorum" indicates that the scribe was not referring to the singular Bartholomew in his original wording. We have elected to follow the sense of the passage with the crossed-out words omitted.

[153] See Le Comte Beugnot, *Les olim, ou registres des arrêts rendus par la cour du Roi*, vol. 1 (Paris: Imprimerie royale, 1839), p. 502, no. xxvii for mention of Radulphus de Sancto Laurentio. The parish of Saint-Merri was on the Right Bank, just east of the rue Saint-Martin.

[154] Later versions in *BL* 13.17; WSP, *Miracles*, no. 52.

[155] This feast was 11 June, a Thursday in 1271. This date would be Saturday, 13 June 1271.

[156] *RHGF* emends to "Labiche."

use of] one of her lower legs since the Winter Feast of Saint Martin,[157] so that she was unable to walk without a cane, dragging the said limb behind her. She came to the oft-mentioned tomb and got back her whole and complete health through the merits of the said king.

[59: Mir. 16][158] Again, in the same year, on the Tuesday before the Feast of the Blessed Apostle Barnabas,[159] Gila of Senlis, abiding in Paris in the parish of Saint-Paul, was unable to move for four years without two crutches, held back by infirmity. She came to the oft-mentioned tomb on the previously mentioned Tuesday and got back her complete health.

[60: Mir. 17][160] Again, in the same year, on the Sunday before the Feast of the Blessed Apostle Barnabas,[161] Alice, the daughter of Robert called Poelecoc,[162] all her life had a crooked hand which she could not raise to her chest or incline over her knees except with the help of her other hand; but, coming to the oft-mentioned tomb, through the merits of the most glorious king, returned liberated from her affliction.

---

[157] 11 November 1270.
[158] Later version in *BL* 13.15.
[159] 9 June 1271.
[160] Later version in *BL* 13.13.
[161] 7 June 1271.
[162] *RHGF* emends to "Peclecoc."

CHAPTER FOUR

Pope Boniface VIII's Bull *Gloria Laus* (11 August 1297)

Boniface, bishop, servant of the servants of God, to all the faithful of Christ,[1] greetings and apostolic blessing.

Let all worshipers of the true faith who aspire to heaven now render glory, praise, and honor, in highest and earnest effort of reverent devotion, to God *the Father of lights,* who gives *every best gift and every perfect gift!*[2] For, overflowing with mercy, generous in graces, munificent in recompense, He cast the eyes of his majesty down from the heights of heaven to the depths of earth and struck with kind consideration upon the noble merits and wondrous works of the blessed Louis, the former renowned king of France and His own most glorious adherent. By these merits and works this king, while stationed in the world, blazed forth like a bright lamp.[3] On account of these things, God as a true judge and praiseworthy rewarder, intending to award fitting recompense, has enthroned him in the ethereal realm, as one who has earned and is most worthy of reward after the prison of his earthly life and the wearisome struggles of this world (which he carried on with strength and patience,[4]

---

[1] We have followed the version of the greeting found in AN J 940 no. 111 ("universis Christi fidelibus"), rather than the version given in *RHGF* (from Ménard, presumably based on Chartres ms. 226) "venerabilibus fratribus, universis archiepiscopis et episcopis, exemptis et non exemptis per regnum Francie constitutis." A version with the latter wording directed to the clergy of France may well have been issued, but a universal announcement to all Christians was the most appropriate language for canonization.
[2] James 1:17.
[3] Cf. Luke 11:36.
[4] The Latin has two alliterative adverbs, "potenter et patenter."

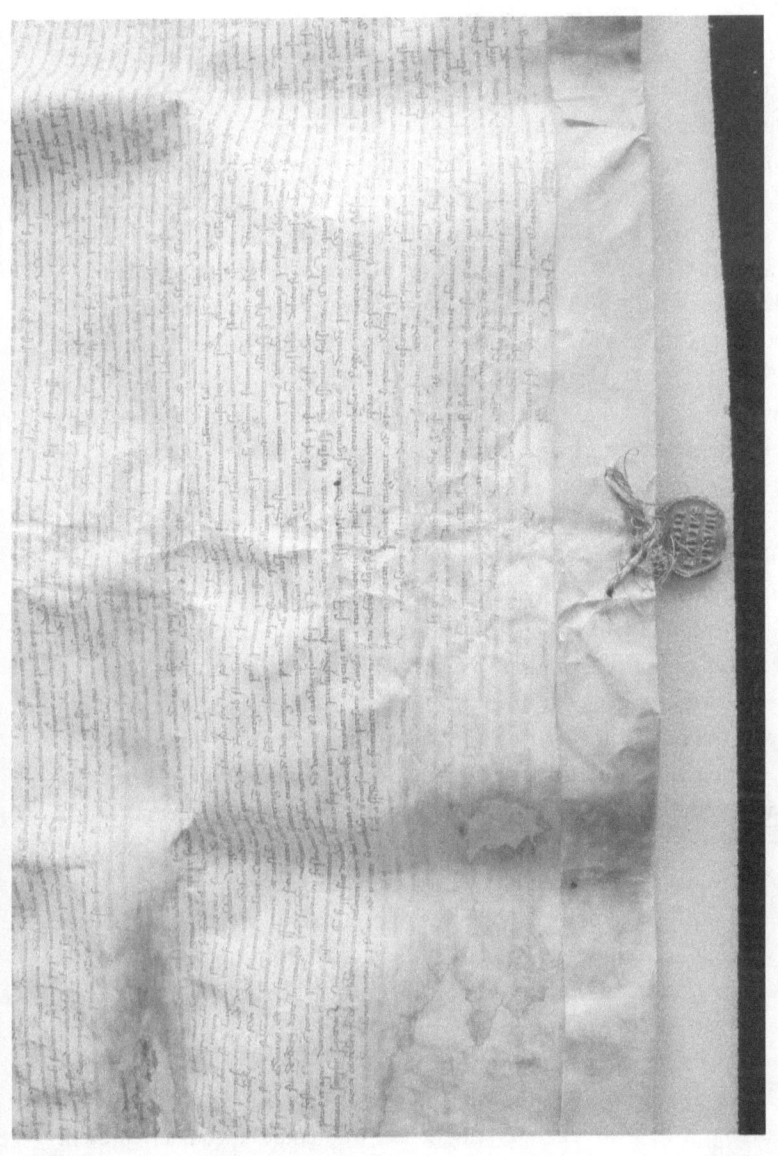

Figure 5. AN J 940 no. 111. Bottom portion of the sealed original of Boniface VIII's canonization bull sent to the court of Philip IV. Damage to the document can be seen on the left-hand side. Photograph by Sean Field. Reproduced by permission of the Archives nationales, Paris.

burning in his obedience to the divine), *that he may sit with princes and hold the throne of glory*[5] to enjoy the sweetness of eternal happiness.

Let mother Church therefore exult, and let her celebrate solemn feasts of joy, because she has brought forth a son of such kind and quality, produced a child, instructed an offspring, who is now resplendent among the glorious host of heavenly kings! Let her rejoice, I say, and sing out, and raise voices praising the Almighty, for she is now seen adorned and clearly illuminated by the mighty lightning flash of such an exalted and illustrious offspring! The Church, which is to be exalted in public harmony and fostered by the exhibition of true veneration, reveals more clearly, explains more openly, that those who by manifest evidence of works and faith profess the said Church—mother of the faithful, the bride of Christ—are to be admitted to the joys of eternal blessedness and partake of eternal inheritance, and that none enter into the heavenly homeland except through her virtuous assistance (inasmuch as she is the keeper of the keys of heaven) in unlocking the high gates.

Let the heavenly throngs rejoice at the arrival of so lofty a shining inhabitant, and that such a tested and proven cultivator and outstanding supporter of the Christian faith has been gathered to them! Let the glorious nobility of the citizens of heaven sound forth a song of joy in recognition of the addition of a fellow citizen of such a kind and quality! Let the venerable crowd of the saints bloom again in joyous exultation upon the new admission of a most worthy companion! Rise up then, vast congregation of the faithful! Rise, you who are zealous for the faith, and together with the Church sing a hymn rich in praise! Let your hearts overflow with the full flood of joy, and let your innermost spirits be full of the fertile dew of sweetness on account of the heavenly advancement of such a worthy and powerful earthly prince, an advancement premised on a wealth of certain hope! For a dweller on earth from among us who has become a citizen of heaven has now risen to be with the Son of the eternal Father; an effective patron who, in His presence, acts as a skillful advocate for the advancement of our salvation.

Moreover, who could there be, no matter how powerfully renowned, flashing forth with whatever eloquence, who could adequately present

---

[5] 1 Kings 2:8. In the biblical passage it is "the poor" that God raises up.

such lofty signs of sanctity and the excellence of the countless merits for which the aforesaid blessed Louis was distinguished while on this earth? For the more pens portray, lips make known, and tongues tell, the more of his laudable deeds come forth for consideration. Nevertheless, lest the brilliance of the deeds themselves lurk beneath a cloud and be shrouded in shadow, we deem it worthy that our words reveal them somewhat and present them for public notice.

He clearly stood out as a man of most famous lineage, supreme power, rich in abilities, exceeding in virtues, exquisite in character, renowned for honesty, with all foul dishonesty banished from his presence. He was so given to efforts of modesty and strove so to avoid corruption of the flesh that many had the certain belief that, were it not for the bond of marriage, he would have been illustrious for virgin purity. Indeed, for a long time he ruled his realm, whose helm, so full of care, he steered with cautious circumspection. Without enmity, harm, or violence to anyone, he labored mightily to preserve and extend the boundaries of justice, never forsaking the path of equity. With the sword of due punishment he suppressed the evil efforts of the wicked, thwarting criminal endeavors, reining in the unlawful intentions of the depraved. Prominent in his zeal for peace, a warm lover of harmony, he worked hard to achieve union, fleeing strife, avoiding scandal, hating disagreement. And because of this, during the period of his happy reign, the seas became calm,[6] the dangers subsided, the storms dispersed, and a dawn of sweet flowing tranquility shown forth for his people and the happy serenity of promised prosperity beamed its smile upon them.

And now, so we may review some of the facts of his life (though, truly, the lengthier the narration, and the more closely it is examined, the sweeter it becomes to the taste of the teller and the more striking to the minds of the listeners), from the very start of his earliest years he loved the Son of God with tender affection, and he did not flag in this love, carrying on with salvific zeal while enjoying the ease of youth. But, as he grew and came into the age of his majority, by so much the more did his spirit burn with greater passion in love.

His father died when Louis was twelve years old and, bereft of his father's aid, he remained under the care and guidance of his mother

---

[6] The metaphor here may owe something to Virgil, *Aeneid* 1.142–56.

Blanche, the queen of France, of illustrious memory. She was given to devout obedience in divine matters and fervently intent on educating him diligently and guiding him prudently so that he would become worthy and competent and be suitable for the governance of the aforesaid realm which was known to await the careful foresight of his rule. Eventually, when the king reached the age of fourteen, the said queen appointed for him his own teacher to instruct him in the knowledge of letters and form him to good character. Placed under the rod of this master, the king was so obedient to him and so reverent and so humble in receiving instruction, that, propelled by heavenly grace, he achieved perfection in both endeavors. And he was also so given to divine prayers that he simply could not just hear them spoken; but rather those prayers, which he had solemnly celebrated by his clerics night and day in his presence, were also recited carefully by himself together with one of the clerics.

When in the course of time he reached the age of thirty,[7] and suffering from a serious illness, in the presence of the bishops of Paris and Meaux[8] he asked with great urgency that the sign of the living Cross be given to him in order to aid the Holy Land. And although these same bishops argued against it for good and sound reasons, he himself—as one whose spirit burned for God, and fervent in the desire to serve Him and for his own salvation—ignored their concerns, and with great and happy exultation received the sign of the Cross from the hand of that same bishop of Paris while a host of prelates, nobles, and knights took the Cross with him.

Finally, when he had reached the age of thirty-four, and when the great expedition was prepared and all of the equipment needed for such an undertaking was assembled, he sailed overseas to bring the aforesaid aid. He took with him his wife and his three late brothers—Robert of Artois, Alfonse of Poitiers, and Charles, king of Sicily, of illustrious memory (at the time, count of Anjou),[9] while all were still living—enduring

---

[7] J 940 no. 111 reads "vicesimo" (twenty) but the *RHGF* editors correctly indicate that these events happened in 1244, when Louis was thirty.

[8] The bishop of Meaux 1223–55 was Peter of Cuisy; the bishop of Paris 1228–49 was William of Auvergne.

[9] Robert, count of Artois, died during Louis' first crusade in 1250 (as Boniface will shortly recount); Alfonse, count of Poitiers, died just after the return from Louis' second crusade in August 1271; Charles had been count of Anjou since the time of his marriage in 1246, and was proclaimed king of Sicily in 1265. He died in 1285. The passage says that Louis took

the many grave perils of the ocean's waves. When he had arrived in those parts, supported by his mighty force he triumphed over the fall of the city of Damietta, and then moved inland. And then (as was pleasing to God), a general plague overtook, as it were, the entire army. And, threatened with other setbacks, the king, together with almost the entire army, fell into the hands and the power of the sultan and his Saracens. Many taunts and many injuries were then patiently and humbly endured, made worse by the foul nature of those inflicting them, and by the death of Count Robert, cruelly slain by them for the faith of Christ.

After some time, negotiations were undertaken with the sultan, who was still alive, for the ransom of the king and his army, requiring a huge sum of money. At this point the sultan was slain by his own vassals. The Saracens who overthrew him lusted for this wealth but they were also most adamant in their insistence that this addition be clearly affirmed in the terms of the ransom agreement to be sworn to by both parties: that should they themselves not abide by it, they would wholly renounce Muhammad, whom, as it is said, they worship;[10] and likewise that the king would add to his own oath, that, should he fail to completely abide by the said agreement, he would renounce the Son of God and abjure the faith. This the king flatly refused to do, utterly horrified. On the contrary, he openly announced with complete indignation that such unspeakable things would never pass his lips, nor would he utter such a wild and base denial. No matter that the counts of Poitiers and Anjou and very many others gathered around were urging him, since they saw that quite likely they and every other Christian would be killed, especially since this happened as they were then bargaining with the Saracens who had killed the sultan and were usurping power for themselves (as has been

---

along "consortem et quondam Robertum ..." "Consortem" can mean companion, brother, sister, or wife, and Carolus-Barré seems to have treated it is a redundant reference to Louis' brothers who are then listed by name. It seems more likely to us, however, that in this context "consortem" refers to Louis's wife Marguerite of Provence (William of Saint-Pathus understood the passage this way in his French life of Louis) who did indeed accompany Louis on the crusade.

[10] The idea that Muslims worship Muhammad in a fashion analogous to the way Christians worship Jesus Christ was a common misconception among medieval European Christians. By 1297, however, educated Europeans did have enough accurate information available to correct this misapprehension, if and when they wished to do so.

explained), and the king was patently told that if he did not do as they asked, they would not hesitate to crucify him and his men. The king's bold, unshaking response was that these Saracens might kill his body, but they would never take his soul.

Indeed, already at the time of this expedition, when the Christian army had been returning to Damietta—after a number of serious conflicts, extreme and severe famine, the dire wounds that the Christians had endured, and with the king at the time afflicted with dysentery and other illnesses—the king had been unwilling to abandon [the army], but rather fully intended to share mercifully its hardships and to undergo its perils, which by then were quite reasonable to fear.[11] He returned there with the army, effectively interposing the protection of his defense against the rabid madness of the Saracens and the evil attacks against [the army], so that it might be preserved from the wicked plots of such an enemy. Then, finally, when with cunning wickedness and deceitful shrewdness the Saracens had surrounded the Christian army (then hampered and disease-ridden as has been mentioned) with a great number of fighters, and had most grievously beset the king, the king and army (as described already) had no choice but to yield to the Saracens. The king, had he not imposed his own will, could have escaped to a ship that was ready at hand for his flight, as most of the great lords around him urged him to do. But because of the ardor of the great love with which he was so warmly burning, he preferred to face bodily peril so that the Christian people might be preserved unharmed. Even though the weak state of the Christian army was not hidden from the Saracens, nor was the power of the Saracens unknown to the Christians, still he would not flee and leave others bound in captivity. But rather he proclaimed all the more clearly that he intended to lead back with him the army that he had led in with him, if possible, or to be captured and die together with it.

When an agreement had at last been reached between the king and the Christians and the Saracens as to the terms of ransom for the release of the king and the Christians, and the treaty was in hand, the Saracens, intending to have sufficient security to guarantee payment of the amount

---

[11] Boniface has here, somewhat confusingly, doubled back to describe Louis' steadfastness before his capture.

of money still owed in ransom, gave this choice to the king: he could either go free and other Christians would stay in chains as security for the money, or he himself could remain a prisoner while the Christians themselves went entirely free. To this the king immediately and without delay responded that he intended to remain a prisoner until every last penny was paid and every Christian would be returned to freedom, even though the aforementioned Alfonse and Charles and the other nobles there at the time spoke out and openly asserted that they disagreed completely, earnestly imploring that instead the king himself leave and the others remain; but the king would have none of this and flatly refused. In the end, the king and the other captives were returned to complete freedom, with Alfonse given as a hostage to secure full payment. The king refused to leave the galley where he was staying until the payment due was completely paid, and Alfonse returned again to his presence, and all the Christians who were at the time detained in local prisons and whom the enemy had not taken to Babylon were released from their chains, and even those people who were being held in Damietta were put on board ship.

Finally the king, set free with his army and falling back on the city of Acre, remained there for some five years. And as an ardent lover of human salvation, he converted to God the minds of many Hagarenes[12] (however hardened), not only by his eloquent, salvific persuasion, but also by the example of his own praiseworthy life. He had these people honorably baptized in praise of the Holy Name and exaltation of the catholic faith, presenting them with generous gifts and fostering them with gracious favors. He redeemed through ransom many knights and other Christians and bestowed upon them from the royal munificence garments and other necessities in accordance with the particular needs of each one. He solemnly saw to the repair of the walls and the fortifications of cities and as many as possible of the camps which were occupied by the faithful in those parts, building them as strongly and soundly as was necessary.

---

[12] Hagarenes, that is, the descendants of Hagar (Abraham's second wife, cf. Gen. 16.3). This was a term European Christians often used for Muslims in the Middle Ages.

In due course, the king, learning that bitter death had carried off his mother and that grave peril threatened his kingdom, on the advice of his nobility returned to the kingdom of France. Now he began works of sanctity, ordering the construction of monasteries, hospitals for the poor, houses for different holy orders (it would take long to list each one), and amply endowed these from his own purse. Now he went personally to visit the sick and the weak who lay in various monasteries and hospices, tending them with words of consolation and with his own hands, and on bended knee ministering to them with food and drink.

A certain monk named Leger was staying at the monastery of Royaumont in the diocese of Beauvais, which the king himself had built and endowed very beautifully. Leprosy had attacked this monk so that he was wretched, indeed abominable, and he was sequestered from the others in a certain room of the monastery. He was quite blind, his eyes ruined by disfigurement or wasted by disease, and his eye sockets were ghastly and red. His nose was gone. His swollen lips were deeply cracked. But the king, in the presence of the monastery's abbot, came to see the monk in person and found him eating as best he could. And the king, after a gentle word of greeting, went down on his knees in front of him and, cutting up his meat with his own hands, carefully placed little pieces into his mouth. Not content with this kind of service, he ordered that dishes be brought over from the royal table, and he attended to the monk from these, not avoiding the horrible quality of the diseased part or place. All the while the abbot was utterly speechless at the loftiness of such a prince who would undertake such efforts and busy himself with such beneficial ministrations.

Moreover, when the king entered the hospital at Compiègne to serve the sick lying there, although he was quite weary from exertion, he caught sight of a certain sick man close by who was suffering from what is called the disease of Saint Eloi. As the king knelt before him and was putting a bit of peeled pear in his mouth, puss flowed down from the poor man's nose, foully soiling the king's hands. The king kindly and piously endured this, utterly unaffected by it, and, after washing his hands, he carefully finished the considerate service he had begun.

Truly, with compassion for the servants of Christ, the poor, the wretched, and the downcast, through his almsgiving, he behaved most generously toward them all. He provided appropriate dowries for young maidens whose poverty prevented the prospect of marriage, doing this lest they slip into prostitution. And he considered this royal expense laudable and beneficial, knowing that in the long run it all led to pious and charitable results.

He paid great attention to preaching and spreading the word of God. He was no idle listener but endeavored to help in the work. He abhorred those infected with the stain of heretical depravity. And so that these people not spread the stain of this contagion to the true believers of the faith, he took effective steps to expel them from the limits of his kingdom; with careful foresight for the status of the realm, such fomentations were kept far off so that the earnest purity of the true faith should shine forth brightly. When the threat of a famine loomed in certain regions of the kingdom because of a crop failure or bad weather, the moment he learned of it, he dispatched fixed sums of money through a trusted agent as the nature of each area required for distribution among the poor.

He was perfect in his humility and humble in his perfection, and after returning from overseas he gave patent outward signs of this great humility in his dress and trappings, which he often later donated to the poor. He wore no ornaments of gold or silver, no regal garments, colored or even gray, but only simple pelts, eschewing all worldly pomp. And so that the ardor of the flesh not dim the fervor of the spirit, but to arouse it by mortification and suppression, he mastered the flesh itself, as it has been widely reported, through the use of a hair shirt's harshness, tightly binding and constricting the will of the wanton flesh by the bridle of strict abstinence so that his spirit would go safely in the proper paths with safe guidance and watchfully keep away from all wrong, led not by mere will or the guiding force of desire. He taxed his body with strict fasting, adding the harshness of new fasts to those established by the holy Fathers, as suggested by his own will. For throughout Lent and the forty days before Christmas and on the vigils of all the feasts, also during the four periods which the Catholic Church has set out, he remained deep in prayer and fasting, utterly rejecting all indulgence in choice and succulent foods. On the above-mentioned vigils of the feasts of the glorious Virgin and of the Lord's birth and on the Friday of Holy Week he would fast, content with bare sustenance of bread and water. On any Friday in Lent (as mentioned) and during all of Advent he ate no fish, devoting himself to long vigils lest some hour be lost in idleness. Upon his return from overseas, as stated above, he slept not on beds of feather or straw but lay only upon a bare cot on a mat with no mattress.

Moreover he was radiant in the purity of his life, a plain friend of truth and absolute enemy of deception. Every word he spoke promoted saving works and encouraged salvation, softening the hearts of his listeners and sweeping them to edification in many ways.

Since he ardently yearned for the increase of the catholic faith and the swift liberation of the Holy Land, he again took up the sign of the Cross in aid of that Land. Backed by a strong and powerful fleet, a great and powerful army, he once again sailed overseas, this time accompanied by his children, including the queen of Navarre, his own daughter who died upon her return, and the count of Poitiers, with Charles, who was then in Italy, following in the king's tracks.[13] Arriving at last after a favorable voyage to the region of Tunis, the king pitched camp, following the advice of his lords who were there, and deployed his forces against Saracen attacks. After the countless labors which he continually endured, he fell gravely ill. Overwhelmed by the force of illness, after a few days he received the holy sacrament and, seemingly at the hour of death, offering a prayer for the Christian army, commending his soul to God with devote prayers, uttering specifically these words: *Father, into your hands I commend my spirit*,[14] he happily went to Christ to henceforth enjoy the delights of heaven.

The Son of the Almighty (whom the king loved with all the affection of his heart) was unwilling that the sanctity of such a pious prince and defender of the orthodox faith be hidden from the world, since having finished the course of this life [the king] was now truly more alive than before when he was living. And thus, just as he had shone forth by the abundance of his merits before, so now by a wide range of miracles may he blaze up; and may this king, who had worshipped Him in a plenitude of devotion, receive homage now [that he is] established with Him in the

---

[13] That is, Louis' daughter Isabelle and his brothers Alfonse of Poitiers and Charles of Anjou.
[14] Luke 23:46.

heavenly palace. For he has brought movement to the limbs of the paralyzed, he has restored the full health of upright posture to those so bent over that their faces almost scraped the ground, he has freed those burdened by goiterous tumors. He has liberated from her affliction a certain woman whose withered arm lay useless. A certain man whose arm hung lifeless received the gift of remedy through the power of this saint, while many, many others struck by paralyzing disease and others laboring with various other afflictions were restored to health. The blind see, the deaf hear, the lame walk, cured by the invocation of his name. This same saint shone forth through these and so many more glorious miracles, the full list of which we do not think needs to be included here.

Let the illustrious House of France rejoice, which has brought forth such a prince, by whose merits it is loftily made famous![15] Let the most devout people of France be happy, for they have merited so chosen and virtuous a lord! Let the hearts of the prelates and clergy exult, because this kingdom is more favorably adorned by the glittering signs of this king's miracles! Let the hearts of the barons, the magnates, the nobility, and the knights shine, because through the most saintly works of the said king the status of his kingdom is elevated with the prerogative of manifold honor and illuminated as by the rays of the sun!

Then, since it is fitting that those whom the mercy of the highest King honors with the crown of glory in heaven be devoutly venerated by the faithful in our terrestrial home, we—reaching absolute certainty through the diligence of careful and solemn inquiry and review of the earlier extended examination concerning the truth of the holy life and miracles of this most blessed Louis, and by the advice and with the assent of the community of our brothers and all the prelates then at the Apostolic See—do hereby hold that he is, on Sunday, the eleventh of August, to be enrolled in the catalogue of the saints.

We therefore advise and strictly urge every one of you, directed by apostolic letter, to celebrate the feast day of this saint devoutly and solemnly on the day following the Feast of the Apostle Saint Bartholomew, for that

---

[15] Note the parallels here with the third paragraph ("Let the heavenly throngs rejoice …"). The French royal family and the French people are now addressed in the way the denizens of heaven had been exhorted at the beginning of the bull.

is the day that his joyous soul then broke its bodily chains, seeking the stars, and went to the heavenly court to enjoy eternal happiness;[16] and arrange for the feast to be celebrated through your cities and dioceses by faithful Christians with appropriate veneration, so that you will be able, through his interceding prayers, to be free from imminent dangers here and obtain the reward of eternal salvation in the future.[17] So that a more abundant and more fervent multitude may flow to his venerable tomb, and so that his ritual solemnities may be more widely observed, to all those truly penitent and confessed who will have journeyed there reverently on his annual feast day to seek his help, we, relying on the mercy of God Almighty and the authority of his saints Peter and Paul, grant one year and forty days dispensation from the penalty imposed; and to those going to the said tomb each year throughout the octave of his feast, forty days.

Given at Orvieto on the eleventh day of August in the third year of our pontificate.[18]

---

[16] The Feast of Saint Bartholomew the Apostle is on 24 August. The feast for Louis should thus be celebrated on 25 August, the anniversary of the day he died.

[17] As the *RHGF* editors indicate, this sentence might seem better suited to a version of the bull directed to the prelates of France, than to "all the faithful." J 940 no. 111 is badly damaged at the bottom of the document (see figure 5), so that only some portions of this last paragraph can be made out (as, again, the *RHGF* editors indicate in a note). But the legible passages fit exactly with the text as printed earlier by Ménard, and so we assume that this version represents the original text even as the bull was issued to "all the faithful."

[18] 11 August 1297.

Appendix

The Manuscript and Printing Histories of the Texts

The *vitae* by Geoffrey of Beaulieu and William of Chartres have almost always been copied and printed together. The printed tradition goes back to the first edition of these works, published in Paris by Claude Ménard in 1617,[1] and extends to the one prepared by Pierre Daunou and Joseph Naudet for volume 20 of the *Recueil des historiens des Gaules et de la France* in 1840, which is surprisingly the most recent. Surveying this tradition, it seems evident that a single manuscript containing both texts, today BnF ms. lat. 13778, lies behind every edition. Because this fact has been obscured by previous commentators, and because a second important manuscript of Geoffrey of Beaulieu's work (BnF ms. lat. 18335) has never been used for any edition, some detailed remarks are necessary here.

BnF ms. lat. 13778 [= A] is a small volume (158 x 119 mm) copied at the end of the thirteenth century, perhaps in the 1290s,[2] in or near Paris.[3]

---

[1] Claude Ménard, *Sancti Lvdovici Francorvm regis, vita, conversatio et miracula, per F. Gavfridvm de Bello-loco Confessorem, et F. Guillelmum Carnotensem Capellanum eius, Ordinis Praedicatorum, item Bonifacii papae VIII. sermones duo in Canonizatione, Bulla Canonizationis, et Indulgentia in translatione corporis ipsius* (Paris: Cramoisy, 1617), 1–81 (Geoffrey of Beaulieu), 85–130 (William of Chartres). This edition was apparently printed as a separate volume, but also appears (still with these page numbers) appended to Ménard's 1617 quarto edition of Joinville. Conversely, not all printings of Ménard's Joinville appear to have Geoffrey and William appended, to judge from the several digitized exemplars available, as of 2012, on the internet.

[2] Léopold Delise, *Inventaire des manuscrits de Saint-Germain-des-Prés, conservés à la bibliothèque impériale, sous les numéros 11504–14231 du fonds latin* (Paris: Durand and Pedone-Lauriel, 1868), 114, simply labeled the manuscript fourteenth-century (followed by Kaeppeli). But we thank Patricia Stirnemann for examining the manuscript and giving us her expert opinion, to the effect that the manuscript probably dates from before 1300.

[3] Manuscript of iii (paper) + 72 (parchment) + iii (paper) folios, bound in plain brown leather (no title on spine), made up of nine eight-folio quires with evidence of trimming. At bottom of fol. 1r in later hand: "Sancti Germani a Pratis N. 1610." Fols. 1–64 are ruled in one column, with 21 lines per page (except fol. 36r where the scribe wrote above the first line and hence created 22 lines). Decoration is simple, with only red and blue used. The initials beginning Geoffrey's text (fol. 1r) and William's (fol. 41v) are more intricately

The exact circumstances of its creation are unclear, but it was purchased for the Dominicans of Evreux in 1463,[4] and was still in their possession in 1613.[5] After 1617 it entered the collection of Saint-Germain-des-Prés, where it was given the manuscript number 1610, and then passed to the French national library by the early nineteenth century. Geoffrey of Beaulieu's text occupies folios 1r–39v of the manuscript, with a French version of Louis' *Enseignements* immediately following (in the same hand and without any break) on folios 39v–41v. The same hand then copied William of Chartres' *vita* on folios 41v–64v. A later (presumably fifteenth-century) hand added an account of the "Miracles effected in the house of the Preaching Brothers of Evreux" on fols. 65r–72v.[6] This eight-folio quire may originally have been separate and bound into the manuscript sometime after 1463.

Since Ménard indicated in his table of contents that he edited both Geoffrey's and William's texts "from the library of the Preaching Brothers of Evreux" (*ex Bibliotheca Fratrum Praedicatorum Ebroicensium*), there would seem a strong presumption that it was this very manuscript that provided his text. That presumption becomes a near certainty in light

---

ornamented. The incipits of both works are in red, as are chapter headings in Geoffrey's text. First initials of each chapter alternate red and blue. Paragraph markers are always red, and some capitals have light red shading. Several later hands have added marginal corrections and notes, which we have not attempted to study here. The original scribal hand (or a close contemporary) did make a few corrections as well. The final quire (fols. 65–72) containing the Evreux miracles is of slightly different parchment, has different ruling (one column, twenty lines) and no ornamentation at all (with some capitals never having been filled in). It seems likely that this quire was created separately and then bound into the manuscript after 1463.

[4] At the bottom of fol. 64v is found the following note: "Istum libellum emit anno domini m.º cccc.º lxiiiº frater Johannes Brehalli in sacra theologia magister pro conventu sancti Ludovici Ebroicensis ordinis fratrum predicatorum."

[5] A letter from Jacques Le Batelier to Pierre Dupuy in October 1613 states that the former was not able to get permission from the Dominicans to remove the manuscript from the city of Evreux, but was able to make a partial copy (and indicates that he intended to copy the rest). The manuscript was thus certainly still held by the Dominicans of Evreux only four years before Ménard's edition. See Armand Bénet, "Un savant Ebroïcien au XVIIe siècle. Deux lettres de Jacques le Batelier, Sieur d'Aviron," *Bulletin de la Société des Antiquaires de Normandie* 14 (1886/87): 464–65. The letter in question (discovered by Léopold Delisle and given to Bénet to analyze) is copied in BnF Dupuy vol. 714, fol. 155.

[6] The incipit reads "Hec sunt miracula facta in domo fratrum predicatorum ebroycensium presidio beati Ludovici confessoris, que fuit prima ecclesia in regno Francie dedicata in nomine sancti regis, anno domino m.º cc.º lxxxxix in festo beati Ludovici."

of the fact that following the two *vitae* he then printed the "Miracles effected in the house of the Preaching Brothers of Evreux" taken "from the same library." No other medieval manuscript copy of this miracle collection is known to exist or to have existed, and his printed edition appears to reproduce the version found in lat. 13778 with only minor differences explicable as editorial decisions or errors. Thus Ménard must have used either the manuscript now known as lat. 13778, or a copy made directly from this manuscript. The second option might seem possible, since an early seventeenth-century copy of this manuscript does survive as BnF ms. lat. 10409, fols. 114r–131v. Close examination, however, shows that this copy cannot have served as the basis of Ménard's edition.[7] Moreover a local savant writing in 1722 stated that the Dominicans of Evreux had not

---

[7] This manuscript, which entered the Bibliothèque nationale by 1848–52, is a collection of miscellaneous copies and notes from the seventeenth to nineteenth centuries. The copies of Geoffrey's and William's *vitae* were noted by Kaepelli, but they have never been studied (to our knowledge), so the fact that this copy was made directly from lat. 13778 has not before been established in print. We have not identified the *érudit* who is responsible for this copy (though see note 5 above on Jacques Le Batelier for one possibility), and this hand does not appear elsewhere in the manuscript. There is no doubt, however, that the copyist worked directly from what is now BnF ms. lat. 13778: fols. 114r–123r contain a copy of (most of, see below) Geoffrey of Beaulieu's *vita;* fols. 123r–v have the *Enseignements;* 123v–130r are William of Chartres' *vita*, and 130r–131v have the miracles done at the Dominican house of Evreux; all exactly following lat. 13778. The copy cannot have been made from one of the seventeenth-century editions: not only does the copyist include a few revealing notes such as "deest in ms" (fol. 117v), but he gives the purchase note of *frater Iohannes Brehalli* (fol. 130r), which is found in lat. 13778 but not in the editions. The copy of Geoffrey of Beaulieu, however, is incomplete, in two ways. First, between what are now numbered as fols. 116 and 117 several folios have been lost (probably two folios out of what would have been an eight-folio quire) corresponding to Geoffrey's chs. 14–20. Second, and more interestingly, at times the copyist decided simply to refer to identical text in William of Nangis's *vita* of Louis (because William of Nangis had used large chunks of Geoffrey's text), instead of giving a complete transcription of Geoffrey's text (the copyist never engaged in a similar process of replacement with William of Chartres or the Evreux miracles, since these were not used by William of Nangis). Given these omissions this manuscript cannot be a copy actually made in preparation for Ménard's edition. And given this close attention to a comparison with the printed edition of William of Nangis, the lack of any awareness of a printed edition of Geoffrey of Beaulieu and William of Chartres certainly indicates a copying date before 1617. Since the edition of William of Nangis's *vita* referred to must be Pierre Pithou, *Historiae Francorum ab anno Christi DCCCC. ad ann. M.CC.LXXXV. scriptores veteres XI* (Frankfurt: Apud Andreae Wecheli heredes Claudium Marnium & Joannem Aubrium, 1596), 400–471 (we have verified the page and line numbers the copyist gives, leaving no doubt), the copies in lat. 10409 must therefore have been made after 1596 and before 1617.

received their manuscript back after they lent it for Ménard's edition.[8] We are thus convinced that Ménard worked directly from what is now BnF ms. lat. 13778.

Geoffrey's and William's *vitae* were next printed in 1649 by André Duchesne in volume 5 of his *Historiae Francorum scriptores*.[9] Duchesne again indicated (p. 444) that Geoffrey's text was taken "from the manuscript codex of the convent of the Preaching Brothers of Evreux" (*Ex Codice MS. Fratrum Praedicatorum Conuentus Ebroicensis*) and William "from the same codex" (*Ex eodem Codice*). Again Duchesne followed immediately by printing the "Miracles effected in the house of the Preaching Brothers of Evreux" though here he does not give a source. A comparison of the editions strongly suggests that Duchesne simply worked from Ménard's printing, rather than returning to the manuscripts himself.[10] Still, Duchesne's description further indicates that both editions ultimately rested on ms. lat. 13778, since he specifies (where Ménard did not) that the two texts were found in a single manuscript, and in the form of a codex (as opposed to a roll). Duchesne's editions were then reprinted, with new editorial notes but again without any fresh recourse to manuscripts, by J. Stilting in the *Acta sanctorum* series in 1741.[11]

The most recent edition—though at this point 1840 is hardly very recent—was also based on ms. lat. 13778, as its editors Daunou and Naudet made clear by identifying their base text as manuscript 1610 from the collection of Saint-Germain-des-Prés. However, they introduced a certain amount of confusion by suggesting that this manuscript was not the same as the manuscript from the Dominicans of Evreux that had served for all earlier editions. They made this suggestion in spite of knowing

---

[8] Pierre Le Brasseur, *Histoire civile et ecclésiastique du comté d'Evreux* (Paris: Barois, 1722), 202.
[9] André Duchesne, *Historiae Francorum scriptores* . . . , vol. 5 (Paris: Cramoisy, 1649), 444–65 (Geoffrey) and 466–77 (William). In fact this volume was completed and published by André Duchesne's son François, since André had died in 1640.
[10] Among many other examples, see Duchesne's indication (*Historiae Francorum scriptores*, 5:459) regarding an apparent lacuna in Geoffrey's text, that "Desunt haec statuta in MS. Codice, sed habentur apud Ioannem Ionvillae Dominum," which is exactly (letter for letter and with identical capitalization and punctuation) what Ménard had noted (*Sancti Lvdovici Francorvm regis, vita*, 58). Moreover, both editions then insert five stars to mark the lacuna.
[11] J. Stilting in *Acta sanctorum*, Aug. 5 (Antwerp, 1741), 541–58 (Geoffrey), 559–68 (William), 569–71 (Evreux Miracles).

full well that ms. 1610 (that is, the BnF's lat. 13778) had indeed come from the Dominicans of Evreux. Their belief was that their manuscript contained enough readings that differed from those found in the older editions to indicate that they must be dealing with a new, never before edited manuscript.[12] In our judgment (and we are not the first to reach this conclusion),[13] this was a misguided interpretation of the evidence. Differences from Ménard's edition, then passed on to Duchesne and the *Acta sanctorum*, result from Ménard's understandable misreadings and silent emendations. The *RHGF* editors, however, created confusion by referring in some footnotes to "ms. Prat" (for *a Pratis*, the Latin rendering of *des Prés*) when they wished to draw attention to a reading in their base manuscript, but elsewhere to both the "ms. ebroic." and to "Chesn." when they wished to point out a discrepancy with earlier editions. The latter two terms are interchangeable references to Duchesne's edition (*Chesn*), under the belief that it was based on a separate manuscript from Evreux (in Latin abbreviation *ms. ebroic.*). Since, however, the manuscript from Saint-Germain-des-Prés, the manuscript from Evreux, and the base manuscript for the seventeenth-century editions were all in fact one and the same, the editors' observations are often less than helpful.

In sum, all existing editions of these two *vitae* have been based on a single manuscript. For our translation of William of Chartres, this fact does not present great difficulties, because lat. 13778 remains the only known manuscript of this text. For William's text, we have therefore simply been able to compare lat. 13778 against the *RHGF* edition and correct misreadings printed there. Given that our aim has been an accurate translation, not a new critical edition (though one is surely needed for both *vitae*), our notes indicate only where misreadings in the *RHGF* edition affect meaning. The edition by Daunou and Naudet is referred to as *RHGF* in these notes, and lat. 13778 as manuscript A. Discrepancies are simply noted in a straightforward sentence style.

For Geoffrey of Beaulieu's text, however, the situation is more complicated. Although at least one manuscript (noted by early modern *érudits*

---

[12] *RHGF*, 20:xxviii–xxxii and 1–2; and see Daunou's entry "Geoffroi de Beaulieu," *HLF* 19 (1838): 235–36.
[13] See Bénet, "Un savant Ebroïcien au XVIIe siècle," 473–78.

as "ornamented with pictures") would seem to now be lost,[14] an additional manuscript copy of the text does survive. It is perplexing that Daunou and Naudet did not make use of BnF ms. lat. 18335, since it had entered the national collection by 1802 and was known and referred to by other French scholars by the 1840s.[15] Daunou and Naudet were aware of older references to this manuscript, but believed that it was no longer extant.[16]

BnF lat. 18335 [= B], however, is an important witness, since it is of roughly the same date as lat. 13778, copied perhaps just a little later, sometime around 1300, in or near Paris.[17] This somewhat larger manuscript (248 x 152 mm) belonged to the Abbaye des Hyvernaux in Brie in the fourteenth century,[18] and by the sixteenth century to the Collège de

---

[14] For reference to a third manuscript "ornée de figures," apparently now lost, see Daunou, "Geoffroi de Beaulieu," 235.

[15] According to Natalis de Wailly, "Il existe à la Bibliothèque royale deux manuscrits de l'ouvrage de Geoffroy de Beaulieu ... le plus ancient ... est conservé dans le fonds Saint-Germain sous le n. 1610." "Examen critique de la *Vie de saint Louis* par Geoffroy de Beaulieu," *Bibliothèque de l'Ecole des chartes* 5 (1844): 207 n. 1. Earlier, Jacques Echard noted "sed & ejus codex MS elegans 400 & amplius annorum a me visus est & expensus Parisiis in Navarr. anno MDCCII." Quétif and Echard, *SoP* 1:270 (the remark is attributable to Echard, since Jacques Quétif died in 1698). The context of this remark seems to indicate that Echard (mistakenly) thought this manuscript had been used by Duchesne.

[16] *RHGF*, 20:xxviii, and Daunou, "Geoffroi de Beaulieu," 235, explicitly indicating he did not know the whereabouts of another manuscript "qui se conservait au collège de Navarre" that had been cited by older authors.

[17] The notice (by Charlotte Denoël) in the BnF's *Archives et manuscrits* online catalogue in fact says "XIIIe s. (fin)." Patricia Stirnemann confirmed this date for us and suggested that this manuscript, in a more liturgical hand than lat. 13778, might be the later of the two, perhaps dating from just after the canonization of 1297. See also *La France de Saint Louis: Septième centenaire de la mort de Saint Louis. Exposition nationale organisée par le Ministère des Affaires Culturelles avec la collaboration du Ministère de l'Education Nationale* (Paris, 1971), 46, no 49, where date is given as "fin du XIIIe siècle." This manuscript is ii (paper) + 60 (parchment) + ii (paper) folios, now in red leather binding, made up of five twelve-folio quires (with fol. 1bis inserted in the eighteenth century, see transcription below), ruled consistently for one column and eighteen lines. Evidence of trimming. Decoration is minimal. Space is left for capitals but they were never added, except for the initial A. Red incipit, chapter titles, and light shading of some capitals are the only use of color. There are marginal corrections in the same hand as in fol. 1bis, noting comparisons with the Duchesne edition.

[18] Fol. 59v, immediately after the end of Geoffrey's text, a later hand has added: "Iste liber est beate marie de Yvernali," followed by an anathema, and "Explicit vita sancti ludovici regis." This monastery near modern Lésigny was some thirty kilometers southeast of Paris.

Navarre in Paris.[19] Geoffrey's *vita* is the only text copied in this manuscript (fols. 1–59v), except for short prayers on the final page (fol. 60r).[20] Moreover, this manuscript provides important alternative—and in some cases, better—readings of the text. Most importantly, it contains one short chapter completely omitted from lat. 13778, which is almost certainly an authentic part of Geoffrey's original text.[21] This fact was noted by an alert reader at the Collège de Navarre in the mid-eighteenth

---

[19] Top of fol. 1r, in later hand: "Pro libraria regalis collegii Campaniae alias Navarrae Parisius fundati." At bottom of folio: "Lit. A 250" and "*Nav. 77.*"

[20] In the middle of fol. 60r, a hand roughly contemporary with the creation of the manuscript has written the prayer: "[D]eus qui beatum Ludovicum confessorem tuum de terreno ac temporali regno ad celestis et eterni regni gloriam transtulisti; eius meritis et intercessione regis nostri Iesu Christi filii tui nos choeredes [*sic, for* coheredes] efficias et eiusdem regni tribuas esse consortes, per eundem." This is the standard collect ("oratio") for Louis, found in all the early offices and frequently transmitted as part of the Mass, and elsewhere independently. See M. Cecilia Gaposchkin, *The Making of Saint Louis: Kingship, Sanctity, and Crusade in the Later Middle Ages* (Ithaca: Cornell University Press, 2008), 257. At the top of this folio, a later hand has added another prayer: "O Rex egregie quondam Rex francie Ludovice pie cum rege glorie triumphans hodie pro pace require regni ecclesie Christum deprecare." This prayer is noted in a fourteenth-century breviary from Corbie, now Amiens BM 117, fol. 425; and see *Analecta Hymnica*, vol. 28 (Leipzig: Reisland), 307, no. 155 (from a Cologne manuscript). A similar (perhaps even the same) hand then continues in a smaller script: "Sancte Ludovice dulcedo pauperum tu pius consolator miserorum ora pro nobis, ora pro nobis beate Ludovice ut digni efficiamur in promissionibus Christi." This prayer is found in the "Hours of Savoy" made for Blanche of Burgundy (countess of Savoy, Louis IX's granddaughter) ca. 1335–40, some folios from which survive as Yale University, Beinecke Ms 390. See P. Blanchard, *Les Heures de Savoie: Facsimiles of Fifty-Two Pages from the Hours Executed for Blanche of Burgundy, Being All That Is Known to Survive of a Famous Fourteenth-Century Ms, Which Was Burnt at Turin in 1904* (London: Chiswick Press, 1910), pl. VI; Paul Durrieu, "Notice d'un des plus importants livres de prières de Charles V: Les Heures de Savoie ou 'Très belles grandes heures' du roi," *Bibliothèque de l'Ecole des chartes* 72 (1911): 525, and Gaposchkin, *Making of Saint Louis*, 209–10. The inclusion of this prayer—otherwise known only in royal manuscripts—raises important questions about contact between BnF ms. lat. 18335 and court circles. At the bottom of the page, an annotation in a sixteenth-century hand (probably the same as on fol. 1r), reads: "Pro libraria Regalis Collegii Campaniae alias Navarrae." Fol. 60v is blank except for a short illegible note at the bottom.

[21] This judgment is based on the intrinsic likelihood of this chapter being accidentally omitted in the manuscript tradition behind *A* rather than invented for *B*, and on the evident confusion in the attempt to create a workable chapter heading in *A*. The chapter headings before and after this chapter in *B* make sense of the flow of the narrative and structure. The chapter evidently was omitted at some point, but the chapter heading remained in slightly garbled form and was copied by the scribe of *A*, before being crossed out by a later reader as nonsensical.

century,[22] but has otherwise gone unremarked to the present. Hence this "missing chapter" is printed here for the first time (ch. 16*bis*). This manuscript also offers several different chapter headings and occasionally inserts chapter breaks at different points. In some instances, these headings and breaks make better sense of the text (though in others, less).

Due to the existence of this previously unused manuscript, our notes for Geoffrey's text are more extensive than for William's. In these notes we indicate corrections to the edition in the following cases: when both manuscripts agree against the edition, even in the case of fairly minor misreadings (but not simply in cases of differing orthography); when *A* [= 13778] does not read as the edition indicates it does, in cases that affect meaning; when *B* [= 18335] has a reading different from *A* and we have followed the reading in *B* for the translation; when *B* has a reading different from *A* that has not been adopted for the translation, but is

---

[22] We have not identified the *érudit* whose remarks were bound in the manuscript as fol. 1*bis* r–v. He wrote after 1722, however, since he refers to Jacques Le Long's *Bibliotheca sacra*, the first edition of which appeared in 1709, and to Pierre Le Brasseur, *Histoire civile et ecclésiastique du comté d'Evreux* (Paris: Barois, 1722); and surely before 1790, when the Maurists (his "P.P. Bénédictins") were suppressed. These remarks, titled "Sur le ms A 250 de la Bibliothèque du Collége de Navarre," seem worth giving in their entirety here (orthography and accents follow the manuscript):

> Ce ms in 4° sur velin, cuntient l'histoire de St Louis composée par Geoffroi de Beaulieu dominicain Confesseur du St Roy & qui l'accompagna dans son Expédition d'outremer. Claude Menard publia le premier cet ouvrage en 1617, à la suite de l'histoire de Joinville, Sur un Ms des freres Prêcheurs du convent d'Evreux. Francois Duchesne, fils d'André, le donna de nouveau dans le 1ᵉʳ Volume de la Collection des historiens de france en 1649, & dit de même dans le titre qu'il le donne d'après le Ms que je viens de nommer. Cependant suivant l'historien du Comté d'Evreux (p. 202), ce ms étoit perdu depuis la communication qui en avoit été accordée par les freres Prêcheurs, pour l'Edition de 1617. C'est à dire qu'il ne leur avoit pas été rendu. S'il est en effet perdu comme le dit cet Ecrivain, celui de Navarre en devient encore plus précieux. Il me paroit à peu près du tems où vivoit l'auteur, ou tout au plus tard de la fin du XIVᵉ Siécle. // Je l'ay comparé très exactement avec le texte imprimé, & j'en ai plusieurs variantes, dont quelques unes sont importantes. Elles pourront être utiles aus P.P. Bénédictins qui travaillent à la collection des Monumens de Notre histoire. Dans cette vüe je les ai transcrites à la marge de mon exemplaire de Duchesne. Le morceau le plus considérable est un chapitre entier qui manque dans tous les imprimés. J'en ai fait note, sur un papier volant que l'on trouvera dans le ms. J'avertis qu'en quelques endroits ce ms est fautif. Lorsque les fautes m'ont paru de nature à rendre le sens obscur, j'ai pris la Liberté de les corriger à la marge d'après l'imprimé, c'est le moyen d'en rendre la lecture plus utile à ceux qui le voudront consulter. Je crois que Personne jusqu'ici ne l'a connu, il n'est point indiqué dans la Bibliothèque du P. Le Long & Je ne sache aucun Ecrivain qui l'ait cité.

significant enough to be of interest; and in the very few cases when the edition and *B* agree against *A* (we believe these rare instances can be explained as obvious emendations made by the earlier editors, in ignorance of *B*). For this text, these variant readings are presented in the customary abbreviated style of critical apparatus.

The manuscript and printing histories of our additional texts can be covered more succinctly. The early printing history of Boniface VIII's canonization bull (and his two related sermons for the canonization, not included in our collection) directly parallels that of Geoffrey and William. The bull and sermons were published by Ménard in 1617 (162–83); by Duchesne in 1649 (*Historiae Francorum scriptores*, 5:481–91), and in the *Acta sanctorum* in 1741 (Aug. 5:528–32).[23] Ménard's edition, and those taken from it, were apparently based on Chartres, Bibliothèque municipale ms. 226, which was destroyed in 1944.[24] Boniface's bull, however, was better served by its *RHGF* edition in 1894 than had been the *vitae* by Geoffrey and William in that same series a half-century earlier.[25] Not only was volume 23 of the *RHGF* in the very capable hands of Natalis de Wailly, Léopold Delisle, and Charles Jourdain, but the editors had access to the sealed original sent to Philip IV, now AN J 940 no. 111. Because this original is badly damaged in places, it was still necessary for the *RHGF* editors to use Ménard's edition as a starting point, and make corrections from J 940 no. 111 where required and possible. Our comparison with J 940 no. 111 has found that the *RHGF* edition (also referred to simply by that abbreviation in the notes to chapter 4) is highly trustworthy, with its notes accurately representing differences between the sealed original and Ménard's printing. We have thus been able to follow this edition, except that we give the papal greeting as found in J 940 no. 111, whereas Wailly, Delisle, and Jourdain preferred to follow the alternative version given by Ménard (presumably from Chartres ms. 226).

The text of Philip III's letter from North Africa was first printed by Duchesne in 1649 (*Historiae Francorum scriptores*, 5:440–41), based on

---

[23] A summary is also found in G. Digard et al., *Les registres de Boniface VIII*, vol. 1 (Paris: E. Thorin, 1884), no. 2047.
[24] Carolus-Barré, *Le procès*, 278.
[25] Natalis de Wailly, Léopold Delisle, and Charles Jourdain, eds., *RHGF*, 23:154–60 (Paris: Welter, 1894).

a manuscript he received from Nicolas Camusat (1575–1655), canon of Troyes and well-known *érudit*.[26] Although it is not certain exactly where Camusat procured his copy, it would seem to have been textually close to the one now found in BnF ms. lat. 5526, a thirteenth-century cartulary of Notre-Dame de Paris, where the text is added by a hand that may still be late thirteenth-century on fols. 138r–139v. This manuscript was the basis for editions by Gérard Dubois in 1710 and (more accurately) Benjamin Guérard in 1850.[27] Another early copy, with notable differences from lat. 5526, is found in BnF ms. lat. 9376, fols. 61–72, which are an early fourteenth-century copy of a letter collection dealing with the crusade of 1270 and compiled at Saint-Denis shortly afterward.[28] Philip's letter is found on fols. 65rb–65vb. Another, perhaps better, copy of this collection was identified at Oxford in the Bodleian Library in the 1950s and described by Louis Carolus-Barré in 1966, but—somewhat incredibly—now seems to have disappeared.[29] In any event, the copy in ms. lat. 5526 seems to us

[26] See Donatella Nebbiai, "Pour la bibliothèque de Saint-Germain des Prés au 17e siècle: Nicolas Camusat (1575–1655), ses livres, ses recherches," in *Dom Jean Mabillon, figure majeure de l'Europe des lettres: Actes des deux colloques du tricentenaire de la mort de dom J. Mabillon*, ed. Jean Leclant, André Vauchez, and Daniel Odon Hurel (Paris: Académie des Inscriptions et Belles Lettres, 2010), 517–48, esp. 521–26 for his relationship with Duchesne.
[27] Dubois, *Historia ecclesiae Parisiensis*, vol. 2 (Paris: Muguet, 1710), 467–68; Guérard, *Cartulaire de l'église Notre-Dame de Paris*, vol. 1 (Paris: Crapelet, 1850), 189–92 (no. CCLVII).
[28] This twelve-folio quire was in fact originally part of BnF ms. lat 11867 (between what are now fols. 164 and 165), which belonged to Saint-Germain-des-Prés. The quire was detached in the seventeenth century, probably by Luc d'Achery (who published most of these texts in 1657, though not the letter by Philip under consideration here), and was eventually bound into ms. lat. 9376 in the mid nineteenth century. We thank Elizabeth A. R. Brown for sharing her notes on both manuscripts with us.
[29] See Louis Carolus-Barré, "Un recueil épistolaire composé à Saint-Denis sur la Croisade (1270–1271)," *Comptes-rendus des séances de l'Académie des Inscriptions et Belles-Lettres* 110, no. 4 (1966): 555–68, on the letter collection generally and the Oxford manuscript specifically, as things stood in 1966. Carolus-Barré showed that the letters had been compiled at Saint-Denis, and preserved not only in BnF ms. lat. 9376 but also in a recently discovered copy in the Bodleian Library. This copy was in the form of parchment fragments that had been serving as a paste-down for an incunabulum in the Bodleian collection, brought to the attention of Richard Hunt in the mid-1950s. Hunt signaled the discovery to Jean Richard (see Richard, "Un recueil de lettres sur la huitième croisade," *Bulletin de la Société des Antiquaires de France* [1960]: 182–87) who then left Carolus-Barré to carry out detailed study. Hunt had assigned the recovered fragments to Bodleian lat. Mix b 13, as fols. 47–53, and Carolus-Barré traveled to Oxford to see them in July 1964. Apparently, however, after photographing for Carolus-Barré's further study, the folios were set aside and never actually integrated into lat. Mix b 13. By the mid-1970s other fragments had been assigned to fols. 47–53 of this

clearly superior to that in ms. lat. 9376. Since Guérard's edition contains only very minor deviations from the text found in ms. lat. 5526, we therefore use this edition as our base, and note only those variants in ms. lat. 9376 that represent possible "better" readings.

For the two remaining texts, we have had to rely only on printed editions. Gregory X's letter to Geoffrey of Beaulieu is taken from the 1729 edition by Thomas Ripoll, which we have compared with Marie-Dominique Chapotin's printing of 1898.[30] Jean of Châtillon's letter to the College of Cardinals was first printed by Jean de Rechac in 1647.[31] Because de Rechac placed this letter in the context of the Dominican convent of Chartres and then immediately after the text offered his thanks to Nicolas le Febvre for his zeal in verifying ancient documents of the town, bishopric, and Dominican convent of Chartres, it seems likely that le Febvre had provided him with an original or copy stemming from the

---

manuscript, and when more recent scholars tried to follow up on Carolus-Barré's work (he unfortunately never published his projected new edition of the letters), it became clear that the Oxford copy of these letters had gone missing. Elizabeth A. R. Brown confirmed this fact in correspondence with Martin Kaufmann (whose searches on her behalf were without result) in 2007, and Xavier Hélary's search at the Bodleian in September of that year proved fruitless as well (see Hélary, "'L'épistolaire politique' en XIIIe siècle: Autour d'un recueil de lettres relatives à la croisade de Tunis (1270)," forthcoming in L'Epistolaire politique, ed. Laurent Vissière and Bruno Dumézil (Paris: Presses de l'Université Paris-Sorbonne). Elizabeth Brown also examined Carolus-Barré's papers at the Institut de France, but located no relevant information. We thank Professors Brown and Hélary for sharing information with us on this lamentable (and, one hopes, temporary) disappearance.

[30] Ripoll, Bullarium Ordinis Fratrum Praedicatorum, vol. 1 (Rome: Ex Typographia Hieronymi Mainardi, 1729), 503; Chapotin, Histoire des Dominicains de la Province de France: Le Siècle des Fondations (Rouen: Cagniard, 1898), 648 n. 1. Summaries can be found in Jean Guiraud, Les registres de Grégoire X (1272–1276), deuxième fascicule (Paris: Thorin et fils, 1893), 136, no. 349 (summarized from Reg. ann. I, n° 8, f. 117), and Augustus Potthast, Regesta pontificum romanorum, vol. 2 (Graz: Akademische Druck- u. Verlagsanstalt, 1957), 1652, no. 20511.

[31] La vie du glorieux patriarche S. Dominique, Fondateur et Instituteur de l'Ordre des Freres Prêcheurs, Et de ses premiers seize Compagnons: Avec la Fondation de Tovs Les Couuens et Monasteres de l'vn et l'autre sexe, Dans toutes les Prouinces du Royaume de France, et dans les dix-sept du pays-Bas, vol. 1 (Paris: Huré, 1647), 652–54. In this edition the letter has the heading "Lettre que le chapitre Prouincial de la Prouince de France, de l'Ordre des Freres Prêcheurs, ecriuit au sacré College des Cardinaux, pour la Canonization de saint Louys Roy de France, A la sollicitation et aux poursuittes de Guillaume de Chartres, et Gauffrid de Beau-Lieu, Religieux du Couuent de Chartres." No evidence is provided, however, to show that William or Geoffrey "solicited" the letter (or that Geoffrey was a member of the convent of Chartres).

archives of that community.³² In a similar manner, le Febvre's correspondence with the convent of Le Mans in 1628 probably accounts for the fact that in 1692 the beginning of the letter and the names of those signing it are cited by an anonymous historian of that convent, whose text was later published by Ch. Cosnard.³³ The text of the entire letter was then most recently printed by Marie-Dominique Chapotin in 1898.³⁴ It may be that Chapotin took his text (for which he indicates no source) from de Rechac; there are a number of small differences between the texts but most could be explained as careless errors or obvious emendations. But it is also possible that he found an early modern copy in the archives of the order at Santa Sabina. Our translation is thus based on a comparison between the texts of de Rechac and Chapotin. Generally that of de Rechac appears superior, but where significant differences are found we have indicated them in the notes.³⁵

---

³² De Rechac thanks le Febvre directly following the document in question, ibid., 654. On le Febvre, see introduction, note 45.
³³ *Histoire du couvent des FF. Prêcheurs du Mans, 1219–1792* (Le Mans: Monnoyer, 1879), 6 (see p. 5 for le Febvre's correspondence; the anonymous chronicle is now AD de La Sarthe, H 1153 no. 3).
³⁴ *Histoire des Dominicains de la Province de France*, 648–49 n. 2.
³⁵ We are grateful to Dr. Simon Tugwell, O.P., who kindly signaled to us the existence of de Rechac's edition and that of the anonymous chronicle from Le Mans, as well as the current whereabouts of the latter and its relation to the printing by Cosnard.

SELECT BIBLIOGRAPHY

Primary Sources

Editions of the vitae by Geoffrey of Beaulieu and William of Chartres

Daunou, Pierre, and Joseph Naudet, eds. *Recueil des historiens des Gaules et de la France*, 20:3–27 (Geoffrey), 28–41 (William). Paris: Imprimerie royale, 1840.

Duchesne, André, ed. *Historiae Francorum scriptores coaetanei... Quorum plurimi nunc primum ex variis codicibus mss. in lucem prodeunt: alij vero auctiores & emendatiores. Cvm epistolis regvm, reginarvm, pontificvm... et aliis veteribus rerum francicarum monumentis*, 5: 444–65 (Geoffrey), 466–77 (William). Paris: Cramoisy, 1649.

Ménard, Claude, ed. *Sancti Lvdovici Francorvm regis, vita, conversatio et miracula, per F. Gavfridvm de Bello-loco, Confessorem, et F. Guillelmum Carnotensem, Capellanum eius, Ordinis Praedicatorum, item Bonifacii papae VIII. sermones duo in Canonizatione, Bulla Canonizationis, et Indulgentia in translatione corporis ipsius*, 1–81 (Geoffrey), 85–130 (William). Paris: Cramoisy, 1617.

Stilting, J., ed. *Acta sanctorum*, Aug., 5: 541–58 (Geoffrey), 559–68 (William). Antwerp, 1741.

Editions of Other Texts Translated in this Volume

Chapotin, Marie-Dominique. *Histoire des Dominicains de la Province de France: Le Siècle des Fondations*, 648 n. 1 (Gregory X's letter) 648–49 n. 2 (Jean of Châtillon's letter). Rouen: Cagniard, 1898.

De Rechac, Jean. *La vie du glorieux patriarche S. Dominique, Fondateur et Instituteur de l'Ordre des Freres Prêcheurs, Et de ses premiers seize Compagnons: Avec la Fondation de Tovs Les Couuens et Monasteres de l'vn et l'autre sexe, Dans toutes les Prouinces du Royaume de France, et dans les dix-sept du pays-Bas*, 1: 652–54 (Jean of Châtillon's letter). Paris: Huré, 1647.

De Wailly, Natalis, Léopold Delisle, and Charles Jourdain, eds. *Recueil des historiens des Gaules et de la France*, 23: 154–60 (Boniface VIII's bull). Paris: Welter, 1894.

Dubois, Gérard. *Historia ecclesiae Parisiensis*, 2: 467–68 (Philip III's letter). Paris: Muguet, 1710.

Duchesne, André. *Historiae Francorum scriptores*, 5:440–41 (Philip III's letter); 481–91 (Boniface VIII's bull).
Guérard, Benjamin, ed. *Cartulaire de l'église Notre-Dame de Paris*, 1: 189–92 (Philip III's letter). Paris: Crapelet, 1850.
Ménard, Claude. *Sancti Lvdovici Francorvm regis, vita*, 162–83 (Boniface VIII's bull).
Ripoll, Thomas. *Bullarium Ordinis Fratrum Praedicatorum*, 1: 503 (Gregory X's letter). Rome: Ex Typographia Hieronymi Mainardi, 1729.
Stilting, J. *Acta sanctorum*, Aug. 5: 528–32 (Boniface VIII's bull).

Editions of Selected Other Early Writings on the Life of Louis IX

Daunou, Pierre, and Joseph Naudet, eds. *Recueil des historiens des Gaules et de la France*, 20:310–465 (William of Nangis's *Gesta sancte memorie Ludovici*). Paris: Imprimerie royale, 1840.
Delaborde, H.-François, ed. *Guillaume de Saint-Pathus. Vie de Saint Louis*. Collection de textes pour servir à l'étude et à l'enseignement de l'histoire 27. Paris: A. Picard, 1899.
———. "Une oeuvre nouvelle de Guillaume de Saint-Pathus." *Bibliothèque de l'Ecole des chartes* 63 (1902): 261–82.
Fay, Percival B., ed. *Guillaume de Saint-Pathus, confesseur de la reine Marguerite, Les miracles de saint Louis*. Paris: Champion, 1932.
Field, Sean L., ed. *The Writings of Agnes of Harcourt: The Life of Isabelle of France and the Letter on Louis IX and Longchamp*. Notre Dame, Ind.: University of Notre Dame Press, 2003.
Gaposchkin, M. Cecilia, ed. *Blessed Louis, the Most Glorious of Kings: Texts Relating to the Cult of Saint Louis of France*. Translations with Phyllis B. Katz. Notre Dame, Ind.: University of Notre Dame Press, 2012.
Monfrin, Jacques, ed., *Jean de Joinville, Vie de saint Louis*. Paris: Garnier, 1995.
Smith, Caroline, trans. *Joinville and Villehardouin, Chronicles of the Crusades*. New York: Penguin, 2008.

Secondary Sources

General Overviews of Capetian France, Crusading, and Medieval Sanctity

Duby, Georges. *France in the Middle Ages, 987–1460*. Translated by Juliet Vale. Oxford: Blackwell, 1991.
Fawtier, Robert. *The Capetian Kings of France: Monarchy and Nation 987–1328*. Translated by Lionel Butler and R. J. Adam. New York: St. Martin's Press, 1960.
Hallam, Elizabeth M., and Judith Everard. *Capetian France, 987–1328*. 2d ed. Harlow, UK: Longman, 2001.

Jordan, William Chester. "The Capetians from the Death of Philip II to Philip IV." In *The New Cambridge Medieval History*, 5: 279–313. Cambridge: Cambridge University Press, 1999.

Klaniczay, Gábor. *Holy Rulers and Blessed Princesses: Dynastic Cults in Medieval Central Europe*. Translated by Eva Pálmai. Cambridge: Cambridge University Press, 2002.

Madden, Thomas F. *The New Concise History of the Crusades*. Updated ed. Lanham, Md.: Rowman & Littlefield, 2005.

Potter, David, ed. *France in the Later Middle Ages, 1200–1500*. Oxford: Oxford University Press, 2003.

Riley-Smith, Jonathan S. C. *The Crusades: A History*. 2d ed. New Haven, Conn.: Yale University Press, 2005.

Smith, Caroline. *Crusading in the Age of Joinville*. Burlington, Vt.: Ashgate, 2006.

Tyerman, Christopher. *God's War: A New History of the Crusades*. Cambridge Mass.: Belknap Press of Harvard University Press, 2006.

Vauchez, André. *Sainthood in the Later Middle Ages*. Translated by Jean Birrell. Cambridge: Cambridge University Press, 1997.

The Reign and Crusades of Louis IX

Jordan, William Chester. "Anti-Corruption Campaigns in Thirteenth-Century Europe." *Journal of Medieval History* 35 (2009): 204–19.

———. "The Case of Saint Louis." *Viator* 19 (1988): 209–17.

———. "Honouring Saint Louis in a Small Town." *Journal of Medieval History* 30 (2004): 263–77.

———. *Louis IX and the Challenge of the Crusade: A Study in Rulership*. Princeton, N.J.: Princeton University Press, 1979.

———. *Men at the Center: Redemptive Governance under Louis IX*. Budapest: Central European University Press, 2012.

———. *A Tale of Two Monasteries: Westminster and Saint-Denis in the Thirteenth Century*. Princeton, N.J.: Princeton University Press, 2009.

Gaposchkin, M. Cecilia. "Louis IX in Captivity." *Questiones Medii Aevi Novae* 17 (2013), forthcoming.

———. "Louis IX, Crusade, and the Promise of Joshua in the Holy Land." *Journal of Medieval History* 29 (2008): 245–74.

Hélary, Xavier. "Les rois de France et la terre sainte, de la croisade de Tunis à la chute d'Acre (1270–1291)." *Annuaire-Bulletin de la Société de l'histoire de France* 118 (2005): 21–104.

LeGoff, Jacques. *Saint Louis*. Translated by Gareth Evan Gollrad. Notre Dame, Ind.: University of Notre Dame Press, 2009.

Little, Lester K. "Saint Louis's Involvement with the Friars." *Church History* 33 (1964): 125–48.

Lower, Michael. "Conversion and St Louis's Last Crusade." *Journal of Ecclesiastical History* 58 (2007): 211–31.

Richard, Jean. *Saint Louis: Crusader King of France*. Translated by Jean Birrell. Cambridge: Cambridge University Press, 1992.

Septième centenaire de la mort de saint Louis. Actes des colloques de Royaumont et de Paris (21–27 mai 1970). Paris: Les Belles Lettres, 1976.

Strayer, Joseph R. "The Crusades of Louis IX." In *Medieval Statecraft and the Perspectives of History*, 159–92. Princeton, N.J.: Princeton University Press, 1971.

Tillemont, Sébastien Le Nain de. *Vie de Saint Louis, Roi de France*. Edited by J. De Gaulle. 6 vols. Paris: J. Renouard et cie, 1847–1851.

Canonization, Cult, Miracles, and Memory of Saint Louis

Allirot, Anne-Hélène. *Filles de roy de France: Princesses royales, mémoire de saint Louis et conscience dynastique (de 1270 à la fin du XIVe siècle)*. Turnhout: Brepols, 2011.

Beaune, Colette. *The Birth of an Ideology: Myths and Symbols of Nation in Late-Medieval France*. Translated by Susan Ross Huston. Edited by Frederick L. Cheyette. Berkeley: University of California Press, 1991.

Brown, Elizabeth A. R. "The Chapels and Cult of Saint Louis at Saint-Denis." *Mediaevalia* 10 (1984): 279–331.

———. "Philippe Le Bel and the Remains of Saint Louis." *Gazette des Beaux-Arts* 97 (1980): 175–82.

Carolus-Barré, Louis. "Les enquêtes pour la canonisation de saint Louis de Grégoire X à Boniface VIII et la bulle *Gloria Laus*, du 11 août 1297." *Revue d'histoire de l'Eglise de France* 57 (1971): 19–31.

———. *Le procès de canonisation de Saint Louis (1272–1297): Essai de reconstitution*. Edited by Henri Platelle. Collection de l'Ecole Française de Rome 195. Rome: Ecole Française de Rome, 1994.

Chareyon, Nicole. "Représentation du corps souffrant dans la Vie et les Miracles de Saint Louis." *Cahiers de Recherches Médiévales (XIIe–XVe s.)* 4 (1997): 175–87.

Chennaf, Sharah, and Odile Redon. "Les Miracles de Saint Louis." In *Les Miracles, Miroirs des Corps*, 53–85. Paris: Université de Paris VIII, 1983.

Delaborde, Henri-François. "Fragments de l'enquête faite à Saint-Denis en 1282 en vue de la canonisation de saint Louis." *Mémoires de la Société de l'histoire de Paris et de l'Ile-de-France* 23 (1896): 1–71.

Farmer, Sharon. *Surviving Poverty in Medieval Paris: Gender, Ideology, and the Daily Lives of the Poor*. Ithaca: Cornell University Press, 2002.

Gaposchkin, M. Cecilia. *The Making of Saint Louis: Kingship, Sanctity, and Crusade in the Later Middle Ages*. Ithaca: Cornell University Press, 2008.

———. "Place, Status, and Experience in the Miracles of Saint Louis." *Cahiers de Recherches Médiévales et Humanistes/Journal of Medieval and Humanistic Studies* 19 (2010): 249–66.

Hallam, Elizabeth M. "Philip the Fair and the Cult of Saint Louis." In *Studies in Church History* 18 (Religion and National Identity), 201–14. Oxford: Blackwell, 1982.

LeGoff, Jacques. "Saint de l'Eglise et saint du peuple: Les miracles officiels de saint Louis entre sa mort et sa canonisation (1270–1297)." In *Histoire sociale, sensibilités collectives et mentalités: Mélanges Robert Mandrou*, 169–80. Paris: Presses Universitaires de France, 1985.

Rathmann-Lutz, Anja. *"Images" Ludwigs des Heiligen im Kontext dynastischer Konflikte des 14. und 15 Jahrhunderts*. Berlin: Akademie Verlag, 2010.

Riant, Paul Edouard Didier. "Déposition de Charles d'Anjou pour la canonisation de saint Louis." In *Notices et documents publiés pour la Société de l'histoire de France à l'occasion du cinquantième anniversaire de sa fondation*, 155–75. Paris, 1884.

Skoda, Hannah. "Representations of Disability in the Thirteenth-Century Miracles de Saint Louis." In *Disability in the Middle Ages: Reconsiderations and Reverberations*, 53–66. Edited by Joshua Eyler. Burlington, Vt.: Ashgate, 2010.

Index

Abraham (biblical figure), 72, 151
Acre, 6–7, 31, 48, 56, 97, 103, 107
Adam of Saint-Leu (abbot of Royaumont) at Louis IX's canonization hearing, 39
Adam of Vale, 68
Agnes "la Maquine," 29, 157
Aigues-Mortes, 6, 13, 116
Alexander III (pope), 15n34
Alfonse of Poitiers (brother of Louis IX), 164–65, 167, 170
Alfonso VIII (king of Castile), 2
Alice (daughter of Robert "called Poelecoc"), 30, 159
Alice of Aube, 156
Ambrose (of Milan, saint), 100
Andrew of Longjumeau, 117n263, 121n285
Aristotle, 19, 118n273
Asa (biblical king), 95
Augustine (of Hippo, saint), 10, 90n109, 100, 118, 133

Baldwin II (emperor of Constantinople), 4
Beatrice of Provence, 122n299
Beaucaire, 37
beguines, 21, 33, 46, 92, 157
Bernard Gui, 41n106, 65n10
Blanche (daughter of Louis IX), 40–41
  father's intentions for, 82
  marriage of, 82n66
Blanche of Burgundy, 179n20

Blanche of Castile (queen of France; mother of Louis IX), 2–3, 6, 46, 47n116, 164
  compared to Idida, 73–74
  death of, 8, 20, 48, 104–6, 168
  praised as regent, 74, 105
Bologna, 124
Bonaventure (saint), 113n245, 118n273
Boniface VIII (pope)
  bull *Gloria laus*, 41
  and canonization of Louis IX, 40–41
  sermons on Louis IX, 41
  themes in his canonization bull, 55–57
Bons-enfants of Paris, 97
Boulogne-sur-mer, 22
Brittany, 153
Brown, Elizabeth A. R., 182n29
Burgundy, 27, 152

Caesarea, 103
Cairo, 7
Calabria, 124
Camusat, Nicolas, 182
Cana, 97
Carcassonne, 117
Carolus-Barré, Louis, 182
Carthage, 13, 43, 62–63, 118–19, 153
Celestine V (pope), 40
Chapotin, Marie-Dominique, 183–84
Charlemagne, 15n34

Charles of Anjou (brother of Louis IX), 13, 24–25, 81n62, 122–23, 164–65, 167, 170
   testimony on Louis IX's sanctity, 39
Chartres, 19, 27, 29, 146, 153
Châteauneuf-sur-Loire, 23n59
Cîteaux, abbot of, 22
Clairvaux, Cistercian monastery of, 78, 141
Clement IV (pope), 115
   death of, 25, 31, 124n305
Clermont, bishop of, 23
Cluny, monastery of, 141
Compiègne, 52, 92, 147, 168
Conrad III (king of Germany), 6
Cosenza, 25
Cosnard, Ch., 184
Crown of Thorns, 4, 46, 50, 81, 100–101, 133, 150n92
Cyprus, 6, 107

D'Achery, Luc, 182n28
Damietta, 3, 7–8, 48, 102, 136, 165–67
Daunou, Pierre, 173, 176–78
David (biblical king), 4, 10, 44, 71
Delisle, Léopold, 171
De Rechac, Jean, 183–84
De Wailly, Natalis, 181
Domfront, 21
Dominic (saint), 45
Dubois, Gérard, 182
Duchesne, André, 176–77, 180n22, 181
Duchesne, François, 176n10, 180n22
Dudo (royal physician), 27, 29, 153–55
Dupuy, Pierre, 174n5

Edward I (king of England), 31
Edward the Confessor (king of England), 15

Elias (biblical figure), 127
Emeline Labrece, 30, 158
Emeline of Chambley, 29–30, 156
Eudes of Châteauroux (papal legate), 16, 98, 102n180, 104–6, 138
   death of, 34
Eudes of Tusculum. *See* Eudes of Châteauroux
Eudes Rigaud (archbishop of Rouen), 22
Evreux, Dominicans of, 174–77

Filles-Dieu of Paris, 46, 92
Francis (saint), 45
Francis Cendra, 117n263
Frederick II (emperor), 2, 122n299

Geoffrey of Beaulieu,
   becomes Louis IX's confessor, 20, 44, 48, 75
   career of, 19–26
   date of his life of Louis IX, 33–34
   death of, 33–34
   influence on Jean of Joinville, 41n107
   influence on William of Saint-Pathus, 40
   recipient of Gregory X's letter, 62
   sent by Philip III to secure prayers for soul of Louis IX, 63
   sermons of, 32–33
   themes in his life of Louis IX, 43–49
   in William of Chartres' *vita*, 131, 139–40, 145, 147
Gila of Senlis, 30, 159
Giles of Saumor (archbishop of Tyre), 104
Gilles de la Chaussée, 34–35
Grandmont, brothers of, 21
Gregory IX (pope), 142n44

Gregory X (pope), 36, 64, 67n26,
  119n274, 124n305
  career of, 31–32
  commissions life of Louis IX,
    31, 43, 131
  death of, 33–34, 37–38
  supporter of Louis IX's
    canonization, 37
Gregory (the Great, pope), 100
Guérard, Benjamin, 182–83
Güyuk (Mongol Khan), 121n285

Hélary, Xavier, 182n29
Henry III (king of England), 2, 9n18
Hodierne of Villetaneuse, 29, 157
Honorius IV (pope), 40
Hôtel-Dieu in Paris, 146–47
Hugh Capet (king of France), 3n3
Hugh of Vermandois, 6
Hunt, Richard, 182n29
Hyvernaux, abbaye des, 178

Idida (biblical figure), 71, 73
Innocent III (pope), 2, 71n11
Innocent V (pope). *See* Peter of
  Tarentaise
Isabelle of Aragon (queen of France;
  first wife of Philip III), 22, 26n71
  death of, 25
Isabelle of France (sister of Louis
  IX), 15
Isabelle of Navarre (queen of Navarre;
  daughter of Louis IX), 16, 170
  death of, 72
  Louis IX's *Instructions* for, 11n25
  Louis IX's letter to, 82

Jacob of Voragine, 41
Jacques (French soldier in
  Egypt), 138–39

Jaffa, 20, 82n66, 103–4, 106
James I (king of Aragon), 9n18, 22
Jean "called Camus," 29, 158
Jeanette of Porte-Baudéer, 30, 158
Jeanne of Châtillon, 81n62
Jeanne of Navarre (queen of France;
  wife of Philip IV), 39
  commissions Jean of Joinville's
    Vie, 41
Jean of Benco, 36
Jean of Chalon-sur-Saône, 152
Jean of Châtillon, 36, 65
  themes in his letter, 53–55
Jean of Essômes, 32n79
Jean of Joinville, 13, 56
  completes his life of Louis IX, 41
  at Louis IX's canonization
    hearing, 39
Jean of Mons
  sent by Philip III to secure prayers
    for soul of
  Louis IX, 24, 63
Jean of Samois, 38
Jean of Tournon, 68
Jean Tristan (count of Nevers; son
  of Louis IX), 26n71
  birth of, 7
  death of, 24, 72, 120
  father's intentions for, 81
  miraculous vision concerning,
    27, 150–51
Jerome (saint), 100
Jerusalem, 6, 53, 149
John (king of England), 1
John "the Englishman," 158
Josias (biblical king), 44–45, 49–50,
  69–73, 87, 96, 111, 126–27, 131–32
Jourdain, Charles, 181

Kaufman, Martin, 182n29

Langres, 22
Lausanne, 37
Le Batelier, Jacques, 174n5
Le Febvre, Nicholas, 183–84
Leger (leprous monk of
    Royaumont), 168
Le Mans, 65, 68, 184
Lihons, convent of, 21
Lombardy, 124
Louis VII (king of France), 3n3, 6
Louis VIII (king of France), 2, 6, 13, 73,
    125, 163
Louis IX (king of France)
    anti-Jewish measures of, 9, 142–43
    attraction to Dominicans and
        Franciscans, 4, 80, 91
    birth of, 1
    burial of, 13, 26–27, 39, 49, 125,
        151, 153
    captivity of, 7, 48, 50, 56, 79,
        102–3, 135–37, 165–67
    compared to King Josias, 69–73, 87,
        96, 111, 126–27, 131–32
    crowning of, 2–3, 10
    death of, 13, 24, 43, 49, 53, 62,
        120–21, 147–49, 170
    Enseignements of, 11, 83–86
    first attempts at canonization
        of, 15–18
    formal canonization hearings
        of, 38–40
    miracles of, 26–31, 125, 150–59, 171
Louvre, 27, 29, 155
Lyon, 37

Maison-Dieu of Paris, 91
Mansura, 7, 79, 138
Mardochai (biblical figure), 126
Marguerite of Provence (queen of
    France; wife of Louis IX), 3, 8,
    24n65, 32, 40, 47, 79–80, 107, 164

Marie of Brabant (queen of France;
    second wife of Philip III), 37
Marmoutier (Benedictine
    monastery of), 141
    abbot of, 22
Martin IV (pope), 38. *See also* Simon
    of Brie
    death of, 40
Martin of Tours (saint), 85
Matthew (nephew of William
    of Chartres), 34
Matthew of Vendôme (abbot of Saint-
    Denis), 17, 24–25, 30, 34n86, 125
    at Louis IX's canonization hearing, 39
Maubuisson, Cistercian abbey
    of, 82n66
Ménard, Claude, 173–77, 180n22, 181
Michael "called Savage," 29, 157
Montpensier, 73n19
Moses (biblical figure), 134
Mustansir, al- (Sultan of Tunis), 116–17

Narbonne, 117
Naudet, Joseph, 173, 176–78
Navarre, Collège de, 178–79
Navarre, queen of. *See* Isabelle
    of Navarre
Nazareth, 46, 97
Nevers, count of. *See* Jean Tristan
Nicholas III (pope), 37n90, 38
Nicholas IV (pope), 40
Nicholas of Auteuil (bishop of Evreux)
    at Louis IX's canonization
        hearing, 39
Normandy, 52, 146

Orgelet, 152
Orvieto, 55

Palermo, 13, 16, 25, 123
Périgord, count of, 36n87

Peronne, 21
Peter Lombard, 19, 105n201, 118n273
Peter Martyr (saint), 153n109
Peter of Alençon (son of Louis IX), 68n32
   father's intentions for, 81
Peter of Aragon (king), 122n299
Peter of Condé, 15, 24n63, 36n87
Peter of Cuisy (bishop of Meaux), 164
Peter of Laon (knight), 27, 29, 155
   at Louis IX's canonization hearing, 39
Peter of Tarentaise, 37, 65n10
Petronilla (daughter of Alice of Aube), 29–30, 156
Philip I (king of France), 6
Philip II "Augustus" (king of France), 1–3, 6, 13, 92
   attempt to canonize, 15
   in Louis IX's *Enseignements*, 85
Philip III (king of France), 11, 22, 24–27, 32, 123–25, 153, 155
   coronation of, 30, 32
   death of, 40
   letter on Louis IX's death, 15–16, 42–43, 49
   plans new crusade, 37–38
   promotes Louis IX's canonization, 36, 38
   at Louis IX's canonization hearing, 39
Philip IV (king of France), 181
   and canonization of Louis IX, 40
Philip (older brother of Louis IX), 2
Poissy, 111–12, 146n60
Pontoise, 92

Ralph, treasurer of Saint-Martin of Tours, 21
Raymond Marti, 117n263

Raymond of Peñafort, 117n263
R. de Yvemesnil, 36n87
Reims, 112
   archbishop of, 36
Richard, Jean, 182n29
Richard of Peleyo, 68
Ripoll, Thomas, 183
Robert "called Poelecoc," 159
Robert of Artois (brother of Louis IX), 7, 164–65
Robert of Nantes (patriarch of Jerusalem), 136
Robert "the Pious" (king of France), 3n3, 112n240
Roland of Parma, 39
Rome, 124
Rouen, 92, 156
Royaumont, Cistercian monastery of, 3, 91
   Louis IX and the leper at, 56, 145, 168
   Louis IX leaves books to, 100

Saint-Benoît of Fleury, Benedictine monastery of, 141
Saint-Denis, Benedictine monastery of, 13, 27, 29–31, 57, 117, 123, 125, 141, 151,
   canonization hearings at, 39
   letter collection compiled at, 182
   miracles at, 152, 155–59
Sainte-Chapelle (Paris), 4, 37, 50, 101–2, 133, 150
Saint-Germain-des-Prés, Benedictine monastery of, 174, 176–77, 182n28
Saint-Germain-en-Laye, 26–27, 153
Salerno, 81n62
Sardinia, 116
Saul (biblical king), 10
Senlis, 21

Sens, 101n178, 133
  archbishop of, 36
Sepphoris, 97
Sheba, queen of, (biblical figure), 127
Sicily, 123–24
Sidon, 103, 106, 137
Simon of Brie (papal legate), 37–38, 109–10, 115.
  See also Martin IV (pope).
Simon of Clisson (bishop of Saint-Malo), 29, 153
Simon of Nesle, 17, 24–25
  at Louis IX's canonization hearing, 39
Simon of Troyes, 68
Solomon (biblical king), 4, 10, 48, 88, 95, 126–27, 136n24
Stephen of Gâtinais, 68
Stilting, Johannes, 176

Tancarville, chamberlain of, 36n87
Tebaldo Visconti. *See* Gregory X
Thibaut of Champagne. *See* Thibaut of Navarre
Thibaut of Navarre (king of Navarre; count of Champagne; son-in-law of Louis IX), 16, 26n71
  death of, 25
  marriage to Louis X's daughter Isabelle, 72n116
Thomas Aquinas, 118n263
Thomas Hauxton, 30, 156n130
Thomas, prior of Vaux-de-Cernay, 25–26
Tobias (biblical figure), 135
Tripani, 25
Troyes, bishop of, 22
Tunis, 13, 43, 49, 56, 62, 72, 116–19, 121, 170

Urban II (pope), 6
Urban IV (pope), 22

Vauvert, Carthusian monastery, 92
Vaux-de-Cernay, 25
Vernon, 92
Villeneuve-l'Archevêque, 101n178
Villetaneuse, 157
Vincennes
  bois de, 21, 108n216
  royal residence of, 47, 108
Viterbo, 25, 31, 64, 124

Walter Cornut (archbishop of Sens), 101n177
Walter of Saint-Quentin, 101n177
William (bishop of Olenos), 21
William Durandus, 114n246
William of Auvergne (bishop of Paris), 164
William of Chartres, 4
  anti-Jewish attitude of, 9, 52, 133, 142–43
  becomes a Dominican, 23, 139
  career of, 19–26
  date of his life of Louis IX, 34
  gathers miracle stories, 26–31
  guardian of the royal seal, 24
  miracles reused in *Beatus Ludovicus*, 42
  nephews of, 20, 34
  niece of, 34
  sent by Philip III to secure prayers for soul of Louis IX, 63
  sermons of, 33
  sisters of, 20
  themes in his life of Louis IX, 49–53
William of Châteauneuf (master of the Hospital), 137

William of Flavacourt, 39
William of Grez, 39
William of Mâcon (canon of Paris), 27, 29, 151
William of Saint-Pathus, 22, 41

vita based on canonization hearings, 40
William of Tournai, 68

Yolanda of Burgundy, 72n16
Yves, abbot of Cluny, 21

www.ingramcontent.com/pod-product-compliance
Lightning Source LLC
Chambersburg PA
CBHW020901230426
43666CB00008B/1266